THE BRAZILIAN SOUND

SAMBA, BOSSA NOVA, AND THE POPULAR MUSIC OF BRAZIL

THE BRAZILIAN SOUND

SAMBA, BOSSA NOVA, AND THE POPULAR MUSIC OF BRAZIL

Chris McGowan
and Ricardo
Pessanha

BILLBOARD BOOKS
An imprint of
Watson-Guptill Publications/
New York

ABOUT THE AUTHORS

Chris McGowan covers music, video, and cultural subjects for *Billboard, The Beat,* and other publications, and has written many articles and special magazine supplements about Brazilian music. He currently resides in Los Angeles.

Ricardo Pessanha has worked as a teacher, writer, and supervisor for one of Brazil's leading institutes of English-language education, serving as a consultant on numerous projects conducted in Brazil by foreign scholars and journalists. He lives in the Tijuca neighborhood of Rio and is a dedicated fan of the Flamengo soccer club.

A Note on the Translations

All song lyrics, most of the interviews with Brazilian musicians and critics, and all quotations from books in Portuguese were translated by the authors. The translations of the song lyrics, in particular, reflect the authors' emphasis on literal accuracy rather than poetic license. *Ed.*

Senior Editor: Tad Lathrop
Book and cover design: Areta Buk
Musical instrument illustrations: Pat Welch
Rhythm charts: Don Giller
Production Manager: Hector Campbell

First published 1991 by Billboard Books, an imprint of
Watson-Guptill Publications, a division of BPI Communications, Inc.
1515 Broadway, New York, NY 10036

Library of Congress Cataloging-In-Publication Data

McGowan, Chris, 1956–
    The Brazilian sound: samba, bossa nova, and the popular music of
  Brazil / Chris McGowan and Ricardo Pessanha.
      p. cm.
  Includes bibliographical references and index.
  Discography: p.
  ISBN 0-8230-7673-3
    1. Popular music—Brazil—History and criticism.   I. Pessanha,
  Ricardo.   II. Title.
  ML3487.B7M4 1991
  781.64'0981—dc20   90-27381
                                          CIP
                                          MN

Manufactured in United States of America

First Printing, 1991

2 3 4 5 6 7 8 9 / 96 95 94 93 92

ACKNOWLEDGMENTS

We would like to thank a number of people who helped us as we worked on this book. Dexter Dwight was our right-hand man and gave us invaluable suggestions and criticism throughout the project. Lígia Campos provided valuable research on the rhythms and genres of Brazilian music. João Parahyba was generous with his percussion instruments and his musical knowledge. Ivan Cordeiro, Karl Garabedian, Cristina Portela, Marcus Lima, Embratur, and Cebitur contributed important artwork and photographs for the book.

Special thanks to Ricardo "Cabra" Bomba, Alda Balthazar, Cecilia McDowell, Rifka Souza, Carla Poppovic, Francisco Rodrigues, Aretuza Garibaldi, Cacaia, Edna Duarte, Carlos de Andrade, Lila Pereira, Renato Costa, Victor Kenski, Antonio Duncan, Luis Boaventura, Mario Aretana, Angela Bosco, Márcio Ferreira, Layra Pessanha, Neusa Braga Ferreira, Paola Vieira, Edgard "Bituca" Rocca, Dayse Sacramento, Paulo Guerra, Zilah Araújo, Luciana Dutra, Cláudio Siqueira Vianna, and Iona Zalcberg.

In the Northern Hemisphere, we were greatly aided by Marv Fisher, Ed Ochs, Jim McCullaugh, Sérgio Mielniczenko, Márcia Garcia, Ben Mundy, Terri Hinte, Nina Lenart, Viola Galloway, Ana Maria Bahiana, Shelley Selover, Bobbie Marcus, Talaya Trigueros, Álvaro Farfan, Maria Lucien, and Judith Wahnon. Tay McGowan's clipping services and enthusiasm were quite important, as was Nancy Ott's constant encouragement.

Thanks to all our interviewees: Alcione, Laurindo Almeida, Carlos de Andrade, Leny Andrade, Mario de Aretana, Geraldo Azevedo, Ana Maria Bahiana, Beto Boaventura, Ricardo Bomba, João Bosco, Charlie Byrd, Lígia Campos, Oscar Castro-Neves, Dori Caymmi, Ivan Cordeiro, Gal Costa, Djavan, George Duke, Dexter Dwight, Engenheiros de Hawaii, Hermínio Marques Dias Filho, Aretuza Garibaldi, Gilberto Gil, Don Grusin, Tim Hauser, Rildo Hora, Antonio Carlos Jobim, Josias of Salgueiro, Victor Kenski, Rita Lee, Téo Lima, Ivan Lins, Lobão, Herbie Mann, Lyle Mays, Mazzola, Zuza Homem de Mello, Sérgio Mendes, Margareth Menezes, André Midani, Sergio Mielniczenko, Airto Moreira, Milton Nascimento, Rique Pantoja, João Parahyba, Paulo Ricardo, Ritchie, Lee Ritenour, Francisco Rodrigues, Lulu Santos, Bezerra da Silva, Ricardo Silveira, Simone, Rifka Souza, Toquinho, Alceu Valença, Herbert Vianna, Paulinho da Viola, and Paul Winter.

A special thanks to our simpatico editor Tad Lathrop, to Herbie Mann for entrusting us with his bossa nova photos, and to Laurindo Almeida for the use of his old photos and discography. And our deepest gratitude to Paul Winter for lending us his only copies of rare albums, for writing the foreword to this book, and for his music.

And, most of all, thank you to Monica Braga Ferreira and Ana Paula Macedo.

CONTENTS

FOREWORD

In a bleak Chicago January, 1962, I heard a new sound that was to change my musical life. My jazz sextet, just out of college, was preparing to leave on a six-month State Department-sponsored tour of Latin America. Gene Lees, then editor of *down beat*, played for us a rare recording that Washington disk jockey Felix Grant had brought back from Brazil. It featured a young singer named João Gilberto, with songs and orchestrations by Antonio Carlos Jobim. This music hit us like a warm breath of fresh air. At a time when most of the sounds in our bebop pantheon were fairly loud, here was a quiet music that we found totally captivating. It was a foretaste of the experience that awaited us in Brazil, which was to be fourteenth on our upcoming twenty-three-country itinerary.

It was June when we finally arrived, and Rio de Janeiro seemed to us like a musical paradise. A whole new genre of music making was in full flower, and it was called *bossa nova*—"new touch." Gorgeous chord progressions, from jazz standards and European composers like Chopin, were woven with exquisite melodies and subtle rhythmic syncopations, into a gentle, swinging tapestry that was absolutely irresistible. The bossa nova groups sang in this sensual and lyrical language of Portuguese, and often they included superb jazz-inspired horn players. We soon made friends with a whole community of young musicians and composers, including Carlos Lyra, Oscar Castro-Neves, Roberto Menescal, Luiz Bonfá, and Jobim, as well as the dean of bossa nova lyricists, Vinícius de Moraes.

This alluring Brazilian music showed me a new path: the possibility of a *gentle* way, in an increasingly noisy world. And it changed my sax playing forever: hearing how João used his voice like a horn, I wondered, "Could a horn be played like a voice?"

I also fell in love with Rio's carnival samba music, which comes from a totally Dionysian tradition. The sound of the *bateria*, the 300 drummers of each *escola de samba*, offers what must be the ultimate power-percussion experience on the planet. (I was enthralled with the sound of their huge *surdo* drums, and on a later trip to Brazil in 1965 I brought back a set of seven, which I've incorporated in all my bands for the last twenty-five years.)

As our tour continued through seventeen other cities around this vast country, we learned that the music of Rio was not by any means the whole Brazilian story. We heard different traditions everywhere,

with rhythms like *frevo, choro, baião, maracatu,* and *marcha rancho.*
Each region has its own music, but wherever you go, rhythm is part of
life's sustenance. This is a culture born of living outdoors, with people
dancing, drumming, and singing, as if life were a perpetual celebration
of the wedding of land and sea.

In *all* these traditions, I hear that distinctive, characteristically
Brazilian flavor—in the deep-chested Bahian songs of Dorival Caymmi,
in the gentle bounce of João Gilberto's guitar, the cello choirs of
Villa-Lobos, the heartbeat of the surdo drum, and the little-girl edge in
the voice of Nara Leão. It's a certain poignance, a soulfulness, coming
from what Brazilians call *saudade*—a kind of bittersweet longing, which
means, in a way, "glad to be feeling." (We have no word in English for
this concept.) All Brazilian music seems to be imbued with *saudade.*

Since that first wondrous tour, Brazil has been my "vitamin B" of
the soul, luring me back again and again. Coming down from our cold
northland, where we ration our smiles, to this world where human
instincts live in full bloom, I always feel like I'm landing in heaven.
Though, to be sure, heaven it's not.

Brazil remains a fertile garden of music, as lush and as varied as the
rainforest of the Amazon. And even there, in Brazil's symphony of
nature, the voices are extraordinary: the Amazon musical wren, *uirapuru,*
sings a song so intricate, so rapturous, you would think Charlie Parker
had been reborn as a bird. According to Maué legend, he who hears
that song will live forever.

Finally, now, here is a wonderful new book which celebrates this
vast treasure trove of Brazilian popular music, and tells how this music
has radiated outward, in recent decades, to charm and enchant the
world. Long overdue, there has never been a survey like this one, and
I'm grateful. Ricardo Pessanha and Chris McGowan have taught me
much, in *The Brazilian Sound,* about this amazing culture that has been
part of my life for almost thirty years.

What *is* it, in all this music of Brazil, that lightens my life the
instant I hear it? Some promise . . . of life's fullness, life's grace. Samba
songs of eternal summer, of sun and suffering, of the sea, and life's
shadows. I have *saudade.*

Muito obrigado, Brazil
Paul Winter
December, 1990

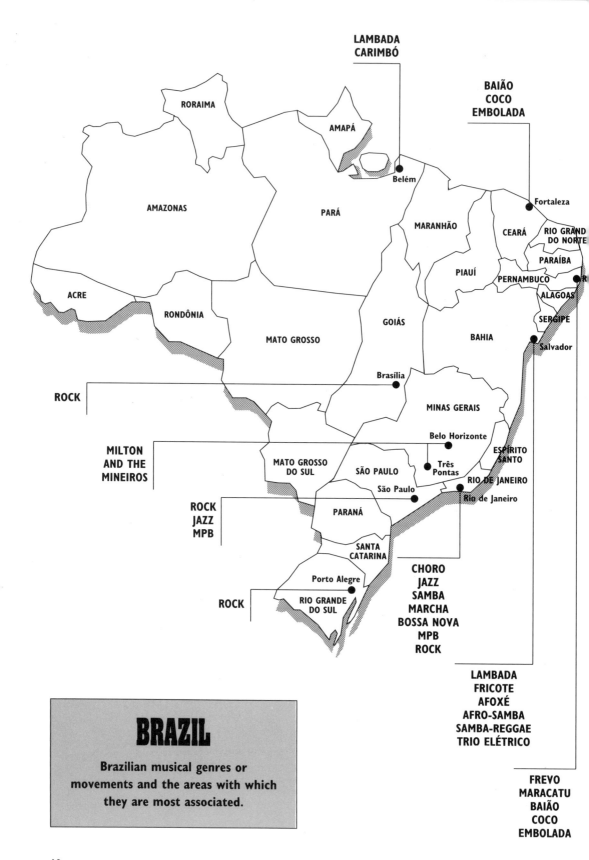

LAMBADA
CARIMBÓ

BAIÃO
COCO
EMBOLADA

RORAIMA

AMAPÁ

Belém

Fortaleza

AMAZONAS

PARÁ

MARANHÃO

CEARÁ

RIO GRANDE
DO NORTE

PARAÍBA

PIAUÍ

PERNAMBUCO

ACRE

RONDÔNIA

ALAGOAS

SERGIPE

MATO GROSSO

GOIÁS

BAHIA

Salvador

Brasília

ROCK

MINAS GERAIS

Belo Horizonte

MILTON
AND THE
MINEIROS

MATO GROSSO
DO SUL

SÃO PAULO

Três
Pontas

ESPÍRITO
SANTO

RIO DE JANEIRO

São Paulo

Rio de Janeiro

ROCK
JAZZ
MPB

PARANÁ

SANTA
CATARINA

CHORO
JAZZ
SAMBA
MARCHA
BOSSA NOVA
MPB
ROCK

Porto Alegre

ROCK

RIO GRANDE
DO SUL

LAMBADA
FRICOTE
AFOXÉ
AFRO-SAMBA
SAMBA-REGGAE
TRIO ELÉTRICO

BRAZIL

Brazilian musical genres or
movements and the areas with which
they are most associated.

FREVO
MARACATU
BAIÃO
COCO
EMBOLADA

INTRODUCTION

In Brazil, music is everywhere. You can find it in a complex rhythmic pattern beaten out by an old man with his fingers on a cafe table; in the thundering samba that echoes down from the hills around Rio in the months prior to Carnaval; and in the bars where a guitar passes from hand to hand and everyone knows the lyrics to all the classic Brazilian and international songs played late into the night.

Music is part of the Brazilian soul, and rhythm is in the way people speak, in the way they walk, and in the way they play soccer.

In Rio de Janeiro, after the national team has won an important soccer game, fireworks explode in the sky and samba detonates in the streets. On sidewalks and in city squares, the celebration begins. Impromptu percussion sections appear, made up of all types of Brazilians, rich and poor, black and brown and white. As participants pick up instruments—a drum, a scraper, a shaker—an intricate, ebullient samba *batucada* (percussion jam) builds. Each amateur music-maker kicks in an interlocking rhythmic part to create a groove that would be the envy of most professional bands in other parts of the world. The singing and dancing inevitably go on for hours.

It has been said that Brazil is composed basically of three sad, nostalgic groups of people: the Portuguese, the Africans, and the Indians, each yearning to return to a former land or way of life. Yet the final result is not all sad, partly because of music, which is a passport to happiness for Brazilians, an escape from everyday frustrations and (for most) a hard and difficult material life. "There's an amazing magical, mystical quality to Brazilian music. Their music is paradise," jazz flutist Herbie Mann has said.

In the twentieth century more than a little of this paradise reached the outside world, and Brazil arguably had more of an impact on international popular music than any country other than the United States and—possibly—Cuba. It was successful abroad for as many reasons as there are types of Brazilian music. Just as the U.S. has exported a wide variety of musical genres, so too has Brazil, even though very few countries speak its national language, Portuguese.

Most Brazilian music shares three outstanding qualities. It has an intense lyricism tied to its Portuguese heritage that often makes for beautiful, highly expressive melodies, enhanced by the fact that Portuguese is one of the most musical tongues on the earth, and no small gift to the ballad singer. Secondly, from the 1920s through the 1980s, a high level of poetry has been the rule in Brazilian song lyrics

Rio's famed Copacabana beach.

rather than the exception (as is the case with the pop music of most countries). Lastly, a vibrant palette of Afro-Brazilian rhythms enliven and energize most Brazilian popular songs, from samba to coco to bossa nova.

Brazilian music first grabbed international attention with the success of the dance-hall style *maxixe* in Europe between 1914 and 1922. The public was captivated by this vivacious and provocative song and dance, much as Europeans were taken with *lambada* in the 1980s.

The 1940s saw the first export of *samba*, as songs like Ary Barroso's marvelous "Aquarela do Brasil" (known to most of the world as simply "Brazil") reached North America. Ary's tunes were featured in Walt Disney films and covered in other Hollywood productions by a playful, exotic young woman who wore colorful laced skirts, heaps of jewelry, and a veritable orchard atop her head. Her name was Carmen Miranda, and she sang catchy sambas and marchas by many great Brazilian composers in a string of American feature films, like *That Night in Rio*, *The Gang's All Here*, and *Copacabana*. (Carmen was actually born in Portugal, but she moved to Brazil at the age of one.) For better or worse, she would symbolize Brazil to the world for decades and become a cultural icon in North America and Europe, a symbol of fun and extravagance. She inspired legions of Carmen imitators (actor

Mickey Rooney was one of the first—in the 1941 film *Babes on Broadway*), and decades later she is still a popular "character" for costume parties.

Samba would survive Carmen's fame (and infamy) and become a fundamental part of the world's popular music vocabulary. The genre would get a boost when one of its variations, a sort of ultra-cool modern samba called bossa nova, entered the world spotlight through the 1959 movie *Black Orpheus*, which won the Cannes Film Festival grand prize and the Academy Award for best foreign film. In North America, a bossa craze was ignited by the 1962 smash hit album *Jazz Samba*, recorded by guitarist Charlie Byrd and saxophonist Stan Getz.

Jazz artists Herbie Mann, Paul Winter, Cannonball Adderley, and others helped globally popularize the new sound, which had a breezy syncopation, progressive harmony, and a deceptive simplicity. Recalls flutist Mann, "The two most important things that ever happened to me musically were when I decided to play jazz on the flute and when I discovered the music of Brazil." Bossa nova would be the big pop-music trend of the early 1960s, until it was supplanted by the English rock invasion led by the Beatles.

Bossa, like samba, is now a solid part of the international repertoire, especially in the jazz realm. Bossa's leading songwriter, Antonio Carlos Jobim, has had his engaging melodies recorded hundreds of times by musicians all over the world, and his stature now rivals that of George Gershwin, Duke Ellington, and other leading composers of Western popular music in this century. Everyone was inspired by bossa nova, from Coleman Hawkins to Frank Sinatra, and it initiated a widespread infiltration of Brazilian music and musicians into North American music.

From the late 1960s on, Brazilian percussion became an essential element of many jazz and pop recordings. And a new generation of talented Brazilian musicians began a long-term interchange with jazz artists that would put Americans on dozens of Brazilian albums and Brazilians on hundreds

Musical notes in a sidewalk in Vila Isabel, a neighborhood in Rio known as the home to many great samba composers and musicians.

Astrud Gilberto, whose vocals on "The Girl from Ipanema" helped begin a Brazilian music boom in the U.S. in the early sixties, pictured here on her 1987 Verve release.

of American albums in the seventies and eighties. Airto Moreira and Flora Purim were two of these artists, and they would perform (separately or together) on groundbreaking albums by Miles Davis, Weather Report, and Return to Forever that helped establish the new sub-genre called "jazz fusion."

Most of the other influential Brazilian artists from the 1970s on were singer-songwriters whose careers began after the bossa era and who fashioned remarkable new sounds from an eclectic variety of sources in and outside of Brazil. Their music came to be referred to as *MPB* (an acronym that stands for *música popular brasileira*), a new catch-all category, and their ranks included the talents of Milton Nascimento, Ivan Lins, João Bosco, and Djavan. Their music demonstrated a superb integration of rhythm, melody, harmony, and lyrics; many critics and musicians consider MPB one of the most sophisticated popular music movements of its time in the world.

At the end of the 1980s, yet another new Brazilian song and dance gained international currency: the notorious *lambada*. Conquering Europe in 1989 with its sexy moves, lambada sent a million hips swaying suggestively into the continental night.

As the 1990s began, foreign interest in Brazilian sounds lay not just in one genre—such as bossa nova or lambada—but in a diverse spectrum of Brazilian artists and styles. A seemingly inexhaustible natural resource (one that is always renewing itself), Brazil's popular music includes a dazzling variety of song forms and musical traditions.

There are troubadours from the Northeast who strum guitars and trade improvised stanzas back and forth, each trying to top the other, in

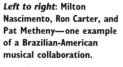

Left to right: Milton Nascimento, Ron Carter, and Pat Metheny—one example of a Brazilian-American musical collaboration.

An elaborately costumed
Carnaval participant.

traditional *desafio* song duels. There are the accordion virtuosos who
lead their bands in rollicking *forró* music. There are languid *maracatus*,
ritualistic *afoxés*, festive *marchas*, frenetic *frevos*, and the leaping
instrumental improvisations of *choro*. And there are the types of samba
you need to go to Brazil to see and hear: the walls of sound and waves
of color that are the *escola de samba* (samba school) parades during
Rio's Carnaval. The greatest polyrhythmic display on earth, their rhythm
sections—roughly 300 drummers and percussionists in each escola—
work in perfect coordination with thousands of singers and dancers to
create an awe-inspiring musical spectacle.

Whether manifested in these or other forms, Brazilian music above
all has heart, a profound ability to move the human soul. In its
sounds and lyrics, it reflects the Brazilian people: their uninhibited joy
or despair, their remarkable capacity to celebrate, their singular ironic
humor, and the all-important concept of *saudade* (longing, yearning).

To best understand Brazil's rich musical heritage, we must first
journey back several hundred years, to where Brazil and its music
both began.

An early nineteenth-century map of Brazil, included in Frenchman Jean Baptiste Debret's *Viagem Pitoresca e Histórica ao Brasil.*

FIVE CENTURIES OF MUSIC

Brazil has characteristics of the first world and the third world existing side by side. It is highly industrialized in some areas and absolutely medieval in others. Brazil is wealthy and miserable, chic Ipanema and mud-and-stick hut, high-tech engineer and stone-age Indian, computers and bananas. As a common joke goes: if there were no Brazil, someone would have to invent one.

The feeling of uniqueness that Brazilians have (and they are convinced, by the way, that God is Brazilian) may have many sources, but two deserve special mention. One is that all Brazilians (save for isolated Amazonian tribes) speak one language: Portuguese. This is remarkable for such a huge country (larger than the continental United States), a nation that is surrounded by so many Spanish-speaking countries, that has been invaded by the French and the Dutch in its history, and that has received immigrants from all over the world. And Portuguese sets Brazil apart from all but a few nations that share that tongue; Angola, Portugal, and Mozambique are most prominent.

A simple house in Maranguape, Ceará, in the Northeast of Brazil.

Another argument for Brazil's singularity is that nowhere else on the Earth do different races, cultures, and religions coexist as peacefully as they do there. There is prejudice among Brazilians, but on a level that does not interfere with the day-to-day social life of most people. Discrimination in Brazil is, in general, more tied to distinctions of class and wealth than it is to differences of race or religion. It is also a complex subject that few agree about.

In terms of skin color, black and mulattos have indeed suffered disproportionately more from poverty in Brazil than have whites, in part because slavery ended only a little more than a century ago. In cities like Rio, Salvador, and São Paulo, they constitute the majority in the older *favelas* (slums). Yet at the same time, poor non-black immigrants from Brazil's parched Northeast dominate many of the newer favelas.

Nevertheless, dark-skinned and light-skinned people in Brazil generally get along well and do not experience the social barriers that exist between people of different colors in the United States and England, for example. Interracial marriage is commonplace, and it is perfectly ordinary to find people of all colors amiably interacting in the bars, beaches, and streets of cities like Rio. Most everything in Brazil is integrated except for wealth, and even that is slowly changing.

People from different religions also have no problem living and working together in Brazil. A good example is the commercial district in downtown Rio called Saara (Sahara), where Brazilians of Jewish, Lebanese, and Syrian descent all go to the same *botequins* (small, simple bars) at the end of the workday for a beer, a chat, and a little samba on Fridays. Brazil has been a real melting pot for centuries, not a mixed salad like the United States. As such, someone in Brazil of Lebanese or Yoruban or Japanese ancestry usually identifies him or herself first and foremost as *Brazilian.*

Maybe God is Brazilian, indeed.

THE FIRST BRAZILIANS

Brazil's national character and its rich musical tradition both derive from the profound mingling of races that has been going on since April of 1500, when the Portuguese explorer Pedro Álvares Cabral stepped onto the lush tropical coast of what would later be southern Bahia.

Musicians playing pagode samba at a cafe in Rio's Salgueiro neighborhood.

Of course, Cabral was not the first human to discover Brazil, and long before his foot touched Bahian sand, a long musical tradition of a different kind had been at play for thousands of years.

Not counting the sabiá, uirapuru, and other birds, Indians were the first to make music on the continent. The ancestors of today's Brazilian Indians migrated from Asia to the Western Hemisphere more than 40,000 years ago and then eventually made their way down to South America. When Cabral first came to Brazil, there were innumerable tribes there and an indigenous population that probably exceeded two million. When they made music, the different tribes sang songs solo and in chorus, accompanying themselves with hand-clapping, feet-stamping, flutes, whistles, horns, rattles, sticks, and drums.

Their music did not, however, play a major role in the development of Brazilian popular music. This may have been partly due to the influence of Jesuits, who began arriving in 1549 and immediately set about culturally reorienting the Indians, teaching them Catholicism and how to play European instruments and sing chants in Latin and Portuguese. Also, the Indians tended to lose their cultural traditions when they left their native homes and went to live with the whites.

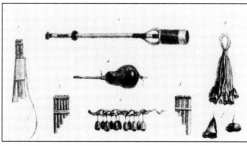

Amerindian musical instruments, drawn by Frenchman Jean-Baptiste Debret, first published in 1839.

From the sixteenth through the twentieth century, the number of Brazil's indigenous inhabitants declined drastically. They were either killed by the Portuguese conquerors, decimated by European diseases, or absorbed into colonial settlements (voluntarily or against their will). The number of Indians remaining in tribes had dropped to perhaps 200,000 by the 1980s. Further losses came that decade as new settlers pushed further into the Amazon rain forest in search of gold and farmland.

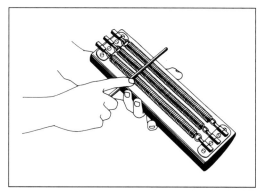

A modern, metal reco-reco (a scraper).

There is Indian influence in some Brazilian popular music, as seen in songs by musicians like Egberto Gismonti, instruments such as the *reco-reco* scraper, and the traditions of the *caboclinho* Carnaval groups, but one generally must journey to the remote homelands of the Yanomâmi and other indigenous groups to hear a lot of it.

THE PORTUGUESE CONQUEST

Cabral encountered a land of great geographic diversity that is now the world's fifth largest nation in terms of land mass. Brazil is a tropical country situated largely between the equator and the Tropic of Capricorn. It possesses 4,600 miles of coastline, as well as the vast Amazon River basin, home to the largest rain forest on the planet. While that humid region can receive up to 150 inches of annual rain in certain spots, Brazil's arid, sprawling *sertão* in the Northeast has areas that may go years with no rain at all. Other regions include a savannah-covered plateau in central Brazil, grassy plains in the South, and a lush coastal belt that was once covered by Atlantic rain forest.

Cabral sailed back to Portugal and the court of King Manuel I, bearing with him monkeys and parrots, but unfortunately no jewels, silks, or spices. However, royal expeditions that returned to the new continent shortly thereafter discovered plentiful stands of brazilwood, a tree that yielded a useful red dye and that gave the country its name. Handsome profits from the brazilwood trade soon increased the number of visiting Portuguese and French traders; naturally, the Portuguese crown decided to expand its exploitation of Brazil and get rid of the French interlopers. In 1532 the first settlement, São Vicente, was established near present-day Santos in São Paulo state. The first sugar mills were constructed there and farther north, in Pernambuco.

There were some respectable Portuguese settlers who came with their families to Brazil. But for the most part, as historian E. Bradford Burns writes, "The Portuguese monarchs customarily sent out on their global expeditions a combination of soldiers, adventurers, and petty criminals condemned to exile. Women were excluded. The Portuguese female was noticeably rare during the first century of Brazilian history. Her scarcity conferred a sexual license on the conquerors, already well acquainted with Moorish, African, and Asian women and, seemingly attracted to dark-skinned beauty." A colony of mixed races was soon in the making, quite different from the civilization that would be created in North America by English Protestants and their families, who came to settle permanently, kept more of a distance from the natives, and maintained an air of moral superiority with regard to other races.

Debret's early nineteenth-century illustration of upper-class Brazilians taking their leisure on a veranda in the tropical heat, trying to beat their "saudades."

Ângelo Agostinho's depiction of an 1880s entrudo in Rio; the rude celebration was a precursor to Carnaval.

The Portuguese brought their culture to this new land, which in the realm of music included the European tonal system, as well as Moorish scales and medieval European modes. There were numerous festivals related to the Roman Catholic liturgical calendar and a wealth of dramatic pageants such as the *reisado* and *bumba-meu-boi* that are seasonally performed in the streets.

The reisado (or *folia de reis*) celebrates the Nativity and the processional bumba-meu-boi dance enacts the death and resurrection of a mythical bull. Both are *autos*, a type of dramatic genre that dates back to medieval times and includes dances, songs, and allegorical characters. Jesuit priests introduced many religious autos that, over time, took on local themes and musical elements.

In addition, many musical instruments came to Brazil from Portugal: the flute, guitar, cavaquinho, clarinet, violin, violoncello, jew's harp, accordion, piano, drums, triangle, and tambourine. The Portuguese had a fondness for brisk, complex rhythms and used a lot of syncopation—two traits that would help their music mesh well in Brazil with that of the African slaves.

There was also the Portuguese tradition of the lyric ballad, often melancholy and suffused with saudade. Portuguese song forms included the *moda*, a sentimental song that became the *modinha* in Brazil in the eighteenth century; the *acalanto*, a form of lullaby; the *fofa*, a dance of the eighteenth century; and *fado*, a melancholy, guitar-accompanied Portuguese ballad that evolved from the *lundu* in the mid-nineteenth century. And, also of great importance, the Portuguese imported the *entrudo*, a rude celebration that was the beginning of Brazil's Carnaval tradition.

As they settled the new land, planted tobacco and cotton, and built sugar mills, the Portuguese looked upon the native Brazilian people as prime candidates for forced labor on the plantations being developed in northeastern Brazil. But the Indians were unsuitable—they either escaped to the forest or died from the hard forced labor. So the Portuguese looked east, across the Atlantic.

THE AFRICANS IN BRAZIL

The first recorded importation of Africans into Brazil occurred in 1538, and from that year until the end of the slave trade in 1850, an estimated 3.5 million Africans survived the crossing of the Atlantic to Brazil (roughly six times more than were taken to North America). The institution of slavery continued until the Brazilian Abolition of 1888.

There were three main ethnic/cultural groups that made the journey. The Yoruban, Fon, Ewe, and Ashanti peoples (the Sudanese groups) traveled from what are now Nigeria, Benin (formerly Dahomey), and Ghana. Bantu groups came from Angola, Zaire (formerly the Congo), and Mozambique. Tapas, Mandingos, Fulahs, and Hausa (the Moslem Guinea-Sudanese groups) were taken from Ghana, Nigeria, and neighboring areas.

The Africans brought their music, languages, and religions, much of which survived in a purer form in Brazil than in North America. This may have been partly due to Portuguese slavery practices. The Mediterranean world had already experienced great religious and linguistic diversity by the time Cabral first came to Brazil. On the Iberian peninsula Christians and Moors had enslaved each other for centuries. African influence in Portugal, in fact, predated the settlement of Brazil by several centuries, and was quite apparent long after Moorish rule ended in A.D. 1249. One result of this was that the Portuguese were relatively more tolerant than Northern Europeans of the native culture of their African captives. They did suppress African religious practices, partly in fear of organized revolts, but slaves by and large managed to keep their drums and dances. In addition, the Portuguese intermarried extensively, partly because—as mentioned above—most of the early settlers came without wives. A racially mixed population was soon formed by the offspring of the Portuguese, Indians, and Africans who intermingled. Even the families of wealthy white officials and planters were exposed to African culture as children by playmates and nurses, and when they were older, by wives and lovers.

The survival of African culture may also have been aided by the establishment of *quilombos*, colonies of runaway slaves in the interior of Brazil. The largest and most famous of these was Palmares, established in the rugged interior of Alagoas state in 1631. It lasted for decades, had a population in the thousands (some say as high as 20,000), and made an effort to organize a society based in African traditions. To the Portuguese, Palmares was a threat to the established order, not to mention the institution of slavery. Numerous armed expeditions were mounted against it, until finally it was overwhelmed and destroyed in 1697.

African heritage survived in modern Brazil in many manifestations. Brazilian Portuguese has incorporated many Yoruban and other African words. The cuisine of Bahia is quite similar to that of West Africa. And Brazilian music and dance are heavily rooted in Africa, as we shall see. Brazil has the largest African-descended population outside of Africa, as an estimated sixty million Brazilians have some ancestry from the continent.

The slaves also brought their animist beliefs to the New World, religions that are probably thousands of years old, far predating Christianity, Islam, or Buddhism. These belief systems were contained for millennia not on parchment or tablets, but maintained as living oral traditions in ritual and music handed down from generation to generation. Carried across the Atlantic Ocean, they were transformed into santeria in Cuba, vodun in Haiti (and voodoo in New Orleans), shango in Trinidad, and a plethora of different sects in Brazil.

In Brazil, slaves from different nations sometimes followed only their own traditions, but most often they mixed their religions together, with the Yoruban belief system having the strongest influence. *Macumba* is a common generic name for all these religions. *Candomblé*, practiced most in Bahia, was the closest to the old West African ways, while *umbanda* is a twentieth-century variation with considerable influence from spiritist beliefs. Other Afro-Brazilian sects include *xangô, catimbó, caboclo, batuque,* and *pajelança*.

The Afro-Brazilian religions were often syncretized into new forms by the slaves because of government and Catholic repression that persisted into the twentieth-century. West African gods, the *orixás*, were secretly worshiped behind Catholic ceremonies. When slaves prayed to a statue of the Virgin Mary, they were often actually thinking of Iemanjá, the goddess of the sea; Saint George might represent Ogun, god of iron and warriors; Saint Jerome could stand in for Xangô, god of fire, thunder, and justice; and Jesus Christ might really signify Oxalá, the god of the sky and universe. Catholicism, with its abundance of saints, meshed well with the orixá tradition and inadvertently sheltered it. Followers of macumba and umbanda today still use plaster-cast figures of Catholic saints to fill in for the orixás in their ceremonies.

In the Afro-Brazilian religions, a follower always has two different orixás, a male and a female that "rule your head"—your spiritual parents, so to speak. For example, you might have Xangô and Iemanjá as the "masters of your head." The head priestess, the *mãe-de-santo* (mother of the saints), might discover this for you, asserting that these two orixás, because of their specific personalities and powers, are the natural guides for you and your life. During the ceremonies, the drums and singing call down the orixás, and they or their intermediary spirits "possess" the bodies of chosen sons and daughters.

While the traditional sect of candomblé focuses solely on the orixás, the eclectic religion of umbanda has incorporated ideas of the French spiritist Alain Kardec and also includes numerous non-African spirits (some of them Amerindian) in its pantheon.

In the late twentieth century, candomblé and umbanda have become an accepted and integral part of Brazilian culture. Novelist Jorge Amado is a well-known follower of candomblé and a son of Xangô. Numerous leading cultural figures are *umbandistas.* Many Brazilian musicians praise or refer to Afro-Brazilian deities in their pop song lyrics. The noted samba-singers Clara Nunes and Martinho da Vila, for example, have included invocation songs for the orixás on their albums.

Ceremonial umbanda drums and figurines in an umbanda supply store, Rio.

Although Brazil is said to be ninety percent Roman Catholic, at least fifty percent of its population also follows Afro-Brazilian religions. Rio, for example, has hundreds of umbanda supply shops that carry plaster-cast figures of St. George and the other "saints," plus dried herbs, beads, candles, and musical instruments. Offerings of food for an orixá can often be found beside flickering candles late at night alongside a road. And every New Year's Eve, millions of Brazilian men and women dress in white and throw flowers and other gifts into the sea as offerings to the goddess Iemanjá.

Music helped preserve Afro-Brazilian religions. Sometimes slaves held drum sessions that on the surface seemed mere celebrations but in reality were religious rites. And, in turn, candomblé and macumba helped preserve African musical characteristics. African songs, musical scales, musical instruments, and a rich variety of polyrhythms (each deity is called by a particular rhythm and song) have survived (in varying degrees) in their rituals.

A wide assortment of African-derived instruments are still played today, including the *agogô*, a double cowbell struck by a wooden stick; the *cuíca*, a small friction drum; and the *atabaque*, a conical single-headed drum. The African influence also reveals itself in Brazil's

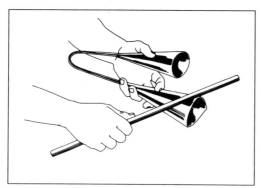

The agogô, a type of double cowbell of African descent, hit with a stick.

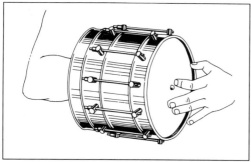

The cuíca friction-drum. One hand rubs a piece of cloth along a reed affixed to the inside of the drumskin.

traditional and folk music (as it does in African-American music in the rest of the Americas) through the use of syncopation and complex rhythmic figures, the importance of drums and percussion instruments, certain flattened or "falling" notes, the so-called metronome sense of West Africa, the use of call-and-response patterns, short motives and improvisation, and—perhaps most importantly—the tendency of music to play an important role in life.

Religious, ceremonial, and festive African music would form the basis of Afro-Brazilian songs and dances that would eventually develop into various musical forms: afoxé, jongo, lundu, maracatu, samba, and more.

THE DEVELOPMENT OF BRAZIL

Brazil's mixed population today reflects its Portuguese, Amerindian, and African ancestors, and has also incorporated large numbers of German, Italian, Japanese, Lebanese, and other immigrants since the nineteenth century. The country's first spurt of development was powered by trade in brazilwood, then sugar, gold, diamonds, coffee, and rubber fueled the country's growth. It was ruled by Portugal until 1822, when Dom Pedro, the heir to the Portuguese throne, declared Brazil's independence and became its first emperor. His successor, Dom Pedro II, was overthrown in 1889 and a republic established. Since the nineteenth century, Brazil has had both authoritarian and democratic governments (it now has a democracy, following military rule between 1964 and 1985).

Industrialization came largely in the twentieth century, accelerating especially during the Getúlio Vargas regimes (1930-45, 1950-54). By the 1980s, Brazil had diversified, becoming an important exporter of soybeans, steel, military weapons, airplanes, shoes, and many other goods (including cultural products such as music, film, and literature). The country had some 140 million people and was the eighth largest market economy in the world at that time.

But the "economic miracle" that followed the military coup of 1964 and greatly modernized Brazil did not benefit the majority of the population. Perhaps it was true, as Brazilians often said, that soccer, beer, cachaça (sugar-cane liquor), and Carnaval were the only things that kept the poor from staging a revolution. As the 1990s began, Brazil was still—as always—the country of the future, a nation of vast potential, the *next* great world power.

A MUSICAL MELTING POT

Over the course of the last five centuries, Portuguese, African, and—to a lesser extent—Amerindian traditions, instruments, harmonies, dances, rhythms, and other musical elements have been mixing together, altering old styles and creating new forms of music. One of the most important early Brazilian musical genres was the *lundu* song and circle dance, which included the *umbigada* movement that was a key part of many Afro-Brazilian dances in their original forms (in the umbigada, two dancers touch navels as an invitation to the dance). Lundu was brought by Bantu slaves from Angola to Brazil, where it began to acquire new influences and shock the Europeans.

The first recorded reference to lundu in Brazil was in 1780, describing it as a rather lascivious dance. By the end of that century it had made an appearance in the Portuguese court, transformed into a salon style sung with guitar or piano accompaniment and embellished with refined harmonies. Both types of lundu would remain popular in Brazil until the early twentieth century.

Another important song/dance, maxixe, was born in Rio around 1880 from the meeting of lundu with Argentinian tango, Cuban habanera, and polka. Created by Afro-Brazilian musicians who were performing at parties in lower-middle-class homes, the maxixe would be the first genuinely Brazilian dance, a synthesis of the above forms with additional voluptuous moves performed by the closely dancing couple. Maxixe would give as erotic and scandalous an impression as lundu had 100 years earlier and lambada would 100 years later. Soon would come other new styles born of many ingredients, including choro, marcha, and samba.

A demonstration photograph of a couple doing the maxixe, from an Italian ballroom dance book published in 1914.

These song types and many more would be recorded by a native music industry that dates back to the first decade of the century. The first recording made on disk in Brazil was the lundu "Isto É Bom" (This Is Good), written by Xisto Bahia and performed by the singer Baiano for the Casa Edison record company in 1902. By the 1970s, the Brazilian music industry would be one of the world's major markets for recorded music (with the multinationals CBS, RCA, PolyGram, WEA, and EMI controlling most of the action there, as elsewhere).

Musically, Brazil has continued to reflect the great racial and cultural miscegenation of its history. Its music is a result of the spontaneity and openness of most Brazilians; new ideas and idioms are accepted, absorbed, and modified. Reflective of this is the long and rich tradition of Brazil's most famous musical form: samba.

PIXINGUINHA AND THE BATUTAS

MARTINHO DA VILA

CENTRO

MANGUEIRA

ESTÁCIO

VILA ISABEL

TIJUCA

AN ESCOLA'S ALA DAS BAIANAS

ISMAEL SILVA

CACIQUE DE RAMOS

ARY BARROSO

RIO DE JANEIRO

SAMBA: THE HEARTBEAT OF RIO

CHAPTER 2

He who doesn't like samba isn't a good guy
He's rotten in the head or sick in the feet
　　　　　—Dorival Caymmi, "Samba da Minha Terra"

On a hot and humid summer night in Rio, a small stage is packed with dozens of musicians playing assorted drums and percussion instruments, engaged in an *escola de samba* (samba school) rehearsal. They are inside a cavernous pavilion that resembles an airplane hanger, and it is crowded with people who all have one passion in common: the samba.

Beer consumption soars as *surdos*—a type of Brazilian bass drum—pound out the heartbeat of Rio de Janeiro. Their incessant drive sets the foundation for the rest of the *bateria*, the core of the huge drum-and-percussion section that will later parade triumphantly during Carnaval. Snare drums called *caixas* rattle away in a hypnotic frenzy, and above them *tamborins*—small cymbal-less tambourines that are hit with sticks—carry a high-pitched rhythmic phrase that sounds like popcorn in an overheated pot. Enter the sad cries and humorous moans of the *cuíca* (a type of friction drum), the crisp rhythmic accents of the *reco-reco*, and the hollow metallic tones of a double cow-bell called an *agogô*. Other percussion instruments add more colors, the ukulele-like *cavaquinho* strums its high-register plaintive harmonies, and the *puxador* (lead singer) belts out the melody.

Dense rhythms cross and dance with each other, each grabbing hold of the crowd in a different way. By now, the sound is deafening and conversations are out of the question. Everyone is dancing, the sweat flows, and the balmy night air carries more than a hint of eroticism with all the men and women wearing so little and drinking so much. The festive atmosphere is euphoric, as worries and cares are sent flying. There's no doubt in anyone's mind: samba is what it's all about.

A Carnaval parader in Rio pounding out samba's rhythm.

A cold technical definition would never express what samba—and the whole universe that revolves around it—is. For one thing, in a musical sense, there are many varieties of samba: from thundering *samba-enredo* played by the escolas during Carnaval to melodious, sophisticated *samba-canção* to earthy, exuberant *pagode samba*. And, if we ask an average Brazilian (especially a Carioca) what samba is, the answer is usually subjective and doesn't always refer to music. "It's something that runs in my veins, it's in my blood," say many samba musicians and devotees.

It is common for Cariocas to say, rather ironically, that everything ends up in samba. If things go wrong there's always samba to lift peoples' spirits. Samba is many things: solace, celebration, escape and abandon, plus philosophy, culture, and tradition. It is a musical form largely created and sustained by the black and mulatto working classes in Rio, but the Brazilian middle-class also lives by it and draws vitality from it. And most Brazilian musicians— MPB stars, jazz artists, even rock bands— record a samba at some point in their careers.

SAMBA'S ROOTS

Samba coalesced into a distinct musical genre in Rio de Janeiro in the early twentieth century, and eventually became one of the most popular types of music in the world. The exact course of samba's early evolution is unknown, but there is no shortage of theories about its origins. The word "samba" appears to come from Angola, where the Kimbundu term "semba" refers to the umbigada navel-touching "invitation to the dance" that was originally a part of many African circle dances. Some scholars feel that samba and the other Afro-Brazilian circle dances that feature or once featured the umbigada are all variants of the same theme.

There are those who feel that lundu, in Brazil since the eighteenth century, was the true musical parent of samba. Others theorize that a primitive type of samba, or at least its essential elements, was brought to Rio from Bahia by slaves and ex-slaves in the late nineteenth century. But it was certainly in Rio that samba was developed, embellished, and transformed into a genre quite distinct from other Afro-Brazilian musical forms.

Many slaves and ex-slaves emigrated to Rio, the nation's capital, in the late 1800s because of a decline in the fortunes of tobacco and cocoa plantations in Bahia state, and because of two important new laws: the "Law of the Free Womb" in 1871 (which declared free all children born to slaves), and Brazil's abolition of slavery in 1888. The immigrants worked at the docks, as street vendors, and as domestic help, struggling to make a living any way they could. They settled in shacks clinging precipitously to the steep hillsides surrounding Rio, and others lived in a central area of the city called Praça Onze.

Praça Onze

Such was the influx of Bahian—and hence Afro-Brazilian—culture that by 1915, Praça Onze (literally, Plaza Eleven) was called "a true Africa in miniature." In their leisure time, many of these immigrants and their children gathered together to make music, dance, and worship their African gods at the homes of old Bahian matriarchs, respectfully called *tias* (aunts). Neo-African culture had survived to a greater extent in Bahia than in other parts of Brazil, in part because of the large black population in Salvador and the ongoing trade between that city and ports in Nigeria and Dahomey. The tias did a great deal to keep their culture alive in Rio once they had emigrated there. They are honored today by the *ala das baianas*, a mandatory section in every samba school's parade.

The most important site in samba's evolution was the home of Tia Ciata, in Praça Onze. Tia Ciata (real name Hilaria Batista de Almeida, 1854-1924) was born in Salvador, but she was renowned in Rio as a maker of sweets and as a party hostess. At her house the orixás were worshiped (she was a daughter of Oxum), and a lot of great music was created and performed. Famed *batutas* (masters) like Pixinguinha, Donga, João da Baiana, and Sinhô gathered at Tia Ciata's place in the early years of this century. There they played music together and began shaping the urban Carioca form of samba that we know today.

At such meetings, samba's musical ancestor received influences from lundu, polka, habanera, and the still developing genres of *marcha* and *maxixe*. Marcha was lively with a fast tempo and a simple ONE-two-ONE-two rhythm. Maxixe was an exuberant dance-hall style that was also quickly paced, jumpy, and derived rhythmically from the tango and habanera.

From out of this rich matrix emerged the samba, a vibrant musical form distinguished by increased responsorial singing, more emphasis on

Pre-1937 Praça XI (Onze), the birthplace of samba in downtown Rio before it was destroyed to make way for Avenida Presidente Vargas.

♩ = 126

Caixa	
Agogô	
Reco-reco	
Surdo e Bombo	

Marcha. The parts shown here are played simultaneously. (The symbol > means the beat is accented.) Other instruments are usually incorporated into this rhythm.

♩ = 100–104

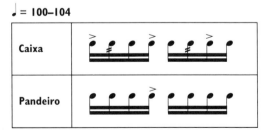

Caixa	
Pandeiro	

A basic maxixe rhythm.

percussive interplay, and a less formal sound than either maxixe or marcha. Technically, samba has a 2/4 meter with its heaviest accent on the second beat, a stanza-and-refrain structure, and many interlocking, syncopated lines in the melody and accompaniment.

The main rhythm and abundant cross-rhythms can be carried by hand-clapping or in the percussion (the *batucada*), which today may be performed by more than a dozen different drums and percussion instruments. Samba is commonly accompanied by the guitar and the four-string cavaquinho and—less frequently—brass.

The first song registered as a "samba" and recorded—"Pelo Telefone" (On the Phone)—was composed at Tia Ciata's house. It was released in 1917, covered by the Banda Odeon. The song's melody was a collective creation and the words were Mauro de Almeida's, but Donga registered it as his alone: "The commandant of fun/ Told me on the phone/ To dance with joy."

At this time, the differences between maxixe, samba, and marcha hadn't completely crystallized. Ismael Silva, one of the founders of the first escola de samba, complained to Donga that "Pelo Telefone" was not a samba but a maxixe.

"What's samba then?" asked Donga rather angrily.

" 'Se Você Jurar,' " answered Ismael, citing one of his own successes.

" 'Se Você Jurar' is not a samba. It's a marcha," replied Donga.

The debate went on for years, and in fact many musicologists today refer to "Pelo Telefone" as a samba-maxixe. But it was a hit Carnaval song that year, and samba took its place alongside marcha as a preferred Carnaval musical style in Rio and much of Brazil.

Pixinguinha (1898-1973) stood out as one of the most important of samba's founding fathers, and was also renowned in the choro and

Pixinguinha and the Batutas in 1919. Top row (l. to r.): José Alves, Pixinguinha, Luis Silva, Jacó Palmieri. Seated (l. to r.): Otávio Viana, Nelson Alves, João Pernambuco, Raul Palmieri, Donga.

maxixe genres. He was an original arranger who enriched the harmony of samba and introduced European brass and wind instruments into his bands. Pixinguinha, whose real name was Alfredo da Rocha Vianna, Jr., wrote famous sambas such as "Teus Ciúmes" (Your Jealousies), "Ai Eu Queria" (How I Wanted It), and "Samba de Negro" (Black's Samba). He composed more than 600 tunes in all.

Pixinguinha's contemporary, Sinhô, was the most popular of the first sambistas. During his short life, Sinhô (José Barbosa da Silva, 1888-1930) wrote big Carnaval hits, love songs, and tunes that were chronicles of nocturnal city life. Sinhô composed the hit sambas "Jura" (Swear It) and "Gosto Que Me Enrosco" (I Like It Bad), the latter co-written with Heitor dos Prazeres, as well as hit marchas such as "Pé de Anjo" (Angel's Foot). Sinhô was a regular in every bohemian spot in town. "Gosto Que Me Enrosco" explored the consequences of his late-night carousing: "One shouldn't love someone if he's not loved/It would be better if he were crucified/May God keep me away from today's women/They despise a man just because of the night life."

Another early sambista, João da Baiana (João Machado Guedes, 1887-1974), the son of famed baiana Tia Perciliana, is credited with introducing the pandeiro as a samba instrument. The police are said to have stolen João's pandeiro when they were cracking down on "batucadas" in 1908, but a senator gave him a new one. He toured Europe with Pixinguinha and Os Batutas, and composed the tunes "Mulher Cruel" (Cruel Woman), "Pedindo Vingança" (Asking Vengeance), and "O Futuro É Uma Caveira" (The Future Is a Skull).

Estácio

Nearby Praça Onze was the Estácio neighborhood, now known as "the cradle of samba." Today, it looks much as it did in the 1920s: narrow streets lined with old, decaying two-story houses and small, simple bars called *botequins* where poor people spend a lot of time drinking, talking, and singing.

The legendary sambistas Ismael Silva, Nilton Bastos, Bide, and Armando Marçal came from Estácio. They were important for two big reasons: they took the fledgling samba genre and clearly differentiated it from maxixe and marcha, introducing longer notes and two-bar phrasing, while making the tempo slower, contrary to the maxixe-like sambas composed by Sinhô and Donga. The form that they codified would become the standard samba reference to which sambistas always return. For a time, in the 1940s and 1950s, these Estácio composers' music was referred to by the media as *samba de morro* to distinguish it from the more middle-class and melodic *samba-canção* and offshoots such as *sambolero* and *sambalada*.

In 1928 these musical pioneers created the first escola de samba: Deixa Falar. Brazil would never be the same, and samba would soon become the unquestioned heart and soul of Rio de Janeiro.

Ismael Silva (1905-1978) was the most important composer of the Turma do Estácio (Estácio Gang) because of his melodic creativity and sophisticated modulations. In addition, his often-ironic lyrics created strong poetic images out of simple, common themes. In "Meu Único

THREE MORE EARLY SAMBISTAS

Caninha (Oscar José Luis de Morais, 1883-1961) was famed for songs such as "Me Leve, Me Leve," (Take Me, Take Me), "Seu Rafael" (Mr. Rafael), and—with Heitor dos Prazeres—"É Batucada" (It's Batucada).

Donga and Pixinguinha at the bust of Villa-Lobos in 1968.

Donga (Ernesto Joaquim Maria dos Santos, 1891-1974) was the son of the baiana Tia Amelia and member of Os Batutas. He co-composed "Pelo Telefone," as well as the hit tunes "Passarinho Bateu Asas" (The Little Bird Beat Its Wings), "Cantiga de Festa" (Party Song), and "Macumba de Oxossi."

Heitor dos Prazeres (1898-1966) composed the famed samba "A Tristeza Me Persegue" (Sadness Follows Me). He claimed Sinhô appropriated many of his best tunes. Heitor was active in the formation of several escolas de samba.

Ismael Silva.

Desejo" (My Only Desire), Silva's sly verse spoke of unrequited love:

> You've returned the photograph
> My letters and my presents
> I didn't accept them
> There's only one thing I really want
> To have you return
> All the kisses I gave you.

Silva left many famous sambas for posterity, including "Se Você Jurar" (If You Were to Swear), "Nem É Bom Falar" (It's No Good Talking About It), and "Antonico." He also co-composed many songs with the hit writers Nilton Bastos, Noel Rosa, and Lamartine Babo, and had a profound influence on later Brazilian composers such as Chico Buarque.

Two other Estácio stalwarts were Bide and Armando Marçal, a powerful songwriting team from the early 1930s until Marçal's death in 1947. Bide (Alcebíades Barcelos, 1902-1975) and Armando Marçal (1903-1947) co-wrote warm, flowing samba masterpieces like "A Malandragem," "Sorrir" (To Smile), and "Agora É Cinzas" (Now It's Ashes).

When Armando died, his family kept the music alive: his only son, Nilton Marçal, is today a famous percussionist and *mestre de bateria* (percussion conductor). And Nilton's son, named Armando for his grandfather, is a superb percussionist as well, highly respected in Brazil and known to North American fans for his work with the Pat Metheny Group.

The musical language elaborated by these Estácio masters was an important form of expression for the Carioca lower classes in the early twentieth century. Samba became a voice for those who had been silenced by their socio-economic status, and a source of self-affirmation in society. As the radio era hit its stride in the 1930s, many of the great songs of the Estácio songwriters reached a wide audience through the interpretations of vocalists like Mario Reis, Francisco Alves, and Carmen Miranda.

Two other important samba composers who supplied hit songs for the radio crooners were Ataulfo Alves and Assis Valente. Alves (1909-1969) married lyrical laments with long, slow musical phrases, a songwriting style that may have been influenced by his youth in slow-paced, bucolic Minas Gerais. Some of his most popular songs were "Ai, Que Saudade de Amelia" (Oh, How I Miss Amelia), "Pois É" (So It Is), and "Mulata Assanhada" (Restless Mulata). Assis Valente (1911-1958) was one of the most popular songwriters of the 1930s and 1940s. His lyrics were witty snapshots of the times in which he lived, and he had an almost naive preoccupation in glorifying what he considered authentically Brazilian. Carmen Miranda recorded many Valente compositions, notably the samba-choro "Camisa Listrada." Other hits included "Recenseamento" (Census) and "Fez Bobagem" (You Were Foolish).

Another important samba singer from this era was Moreira da Silva (born in 1902), who sang sambas when not strolling the boulevards. He invented an original way of singing sambas: he would stop the song, dramatize the situation described in the lyrics or improvise dialogues during the break, then continue. It was called *samba de breque*. His most famous song in this style is "Acertei no Milhar," which tells the story of a man who dreams he won a fortune in a lottery and tells his wife all that they will do with the cash windfall. The tune was written by Wilson Batista and Geraldo Pereira, two noted samba composers from that era, and recorded by da Silva in 1938.

Moreira, who was still performing this song in his eighties, personified the lifestyle of the *malandro*, a type of hustler or layabout that was a romantic bohemian ideal for some in Rio in the thirties and forties. These malandros made their living exploiting women, playing small confidence tricks, gambling. They liked to dress fine, typically in a white suit and white hat, and were proud of their lifestyle. A great cinematic portrait of these characters may be seen in Ruy Guerra's *Ópera do Malandro*, a 1987 film musical based on Chico Buarque's stage play.

Ataulfo Alves.

SAMBA-CANÇÃO

In more respectable neighborhoods in Rio in the 1930s, a brilliant new generation of samba and marcha composers also came of age, most of whom were white. People like Noel Rosa, Braguinha, Lamartine Babo, Ary Barroso, and later, Dorival Caymmi, carried the samba flag on. But the samba they made emphasized the melody more than the rhythm, added more complex harmonies, and had more sophisticated lyrics—usually tied to sentimental themes. It was a cool, softened samba, later labeled *samba-canção*, and it popularized the genre with the middle class. The musicians wrote both Carnaval songs and middle-of-the-year compositions (as the non-Carnaval songs were known), and set the trend for Brazilian music until the advent of bossa nova in the late 1950s.

Noel Rosa

Noel Rosa was born in Rio and is so popular today that he has a statue on the main street of Vila Isabel, the Carioca neighborhood where he lived his short life. During his lifetime he was known only for Carnaval songs like "Com Que Roupa?," a great success in 1931. Rosa composed melodies that were sophisticated and harmonically rich, and also pioneered the use of colloquial language and social criticism. Noel died at an early age from tuberculosis but left more than 200 songs for posterity. Among them were masterpieces like "Último Desejo" (Last Desire), in which he lamented,

> Our love that I can't forget
> Began at the festival of St. John
> And died today without fireworks
> Without a photograph and without a message
> Without moonlight... without guitar
> Near you I'm silent
> Thinking everything, saying nothing....

Noel Rosa as pictured on one of his albums.

For some time Noel Rosa played guitar and sang with a group called Os Tangarás. One of the members of this group was Carlos Braga, a son of a rich man. Back then, being a popular musician was not considered honorable, so Carlos Braga invented another name for himself: João de Barro. Also called Braguinha (Little Braga), he soon would be one of the greatest Carnaval hitmakers, writing light-hearted and lively sambas and marchas whose lyrics featured well-humored and apt social criticism. Born in Vila Isabel, Braguinha composed classic songs such as "Touradas em Madrid," a hit in 1938's Carnaval and known in the U.S. through the recordings of Carmen Miranda, Dinah Shore, The Andrew Sisters, and Xavier Cugat.

Ary Barroso

Ary Barroso, another legendary composer of Carnaval marchas and samba-canção tunes, wrote one of the most famous Brazilian songs of all time: "Aquarela do Brasil" (Watercolor of Brazil), known to much of the world simply as "Brazil." Born in Ubá, Minas Gerais, in 1903, Ary studied classical piano as a youth and played for dance-hall orchestras after moving to Rio in 1920. From 1930 on, he was a successful composer of Carnaval hits and beautiful sambas known for their elaborate harmonies.

Ary wrote "Aquarela do Brasil" in 1939 and today it is one of the best known Brazilian songs in the world. With

Ary Barroso.

"Aquarela," Ary popularized a new subdivision in samba: *samba exaltação*: songs that praise the beauty and richness of Brazil:

> Brazil, Brazil
> For me, for me
> Oh! These murmuring fountains
> Where I quench my thirst
> And where the moon comes to play
> Oh! This brown and beautiful Brazil
> You are my Brazilian Brazil
> Land of samba and tamborins
> Brazil, Brazil, for me, for me.

Walt Disney heard the samba, liked it, and chose "Aquarela do Brasil" to be included in the animated film *Alô, Amigos*, which starred Zé Carioca, a Rio malandro in cartoon parrot form. Another Disney animated movie, *The Three Caballeros*, would include Barroso's "Bahia," a marvelous, languid reverie; "Os Quindins de Iaiá" (Iaiá's Coconut Candies), sung by Carmen's sister Aurora Miranda); and a rousing samba batucada. Ary also contributed the tune "Rio de Janeiro" to Disney's 1944 film *Brazil*, for which he received an Academy Award nomination.

"Aquarela do Brasil" would be remembered for years to come and would be used as the theme song for Terry Gilliam's 1985 black comedy *Brazil*. The song represented a vision of beauty and freedom to the protagonist, trapped in a futuristic, totalitarian society.

SOME STANDARDS FROM THE SAMBA-CANÇÃO TRADITION

Lamartine Babo (1904-1963): "Teu Cabelo Não Nega" (Your Hair Doesn't Deny It), "Eu Sonhei Que Tu Estavas Tão Linda" (I Dreamed You Were So Beautiful), "Moleque Indigesto" (Indigestible Urchin).

Ary Barroso (1903-64): "No Tabuleiro da Baiana" (On the Baiana's Tray), "Na Baixa do Sapateiro," "Inquietação" (Disquiet), "Folha Morta" (Dead Leaf), "Grau Dez" (Grade of Ten) with Babo.

Braguinha (1907-): "Chiquita Bacana," "Copacabana," "Yes! Nós Temos Bananas" (Yes! We Have Bananas), "Balancê" (Swing).

Dorival Caymmi (1914-): "Samba da Minha Terra" (Samba of My Land), "O Que É Que a Baiana Tem?" (What Is It the Baiana's Got?).

Noel Rosa (1910-1937): "Conversa de Botequim" (Bar Talk), "Três Apitos" (Three Whistles), "Palpite Infeliz" (Unfortunate Suggestion), "A-E-I-O-U" [with Babo].

SAMBA FROM THE MORRO

In the 1950s, samba-canção was diluted by contact with boleros, fox-trots, and chá-chá-chá. The musical quality declined and some dissatisfied young musicians, mostly middle-class, made their own revolution: bossa nova. But up on the *morros*, or hills, in the *favelas* where many of the poor people lived, the samba pioneered in Estácio had survived and continued its own evolution, while sticking to the traditional instruments of cavaquinho, pandeiro, and tamborim. At the time, this classic style of samba was labelled *samba de morro*, although today this term has fallen out of use.

In the late fifties, the samba from the morro was too strong a cultural manifestation to remain a neighborhood phenomenon. It invaded the rest of the city and then the entire country. Individuals like Cartola, Nelson Cavaquinho, Clementina de Jesus, Zé Keti, Elza Soares, Monsueto, Silas de Oliveira, and Mano Décio da Viola led the charge.

One of the great "samba de morro" figures of the time was the fiery composer Zé Keti (real name José Flores de Jesus, born in 1921), a writer of songs such as "A Voz do Morro" (Voice of the Morro) and "Opinião" (Opinion). He wrote both romantic songs, as well as outspoken sambas with melancholy and fatalistic lyrics. They denounced the sad poverty in which the majority of Brazilians seemed doomed to live, and lamented the fact that so many died needlessly. One such song was "Acender as Velas" (Light the Candles):

> When there's no samba
> There's disillusion
> It's one more heart
> That stopped beating
> One more angel that goes to heaven
> May God forgive me
> But I'll say it
> The doctor arrived too late
> Because on the morro
> There are no cars to drive
> No telephones to call
> No beauty to be seen
> And we die without wanting to die.

Cartola (Angenor de Oliveira, 1908-80) was another sambista identified with the fifties' term "samba de morro." Curiously, he was a veteran who in 1929 had co-founded the most traditional escola de samba in Rio: Estação Primeira de Mangueira. In the 1930s he composed many hit sambas, some with frequent partner Carlos Cachaça, such as "O Destino Não Quis" (Destiny Didn't Want It). His songs were acclaimed for their artful melodies and poignant lyrics.

In the early 1960s, he and his wife Zica ran a restaurant, Zicartola, where many of the leading lights of samba and bossa nova met and sang together. Cartola's career had a great resurgence in the early 1970s, when singers like Nara Leão, Gal Costa, and Beth Carvalho covered his songs and popularized them throughout Brazil. In 1973, when he was 65 years old, Cartola finally got a chance to record his first album, on the Marcus Pereira label. He is well remembered for the songs "O Sol Nascerá" (The Sun Will Rise), "Acontece" (It Happens), and "As Rosas não Falam" (Roses Don't Talk).

While samba-canção had ruled the Carioca airwaves, many great sambistas from the morros had composed and performed in relative obscurity. But in the late 1950s, the tide had turned. And as played by escolas de samba, which were then expanding into large and formidable institutions, the samba from the morro would develop a stronger and more elaborate rhythmic force and be presented in its most grandiose incarnation to date—with thousands of singers and dancers, and hundreds of drummers and percussionists.

CARNAVAL

From the days of "Pelo Telefone" onward, samba's development would be intimately tied to the popular festivity known as Carnaval, and samba in turn would transform Rio's Carnaval into one of the greatest popular festivals in the world. Indeed, the annual need for new songs to sing and parade to during Carnaval helped accelerate the development of samba and was the mother of much musical invention.

Carnaval is a pre-Lent celebration (Mardi Gras in New Orleans) that has its roots in festivities held by the ancient Greeks and others, such as the Bacchanalia in Rome. It was, and is, a time to make merry, to drink, dance, and be crazy. The normal social order is turned upside down and mocked, and anything goes.

Carnaval arrived in Brazil in the form of the Portuguese *entrudo*, in which celebrants would go to the streets and throw dirty water, flour balls, mud, and suspect liquids at each other, often triggering violent riots. In the mid-nineteenth century, masked Carnaval balls came into fashion, promoted by aristocratic organizations called *sociedades*. Waltzes and polkas were the music of choice. Also around that time, European-style parades were staged that included military bands, horses, and adorned floats. And revelers wearing cat masks, pigs' faces, and huge noses began to prowl the streets during Carnaval.

Jean-Baptiste Debret's drawing of an early Rio de Janeiro Carnaval street scene, with African-Brazilians parading as Europeans while playing such instruments as the reco-reco and the African kalimba.

A cartoon by Ângelo Agostinho depicting the death of the entrudo tradition as it was replaced by Carnaval.

Chiquinha Gonzaga, one of Brazil's greatest composers of popular music, in a nineteenth-century photograph.

In 1848 a young Portuguese man named José Nogueira Paredes walked around Rio beating a big bass drum, thus inaugurating the percussive tradition in Carnaval music. His lead was followed later by Zé Pereira drum-beating groups. Also around this time, Rio's poor people who couldn't afford tickets to expensive masked balls, and who were bored by the orderly parades, formed *cordões*, male-only groups that violently celebrated in the streets. The cordões often paraded to African-based rhythms, marking the beginning of the Afro-Brazilian contribution to Brazil's Carnaval.

In 1899, the cordão Rosa de Ouro (Gold Rose) asked composer Chiquinha Gonzaga (1847-1935) to write a song for their Carnaval parade. She composed a tune that incorporated a boisterous Afro-Brazilian rhythm that she had seen cordões parading to when they passed by her house. The song was "Ô Abre Alas" (Make Way), and it was the first registered marcha as well as the first song to be specifically composed for Carnaval. It was also an enormous popular success, having just what it takes to make a successful Carnaval song: a contagious rhythm and easy-to-memorize lyrics. "Hey, make way/ I want to pass/ I like parties/ I can't deny that."

Today, marcha (or marchinha) is a happy, festive style with lots of horns and drum rolls on the snares. It has a strong accent on the downbeat and typically short, simple, humorous lyrics. From the 1920s on, it would also incorporate horn arrangements and influences from ragtime and North American one-step. Marchas and sambas dominated the Carioca Carnaval from the 1920s to the 1950s, and marchas continue to be popular as Carnaval music today. A slower, more melodically developed variation, called *marcha-rancho* is still paraded to by the co-ed, more civilized cordões called *ranchos* that have been around since 1873. (Bassist John Patitucci used a marcha-rancho rhythm in his 1988 tune "The View.")

The Escolas

Since their beginning in 1928, the *escolas de samba* (samba schools) have been an integral part of Rio's Carnaval and have evolved into a grand spectacle, an overwhelming experience for both participants and observers. The parade of the escolas encompasses dazzling floats, outlandish costumes, thousands of dancers, and veritable symphony orchestras of rhythm. It is like a giant popular opera, one that can give you sensory overload. There is so much happening, musically and visually, that you can't possibly take it all in at once.

As mentioned earlier, the first escola de samba was called Deixa Falar (Let Them Talk), and it was founded on August 12, 1928 in Estácio by Ismael Silva, Bide, Armando Marçal, Nilton Bastos, and others. Apparently, its being called a "samba school" was an ironic reference to a grade school across the street from where Deixa Falar met. Escola means school, but as Noel Rosa sang, "Samba isn't something one learns at school." Deixa Falar was more like a club or fraternity, dedicated to making music and parading during Carnaval.

At the time, the police discouraged blacks and mulattos from celebrating downtown in *blocos*, which are groups of people that parade during Carnaval. This wasn't unusual, because the police were still repressing many manifestations of Afro-Brazilian culture at the time. Deixa Falar defied this repression by going out for a small parade in Estácio and Praça Onze, where a few blocos from other neighborhoods also appeared. Deixa Falar was short-lived: by 1933 it was defunct. But a seed had been planted.

In 1929, a second escola de samba was formed from the fusion of several blocos from the Mangueira neighborhood. It would become the most traditional and longest-lived of them all: Estação Primeira de Mangueira (Number-One Station of Mangueira). Famed composers Cartola and Carlos Cachaça were among its founders. And in 1935, Paulo da Portela (Paulo Benjamim de Oliveira), Heitor dos Prazeres, and others created Portela, which would become the most innovative of the escolas over the next few decades.

Also that year, the Brazilian government—in the form of the Getúlio Vargas administration—stopped discouraging Rio's escolas and officially recognized their parades. Consequently, the festivities moved from Praça Onze to a new home: the wide avenues of downtown Rio. Every year grandstands were assembled, attracting large audiences, generating big expenses, and creating (eventually) terrible traffic hazards. This problem was solved in 1984 with the building on Rua Marquês de Sapucaí of the Passarela do Samba (Samba Path), which Cariocas call the Sambódromo. Designed by acclaimed architect Oscar Niemeyer, it is a 700-meter pathway sided by concrete stands that seat 90,000 people. At its end is the huge, aptly named Praça da Apoteose (Apotheosis Square).

Glamorous women compose the comissão de frente in this escola's Carnaval parade.

Over the last few decades, the escolas have grown to become vital cultural institutions, and their importance stretches far beyond just staging parades. As of 1990, there were fifty-six officially registered escolas de samba in Rio de Janeiro and dozens more in other cities. Although some escolas in Rio are located in middle-class neighborhoods, many are in favelas or working-class areas, with mostly poor people as their members. For them, the escolas are a source of pride and in some cases the center of the community in which they are located. They are often social and recreational clubs; some sponsor schools and nurseries, and give medical assistance and other services to their members. The money for all this comes from spontaneous contributions from the rich (some of whom are engaged in questionable activities such as illegal lotteries and drug-dealing), as well as members' donations and income from dances, open rehearsals, record sales, and performances all over the world.

The 1990 version of the annual "Sambas de Enredo" album, a compilation of that year's Carnaval songs from the sixteen escolas in Group A. The LP often sells over a million copies.

The parade during Carnaval is only a ninety-minute climax, around which life in an escola de samba revolves the whole year. "The parade is the realization of people. They feel like kings for a day," says Hermínio Marques Dias Filho, director of the Arranco do Engenho de Dentro escola de samba.

Another reason for the passion Cariocas display toward their escola's presentation is that, unlike a lot of parades around the world, this one is a competitive event. Parade presentations are judged on a number of criteria, including music, theme, and costumes. The escolas parading at the Sambódromo vie to remain or become one of the sixteen samba schools showcased in the select "Group A," which is the focus of the media's attention. Each year, the two lowest scoring escolas are demoted to "Group B," while the two highest ranked "B" units are promoted, and they will parade with the top group the next Carnaval.

The Parade

Mounting an escola de samba parade is a vast undertaking that involves tens of thousands of people (musicians, dancers, craftsmen, costume-makers, and other contributors), but its basic format is always the same. Every escola's parade has a theme, the *enredo*. As a rule this theme has to be somewhat related to Brazil. It is chosen by the *carnavalesco*, a type of art director who is responsible for the visual aspect of the escola. After the enredo is approved by the board of directors, the carnavalesco writes a synopsis of it, describing the message he wants to visually convey in the parade. The next step is to distribute it among the escola composers for them to write sambas on the theme, which might be political, historical, or a tribute to a particular person. Such a samba is called a *samba-enredo*. This phase happens around June.

When the composers have their sambas ready, they submit them to the directors who choose the three best ones. Around September, rehearsals start in the escola headquarters. In these rehearsals, old popular sambas and the three applicant samba-enredos are played. On a certain night, usually at the end of October, the escola chooses the single winner.

It is a very special night. The escola de samba headquarters get overcrowded and the composers organize groups of rooters that dance and sing loudly, carrying flags adorned with the name of their favorite samba. The three applicant sambas are sung in sequence, and at the end of the evening the winner is announced by the president of the escola. The result is not always welcomed and sometimes it generates fights among members (perhaps understandably: the samba-enredo is important not only for a good parade but it also generates a lot of money for the winner). The samba-enredos from the escolas in Group A are included in an annual album that usually sells more than a million units.

For Carnaval in 1988, Mangueira's samba-enredo was "100 Anos de Liberdade: Realidade ou Ilusão" (100 Years of Freedom: Reality or Illusion"), commemorating the centennial of Brazil's abolition of slavery in 1888 and protesting the poverty of many blacks in the country. The lyrics, written by Hélio Turco, Jurandir, and Alvinho, asked,

> Today, in reality, where is freedom?
> Where is that which nobody has seen?
> Little boy, don't forget that the negro also built
> The riches of Brazil
> Ask the Creator who painted this watercolor
> Free of the plantation's whip
> Imprisoned in the misery of the favela.

Vila Isabel was another escola that explored Afro-Brazilian history that year with "Kizomba, Festa da Raça" (Kizomba, Festival of the Race), which sang of Zumbi (the famed leader of the Palmares quilombo), samba singer Clementina de Jesus, and other aspects of African-based culture. In contrast, other escolas in 1988 took themes like Brazil's deepening economic crisis, Rio's worsening urban problems, the magic of cinema, and the highly popular Trapalhões comedy troupe.

In any year, some samba-enredos are celebratory, others are serious protests or well-humored criticism, but all are meticulously and elaborately illustrated in the floats and costumes of each escola. By the time Carnaval comes round, most people in Rio know many of the songs by heart, having heard the year's samba-enredos on the radio or from the annual album (recorded and released before the parades).

After the picking of the samba-enredo, the energy expended in the preparations and in each rehearsal will build and build until the moment of explosion in the Carnaval parade.

By this time, the carnavalesco has already designed and ordered the making of the costumes for the *alas*—the units into which escolas de samba are divided in the parade. Each ala wears a different costume and plays a specific part in the development of the theme. A big escola like Mangueira has sixty-five alas with an average of eighty members each—that's about 5,200 participants. Most of the people in each ala have to buy their costumes from the escola, which many do through small monthly payments (some costumes are inexpensive; others are quite

An escola's ala das baianas parading in the Sambódromo.

Another escola's ala das baianas. This section is a required element in every samba school's parade.

elaborate and costly). Sometimes rich contributors pay for the outfits of poor but loyal escola members.

There are two alas that are mandatory: the *baianas*—older ladies dressed Bahian-style who wear turbans and broad, long-laced dresses (an ala introduced by Mangueira in the 1930s)—and the *comissão de frente* (front commission), generally comprised of the most important and/or honorable personalities of the escola. The latter open the parade and either walk solemnly or perform a simple, slow choreography.

Practically every Brazilian can dance to samba, but few master its specific steps. Those men and women who do are called *passistas*. The most important passistas in the escola are the *porta-bandeira* (flag-bearer) and the *mestre-sala* (master of ceremonies), characters that made their first appearances with the nineteenth-century sociedades. Dancing elegantly, the former, a woman, carries the escola flag. The mestre-sala, a man, gives her symbolic protection, dancing around her.

In between alas come the *carros alegóricos*—the huge decorated floats that depict important aspects of the enredo. These floats are true pieces of art, a mixture of sculpture, architecture, and engineering. On top of the carros alegóricos stand *destaques*—escola members wearing luxurious, expensive costumes as well as men and women wearing almost nothing. The making of the floats employs hundreds of people for at least six months. Seamstresses, sculptors, carpenters, smiths, and painters work like ants up to the last minute so that everything is ready for the February parade.

Each big escola has an average of 5,000 members who perform in its parade. To organize this many people, not all of them sober, is extremely complicated. That's what the *diretores de harmonia* (harmony directors) are for. They don't have fun. They just work. Hours before the escola actually enters the Sambódromo, the organizing of the parade starts in an outside area—the *concentração* (concentration). Harmony directors are in charge of putting the arriving ala members in their proper places and setting the alas in the right order to start parading.

Some time before the parade, the *puxador* in the sound float begins to sing the samba-enredo. The puxador—main singer—is responsible for keeping 5,000 voices in pace with the drum section, the bateria. He'll sing the same song for almost two hours and can not make mistakes. Slowly the members start singing together with him, stimulated by the harmony directors who also take care of keeping the energy high during the parade. After the whole escola has sung the samba two or three times without accompaniment, the most exciting moment in the parade preparation occurs: the musical entrance of the bateria. Anyone who has witnessed this moment will never forget it: more than 300 percussionists under the command of the *mestre de bateria* start playing perfectly in sync with the singing. The mestre's baton is a whistle. Blowing it, he controls the musicians.

The Bateria

According to Hermínio of the Arranco do Engenho do Dentro samba school, there are variations from escola to escola, but the following is the typical bateria line-up by instrument (see glossary for definitions) and number of musicians playing that instrument in an escola: surdo (30), caixa (40), repique (40), tamborim (70), pandeiro (15), prato (10), cuíca (20), frigideira (20), agogô (20), reco-reco (20), and chocalho (40).

With regard to the surdo, there are three types in escola baterias. The most important one is the *surdo de marcação* (marking surdo), also called the *surdão, surdo de primeira*, or *surdo maracanã*. It is the heaviest surdo, the one that plays on the second beat (of the 2/4 samba). The surdo de marcação holds the rhythm and is the base for the whole bateria.

The second largest surdo is the *surdo resposta* (answering surdo). As its name suggests, it answers the surdo de marcação by playing on the first beat, though less forcefully than the latter. The *surdo cortador* (cutting surdo) is the smallest surdo and it plays on the beats and off-beats, "cutting" the rhythm and adding syncopation. In small samba groups, the percussionist uses one surdo to play all three parts by himself—Airto Moreira provides an example of this technique on the samba-based song "Dreamland" on Joni Mitchell's album *Don Juan's Reckless Daughter*.

The conductor has a truly educated ear: during rehearsals he is able to spot one percussionist making a mistake among thirty playing the same instrument and a hundred playing others. He goes up to the erring musician and shouts instructions or tells him to stop and listen. And he must be able to keep all the percussionists synchronized during complicated *viradas* (changes in percussion

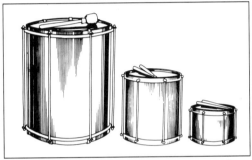

Three common Brazilian drums used in Carnaval parades: (l. to r.) surdo, repique, and caixa.

♩ = 126–132

Caixa	
Agogô	
Reco-reco	
Surdo cortador	
Surdo resposta	
Surdo marcação	

A basic samba as played by an escola bateria. The three surdos provide the rhythmic foundation. Additional instruments typically include tamborim, pandeiro, cuíca, repique, and frigideira.

patterns) and *paradinhas* (stops). In the latter, baterias stop playing during the parade so that everyone can hear other members carrying the rhythm only with their voices. Then the drums resume playing. This operation is the musical equivalent of stopping a jumbo jet's take-off at the end of a runway, and then getting it to take off again, but they do it.

A bateria percussionist is, together with the composers, passistas, destaques, baianas, and directors, part of the elite in an escola de samba. Recording artist/rock musician Lobão, who plays tamborim for Mangueira, says, "I took a test to enter, a very hard one. The technique is very sophisticated. You've got to be very precise with a tamborim. You play together with seventy others, but everybody's got to play at the same time. You've got to hear only one beat. If not, the effect is lost."

In the concentração, when the bateria starts playing, the energy level rises incredibly. As Lobão puts it, "The sound is twice as loud as a heavy metal band." Excitement takes over. Everything is ready for the parade.

Right before the gates open and the clock starts running, fireworks explode in the air. Then the comissão de frente steps into the Sambódromo greeting the people and asking permission to pass. One more parade has started.

The bateria enters the passarela following the first half of the escola. The jury's place is in the middle of the way, on the side where there is a space for the bateria. There, the drummers and percussionists play before the jurors, while the second half of the escola passes. The bateria then closes the parade, following the last ala. By this time the next escola is preparing to get in.

The jury gives grades from one to ten on the following items: theme, samba-enredo, harmony, comissão de frente, mestre-sala and porta-bandeira, costumes, evolution (dance performance of the escola), bateria, baianas, and carros alegóricos. The results are known on Ash Wednesday. The winner celebrates in its headquarters, stretching Carnaval for one more night.

One big escola parade may cost almost a million dollars. It seems absurd for poor people to spend so much money on something that lasts just ninety minutes. But what moves them is passion. Just like they are crazy about soccer, people in Rio love their escolas de samba. People don't say, "My favorite escola is Mangueira" or "I like Vila Isabel." People say, "I am Salgueiro" or "I am Portela." It's part of them. It's in their blood. It's in their souls.

Today there are escolas de samba not just in Rio de Janeiro, but also in São Paulo and many other Brazilian cities. A porta-bandeira from a Paulista escola told us, "Candomblé and escolas de samba are the twentieth century's quilombos" because they remain vital strongholds of Afro-Brazilian culture.

The Most Venerable Escolas

The Portela escola has been responsible for setting most of the patterns that the others have followed. Its founder, Paulo da Portela, and his associates introduced into the parade such now obligatory items as the enredo (theme), the comissão de frente and decorated floats. In addition, many famed composers/singers have been associated with Portela, including Zé Keti, Paulinho da Viola, Candeia, and João Nogueira. Nogueira and Paulo César Pinheiro eventually left to found the new samba school Tradição, while Paulinho and Candeia departed to create the escola Quilombo.

Paulinho da Viola, a major samba figure of the last three decades, left Portela because he felt that the escolas had become overly commercialized and bureaucratized, a common complaint in the 1970s and 1980s. Rio's samba parades are now of an enormous scale and a technical sophistication that would have been inconceivable in 1928 to the founders of Deixa Falar. They are also vital to Rio's tourist business and generate huge sums through broadcast, record, and video rights. Artists like Paulinho feel that something got lost along the way. "Nowadays commercial interests are more important than cultural ones," he observes. "What was spontaneous became official. An escola de samba now has an average of 5,000 members. You can imagine the fights there are to choose the suppliers for this number of people that will need shoes, costumes. That has attracted people to the escolas who don't belong to that cultural environment—people who only want self-promotion or only have economic interests." Today, Paulinho's Quilombo (founded in 1975) doesn't parade in the Sambódromo; instead, it goes out in the streets near its headquarters in Madureira.

Caetano Veloso on guitar and Paulinho da Viola strumming his cavaquinho.

Despite a few notable defections, venerable Portela and Mangueira continue to mount ever more ambitious and grandiose parades each year. Mangueira has attracted innumerable illustrious samba songwriters and singers over the years, including Cartola and Carlos Cachaça (two of its founders), Nelson Sargento, Nelson Cavaquinho, Elza Soares, Alcione, and Leci Brandão.

Another historically important escola, Império Serrano, is located in the neighborhood of Madureira (like Quilombo and Portela). Associated with Império were the important samba composers Silas de Oliveira (1916-1972) and Mano Décio da Viola (1908-1984). Both wrote long sambas with highly descriptive lyrics, a pattern followed by all escolas until the late sixties, when first Martinho da Vila and then other composers moved toward sambas featuring a faster, easier communication. Other important Império members are Ivone Lara, the first woman composer to have a samba-enredo sung by an escola during the parade, and singers Jorginho do Império (Mano's son) and Roberto Ribeiro.

In 1960, the escola Salgueiro hired Fernando Pamplona, the first outside professional designer to be a carnavelesco and design an escola's floats and costumes. His efforts focused around an homage to the

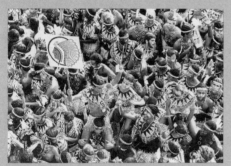
above-mentioned Zumbi of Palmares. It was the first time Zumbi had been so honored, and this enredo had a huge impact. From then on, the escolas would often delve deeply into African heritage for their themes.

Pamplona's participation was of large import in another way: from that point on, the samba school parades would become steadily more theatrical, grandiose, and expensive to stage. This was perhaps the reason for the growing interest of Brazil's TV networks in televising the event. From the 1960s on, the escola de samba parades have been broadcast live from start to finish.

At first, the samba schools received very little of the huge television profits: Riotur, the state tourism agency, had a lock on the ticket sales and TV rights income and handed out only a small percentage of the profits to the schools. Then in 1988 the major samba schools formed an association and demanded a new deal. They got it: forty percent of Sambódromo ticket sales and a one-million-dollar contract with TV Globo (of which Riotur got ten percent). The samba schools also formed their own record company to release the lucrative annual compilation album of samba-enredos from the top escolas.

The escola Beija-Flor is famed (and sometimes criticized) for its visually glittering and luxurious presentation. It has gone the farthest of any escola, creating ever wilder floats and costumes. Beija-Flora also has had talented singers—Neguinho da Beija-Flor, its puxador, has recorded several best-selling samba albums. Mocidade Independente, the champion of 1990, is famed for the perfection of its bateria, generally conceded to be the most precise and creative of any escola. One of its past conductors, Mestre André, was the inventor of the immensely difficult, aforementioned paradinha maneuver.

Today's escolas have a faster, more uniform batucada than the escolas of old, in large part because of time constraints. If an escola takes longer than ninety minutes for its parade, it loses precious points in the final judging. Before the events were so organized, the samba schools played slower, mellower, and more melodic samba-enredo. Nowadays they are faster, jumpier, and less musically differentiated. Still, there are clear differences between the escola's approaches. For example, all of Mangueira's surdos are surdos de marcação, the largest of the three types, and they play only on the second beat of each bar, without the other surdos playing on the first beat and off-beats. Salgueiro's heavier use of cuícas adds more flavor to the general sound and lessens the percussive impact. And Império Serrano's more extensive employment of agogôs gives its sound a more metallic texture.

Escolas de samba are home to many talented individuals, old and young, traditionalists and radicals. The ones examined here are just a sample of the creative power of the Carioca population that, in general, lives in very poor socio-economic conditions.

Aside from the escolas, there are other important Carnaval institutions in Rio. Dozens of clubs hold indoor Carnaval balls on the nights before Ash Wednesday. Live bands perform marcha standards from the 1930s and 1940s, as well as old and new samba hits.

Of course, Carnaval is celebrated not just in Rio, but all over Brazil. There are many hundreds of clubs throughout the country that entertain partiers with marchas, sambas, and other musical styles. Bahia and Recife have great Carnavals (some say the best in Brazil), as we shall discuss later in the book.

THE MODERN SAMBA ERA

Paulinho da Viola (born in 1942), whom we mentioned above, is someone whom music critic Sérgio Cabral considers, together with Martinho da Vila, "a legitimate heir of the Estácio sambistas," meaning that he follows in the footsteps of innovative composers such as Ismael Silva, Bide, and Marçal from the Estácio neighborhood, the "cradle of samba." Paulinho doesn't accept samba mixed with bolero or diluted with other pop currents, and he likes playing it with the traditional instruments: guitar, cavaquinho, pandeiro, tamborim. Said Paulinho to *Nova História da MPB*: "It seems absurd that I have attached myself to these formulas that are considered of the past, but I like them very much. To me the most important thing is the feeling, and this form of music moves me more."

Paulinho da Viola.

Paulinho combines modern arrangements and a subdued, elegant vocal style. His songs are especially known for his clear, clean lyrics that are full of feeling but avoid sentimentality. He has written such important songs as "Recado" (Message), written with Casquinha and a classic today; 1969's "Sinal Fechado" (Red Light), with which he won TV Record's music festival; and Portela's unofficial hymn "Foi Um Rio Que Passou em Minha Vida" (There Was a River That Passed Through My Life). Paulinho has also worked in the choro genre and

Clara Nunes, as pictured on a posthumous compilation album, released in 1989.

Beth Carvalho.

over the last three decades has firmly established himself as one of Brazil's leading singers and composers of popular music.

Clara Nunes (1943-83) was the best-selling samba vocal interpreter of the 1970s, her success propelled by an impassioned, sensual voice, beautiful looks, and a generally strong choice of material. Her big breakthrough came in 1974 with her "Alvorecer" (Dawn) record, the first LP by a female singer in Brazil to sell more than 500,000 units of one album. From then on, all of Clara's releases sold more than 400,000 copies each. She was also an international success who toured Europe and Japan. Her innumerable hit songs covered not only contemporary pop and samba tunes, but also old-guard compositions (by Ataulfo Alves, for example) and songs that explored her Afro-Brazilian heritage. "A Deusa dos Orixás," which delved into candomblé mythology, and "Ijexá (Filhos de Gandhi)," which paid tribute to the Filhos de Gandhi, an afoxé bloco from Salvador, are two examples.

Vocalist Beth Carvalho, who helped launch the pagode movement in the early 1980s, also has had a knack for picking the best work of Brazil's samba songwriters and exploring a variety of genres. A strong defender of Brazilian culture and human rights, Beth features richly rhythmic arrangements in almost all her selections and interprets them with a powerful, smoky voice.

Carvalho's 1987 release *Ao Vivo—Montreux Festival* (Live at the Montreux Festival) shows off her range. On the LP, she recorded the partido alto "Carro de Boi"; the samba de bloco "Cacique de Ramos"; two pagode sambas—"Da Melhor Qualidade" and "Pé de Vento"; "A Vovó Chica," a folkloric jongo; a pagode sendup of Jobim's bossa "Samba do Avião"; and an Edil Pacheco/Moraes Moreira afoxé "O Encanto do Gantois." The latter tune was a tribute to Mãe Menininha, the late "mãe de santo" (head priestess) of the venerable Gantois candomblé temple in Salvador.

Like Clara and Beth, the singer Alcione also covers a wide range of regional styles on her albums and can switch effortlessly between pop romantic ballads perfect for a dark boite nightclub and folkloric excursions that would make an ethnomusicologist leap for his or her tape recorder and notebook. With her robust, commanding voice, Alcione has had numerous hit albums since her first smash, the 1975 album *A Voz do Samba* (The Voice of Samba). Born in 1947 in São Luis, Maranhão, Alcione came to Rio when she was only twenty. But she adapted quickly and joined the Mangueira escola de samba by the early 1970s (she is now a member of its board of directors). Alcione has interpreted many types of samba on her albums, as well a wide variety of other urban and rural styles. An international star, Alcione has toured Europe several times, as well as Japan and the Soviet Union.

Alcione on her album *Ouro & Cobre* (Gold & Copper), released in the late eighties.

Martinho

In the Vila Isabel neighborhood, once the haunt of Noel Rosa, the most famous outstanding name these days is Martinho da Vila (real name Martinho José Ferreira), a singer-songwriter who was born on a Carnaval day in 1938 in Duas Barras, a small town in Rio de Janeiro state.

After Martinho joined the Vila Isabel escola de samba in 1965, he identified so much with it that he attached "Vila" to his name. "Carnaval de Ilusões" (Carnaval of Illusions), his first samba-enredo for the escola, was revolutionary. At that time these sambas had extremely long narrative lyrics and a subdued, mellow tempo. Martinho's 1967 samba, written with Gemeu, was based on *partido alto*, an old kind of samba which features short, light refrains that the singers must follow with improvised verses. Martinho added a narrative to that structure, an innovation that caused no little controversy. And he started a trend towards more concise and colloquial lyrics in samba-enredos.

In the 1970s, Martinho enjoyed enormous commercial success, commonly selling more than half a million copies of each album, and in the 1980s he remained a big pop star. His albums in that decade feature his relaxed, subtle, husky voice, which confidently works softly in and around the intricate, compelling rhythms played by his band. It is a rich sound, one that allows the listeners to savor all the

Martinho da Vila.

rhythmic and textural subtleties of the many song genres, folkloric and modern, that Martinho likes to explore.

Since 1987, Martinho has organized Kizomba, a festival of black heritage in Rio and a reflection of his special concern for African culture in general. And he wants to share his cultural blessings with all. In his song "Axé Prá Todo Mundo" (*axé* is a Yoruban word for "positive energy," "life force," or "peace") he sings: "I, a black Brazilian/ Desire this for all Brazil/ For all races, all creeds... Axé for everybody."

Pagode Samba

The 1970s were a very good decade for samba, commercially and artistically. Record sales for the genre soared and deserving artists like Martinho da Vila and Clara Nunes thrived. Also included in the success were many singers without strong cultural roots, who pleased the public with samba-based songs with romantic lyrics. Using this formula, Benito de Paula, Luis Airão, Agepê, and Wando cumulatively sold millions of albums. But more importantly, at the end of the 1970s, a group of composers who couldn't find an artistic outlet in the escolas de samba started holding meetings in a suburb called Ramos. There they had parties and sang their sambas.

As most of them rode buses, they couldn't carry big instruments, and soon the surdo was replaced by the *tan-tan* (a type of atabaque), which kept a steady beat underneath the patterns of the tamborim and ganzá. The cavaquinho's sound was too quiet for open-air gatherings, so some sambistas started playing the banjo. Their lyrics were unpretentious, focusing on situations from daily life. When recording companies discovered this movement they called it *pagode.*

For many people, "pagode" was not really anything new; it merely meant a party wherein people got together to play samba. But the instrumentation was slightly different, and the music being made was definitely rootsy, colloquial, and shorn of pop overproduction. Pagode samba found its way to the general public through Beth Carvalho. Her 1983 album *Beth Carvalho no Pagode* had songs by Ramos composers like Jorge Aragão, Zeca Pagodinho, and Almir Guineto. Soon these songwriters were contracted by recording companies and made albums under their own names, singing their own songs. Around 1985, their careers took off. They sold millions of records, opening the way for other pagode musicians like Jovelina Pérola Negra and Grupo Fundo de Quintal.

Bezerra da Silva

Also extremely popular in the 1980s was singer Bezerra da Silva, who interprets sambas that he calls "heavy partido alto." Born in Recife in 1937 (later moving to Rio), Bezerra comments, "The authors of the songs are humble people who live in the morros." They write about aspects of life on the morro such as the prejudice and victimization suffered by residents there. "In Copacabana, the police need an authorization to enter someone's house," continues Bezerra, "but on the morro, they enter without one, and rob, kill. Everyone thinks that those who live on the morro are all bandits. So these songwriters live there, and they write about the day-to-day reality of the morro."

Bezerra sings sambas whose lyrics often depict favela problems, police repression, and drug dealing, murders and thefts. In "Preconceito de Raça" (Racial Prejudice), written by G. Martins and Naval, Bezerra sings: "We're blacks from the morro/ But no one stole anything/ This is racial prejudice." And in "Bicho Feroz" (Wild Animal), written by Tonho and Cláudio Inspiração, Bezerra growls, "When you have a gun/ You are real mean/ Without it, your walk changes/ So does your voice." Dicró, another singer, runs on the same track as Bezerra da Silva and their type of samba has been labeled *sambandido* (roughly: bandit-samba) by critics. Both men sing lyrics that are a window into favela life, a sort of ghetto journalism, as are the words of the best rap songs in North America.

Important contributions to samba songwriting have also been made by many musicians who fall more into the bossa nova or MPB categories, such as Tom Jobim, Chico Buarque, and João Bosco (we will cover those three later).

THE SAMBA RESOLUTION

All the people mentioned in this chapter achieved fame for activities connected to samba. But they are just a drop in a samba ocean. In Brazil, millions of people make, sing, dance or just enjoy samba. Its importance in the maintenance of a relative social peace in Brazil is hard to measure, but it is clear.

One doesn't need to wait for Carnaval to see how samba brings people from all social classes and races together and keeps them in harmony. All you have to do is to go to downtown Rio on Friday during "happy hour" after work. The bars and sidewalks in the center of the city are full of secretaries, executives, office boys, bankers— all levels of professionals celebrating the oncoming weekend. They all drink, sing, and dance together. The party music is always samba.

After all, in Brazil everything sooner or later ends up in samba.

♩ = 92

Caixa	
Pandeiro	
Cuíca	
Surdo grave	

Samba partido alto.

Bezerra da Silva's album *Se não Fosse o Samba* (If It Weren't for Samba).

MUSICIANS IN FRONT OF BOTTLES BAR

BADEN POWELL

TIJUCA

ANTONIO CARLOS JOBIM

COPACABANA

LEBLON   IPANEMA

MIÚCHA, GETZ, GILBERTO

VINÍCIUS DE MORAES AND TOQUINHO

RIO DE JANEIRO

BOSSA NOVA: THE NEW WAY

CHAPTER 3

If you insist on classifying
My behavior as antimusical
I, even lying, must argue
That this is bossa nova
And that it's very natural
—*Tom Jobim/Newton Mendonça, "Desafinado"*

"Desafinado" (Off-Key), sung by João Gilberto with his very personal, intimate, whispering style, was an ironic reply to critics who had sarcastically called bossa nova "music for off-key singers."

This negative reaction had been occasioned by Gilberto's previous record, a landmark 78-RPM single with "Chega de Saudade" (written by Antonio Carlos "Tom" Jobim and Vinícius de Moraes) and "Bim-Bom" (by Gilberto himself), released in July, 1958. Much of the Brazilian public was intrigued by the two songs, but others were offended by their unconventional harmonies, the apparently strong influence of American jazz, and Gilberto's unusual vocals.

The prevailing singing style at that time was an operatic one; great loud voices were a must for successful crooners. Although singers like Johnny Alf, Dick Farney, and Lúcio Alves already had developed more introspective vocal styles, it was only with João Gilberto, the young man from Bahia, that people started noticing that something new was happening in the Brazilian music scene.

As for the criticism surrounding "Desafinado" when it was first released, Tom Jobim observes, "Actually it's not an off-key song. It's crooked on purpose. It's tilted. It could be a very square song, except for the endings of the musical phrases which go down unexpectedly. It's a criticism of experts. The guy next door, he's off-key but he's in love with this girl, and he can say that to her because loving is more important than being in tune. Some people are always in tune but they don't love anybody."

"Desafinado," released in November, 1958, became a defiant but good-humored anthem for the emerging Brazilian musical style of bossa nova, which was casual, subtle, and imbued with an infectious swing.

Rio de Janeiro's Copacabana beach at night. Nearby nightclubs and homes were the headquarters of bossa nova musicians.

Bossa would explode in popularity in 1959—in Brazil with the success of Gilberto's album *Chega de Saudade*, and internationally with the release of Marcel Camus' award-winning film *Orfeu Negro* (*Black Orpheus*), the soundtrack of which featured songs by Tom Jobim, Vinícius de Moraes, and Luiz Bonfá.

Bossa nova was a new type of samba in which the genre's rhythmic complexity had been pared down to its bare essentials, transformed into a different kind of beat. It was full of unusual harmonies and syncopations, all expressed with a sophisticated simplicity. Sometimes small combos performed bossa; but it was ideally suited to a lone singer and a guitar. This "new fashion" or "new way" (the approximate translation of "bossa nova") of singing, playing, and arranging songs was born in Rio de Janeiro in the mid-1950s.

Developed by Jobim, Gilberto, and their peers, bossa nova was "off-key" only in relation to the Brazilian (and international) pop music of the time. It had a harmonic richness previously heard only in classical music and modern jazz—for example, the unexpected melodic alterations of "Desafinado" included the use of the tritone interval (an augmented fourth), which many listeners found hard to accept in a pop song.

Speaking of Jobim in the book *Música Popular Brasileira*, keyboardist-arranger Eumir Deodato explained, "He managed for the first time to popularize songs with a harmonic form that was strange for people to hear—'Chega de Saudade' and principally 'Desafinado'—harmonically a very elaborate song."

The international success of bossa nova was the first large-scale global exposure of Brazilian music and musicians. Bossa achieved a huge success in North America in 1962 following the release of Stan Getz and Charlie Byrd's *Jazz Samba* album (which included tunes by Jobim, Bonfá, and Baden Powell). Subsequently, bossa-themed LPs were released by American jazz artists Herbie Mann, Paul Winter, and Coleman Hawkins, among others.

Pop and jazz listeners alike were entranced by the cool Brazilian swing and warm lyrical beauty of the "new way." Over the next three decades, bossa nova had a huge impact on jazz and international pop, as well as on the next generation of Brazilian composers. The genre provided many enduring tunes of remarkable lyricism, musical economy, and harmonic sophistication. One of its most famous hits would be "Garota de Ipanema" (The Girl from Ipanema), one of the best-known songs in the world in the late twentieth century.

BOSSA'S BEGINNINGS

Derived from samba, bossa nova had many musical antecedents, especially in progressive samba-canção tunes written by Noel Rosa, Ary Barroso, and Braguinha. Braguinha's tune "Copacabana," recorded in 1946 by Dick Farney (with arrangements by Radamés Gnatalli), was a suave and sophisticated piece that foreshadowed the bossa sound. And the guitarist Garoto (Aníbal Sardinha, 1915-55), who added altered and extended chords to sambas and choros, had a powerful influence on all bossa nova guitarists.

João Gilberto's 1959 album that launched bossa nova in Brazil.

Closer to the essence of the new style was the music of Johnny Alf, who was on the periphery of the bossa movement, but had a large impact on many of its composers. Alf (real name Alfredo José da Silva), was born in 1929 in Rio's Vila Isabel neighborhood. Heavily influenced by George Gershwin, Cole Porter, Claude Debussy, and bebop jazz, Alf could be heard by the early 1950s in clubs around town such as the Plaza. By then he was already using his sharp harmonic and melodic sense to shape Brazilian songs, notably Dorival Caymmi tunes, in a way that sounded avant-garde to Brazilian audiences accustomed to bolero and samba-canção. His singing was jazzy, with modulations, scatting, and mannerisms typical of bebop, while his piano attack was heavily syncopated. Alf's harmonies and playing style were listened to with avid interest by people like Jobim, Bonfá, Gilberto, and the aforementioned vocalist Dick Farney.

In 1953, Alf cut his first single, "Falsete" (Falsetto), and in 1955 he scored his first hit with the single "Rapaz de Bem" (Nice Guy), which featured new harmonic conceptions and casual-sounding lyrics, and clearly showed Alf prefiguring the bossa nova style.

As the musicians that would form the new movement were getting together in the late 1950s, Alf received an invitation to work in São Paulo. Bad timing, but the money was good and Alf left town for several years. While away, he cut his first album, *Rapaz de Bem*,

Stan Getz and João Gilberto's earlier collaboration *Getz/Gilberto* marked the climax of the bossa invasion of North America. Here the two musicians are pictured with Miúcha, João's second wife, on their 1976 album.

an instrumental work with a trio. He moved back to Rio in 1962, by which time the bossa nova boom had already peaked. He had a big hit song "Eu e a Brisa" (Me and the Breeze) in 1967 but never really received the public attention he deserved.

Two others that helped pave the road to bossa were pianist João Donato and guitarist Luiz Bonfá. (João Gilberto credited both of them as important influences on his innovative guitar sound.) Bonfá (born in 1922) wrote songs that foreshadowed the bossa style—"Perdido de Amor" (Desperately in Love), a hit for Dick Farney in 1951, and the mid-1950s tunes he wrote with Jobim: "Engano" (Mistake), "Domingo Sincopado" (Syncopated Sunday), "A Chuva Caiu" (The Rain Fell), and others.

João Donato (born in 1934 in Rio Branco, Acre) developed a percussive, harmonically adventurous playing style that struck many listeners as decidedly weird. His chords seemed crooked, dissonant, even as his rhythmic sense was secure and precise. Donato's sound had points in common with Thelonious Monk's piano playing, and he took a decidedly jazz-influenced approach to Brazilian tunes. He and João Gilberto became good friends and wrote a song together titled "Minha Saudade" (My Saudade). But in the late 1950s, as bossa nova was about to take over, Donato's oblique piano playing was still not welcome in night clubs—people said he "disorganized the rhythm." Donato went on a tour to Mexico with vocalist Elizeth Cardoso, then moved to California where he lived for thirteen years. But he was not forgotten by those who would gain wide-reaching fame from bossa.

Antonio Carlos Jobim, the most accomplished songwriter of the group, would also cite modern classical music, including Brazil's twentieth-century composer Heitor Villa-Lobos, as a major influence on his work. But Jobim hastens to emphasize that "I had those new harmonies coming from me only. I was always revolting against the establishment, against normal harmonies. It was a very personal thing. Sure I heard Debussy and Ravel, but they didn't have this African beat we have here."

Other bossa composers would draw more from "West Coast" cool jazz, a smooth, relaxed, restrained style of the 1950s that incorporated the melodic and harmonic advances of the bebop movement. For example, Carlos Lyra and Roberto Menescal, who had been exchanging musical ideas since high school, formed a guitar academy in Copacabana that experimented with harmonies influenced by the music of cool-jazz players Gerry Mulligan, Chet Baker, and Shorty Rogers. The academy became a meeting point for future bossa musicians like Nara Leão,

Guitarist/composer Luiz Bonfá's 1970 RCA release.

A basic bossa nova rhythm pattern.

Marcos Valle, Edu Lobo, and Ronaldo Bôscoli. Eventually, the musical careers of Lyra and Menescal overshadowed their music-school efforts, and both became professional performers. So did their students.

These musicians, along with Jobim, Gilberto, and others, absorbed the rich musical currents flowing through Brazil at the time (samba-canção, jazz, Villa-Lobos) and drew from them to create an economical and colloquial new style of popular music.

The rhythm usually came from samba, but on occasion other styles such as baião, bolero, and marcha were used and transformed by the bossa sensibility. Harmonically, bossa nova tunes often included altered chords, inverted chords, and unusual harmonic progressions, along with unexpected melodic leaps and tonal shifts. Yet, as the bossa songwriters applied complex chords, they were also taking out extraneous notes. The net effect was elegant and subtle, deceptively simple and low-key.

This new musical vanguard would find a spiritual and professional center in Rio de Janeiro's most famous neighborhood: Copacabana.

A Cozy Corner and a Guitar

In Copacabana in the mid- to late fifties lived the more sophisticated Carioca middle class, which had a taste for jazz, American movies, and other culture from abroad. They often frequented three hip little Copacabana nightclubs that were squeezed into a narrow sidestreet nicknamed the Beco das Garrafas (Bottles Lane).

Why was it called Bottles Lane? Because Copacabana is a long, narrow strip of tall buildings squeezed between the ocean and the mountains, and sound has only one way to go: up. And a lot of sound did drift up from the Beco das Garrafas, especially since there were often more people milling around outside the small clubs than there were inside. So sometimes people from adjacent buildings, fed up with the late-night carousing and frequent fighting going on in the small lane, would throw bottles down on the noisemakers instead of calling the police.

In these three small clubs (one was called Beco das Garrafas, the other two the Little Club and Bacará) met the musicians who would make up the core of the bossa movement. They had their own slang and code of behavior, and a way of making music that was absolutely unknown outside of Copacabana. Their informal shows sparkled with creativity and lots of improvisation. And they often stayed up all night playing for each other at their homes.

"We did the music because we liked to, nobody was trying to create a movement," recalled guitarist-composer Oscar Castro-Neves. "We just made music and showed it to our friends. We used to go to Jobim's house and we'd leave the place with a fever, because we'd get so excited by the harmonies and everything else."

Nara Leão (1942-1989) was both a muse to the movement and host of guitar sessions that lasted until dawn. Her parents' apartment on Avenida Atlântica, the avenue that runs along Copacabana Beach,

Musicians posing in front of Bottles Bar in Rio in 1962. Standing from the left are Herbie Mann, Kenny Dorham, and a young Sérgio Mendes (clutching an album).

Herbie Mann waiting to take his turn with the flute while two-thirds of the Tamba Trio play: Bebeto on flute and Hélcio Milito on drums. Sebastião Neto mans the bass. The packed crowd of young listeners attests to bossa's hold on that generation in the early sixties.

was a second home to many of her musical friends. A singer with a cool, gentle style, Nara would interpret many of these musicians' bossa classics on disk.

Among those performing and communing in the Beco das Garrafas were Lyra, Jobim, Menescal, Durval Ferreira, Luis Eça, Baden Powell, Sérgio Mendes (he of later fame in the United States), and many others. One of the most dedicated participants was the poet, former diplomat, and bon vivant Vinícius de Moraes, who would become the most prolific if not the most important bossa lyricist. He and his friend Antonio Maria (journalist and lyricist) would stay in these bars until the very last song and then, after many doses of what Vinícius called "bottled dog" (whisky—man's best friend), they would go to the beach and watch the sunrise.

It was a fast-lane life that these bohemians led: getting home with the sun high in the sky, waking up in the late afternoon, lots of drinking and smoking. Their mood reflected that of an optimistic Brazilian middle class in the 1950s, especially those who lived in Rio. The future was bright.

At that time, the country had a popular and democratically elected president, Juscelino Kubitschek, and he was building the new federal capital—the architecturally daring and futuristic city of Brasília—on the high plains of Goiás state. Kubitschek's motto was "fifty years of development in five."

Everyone thought Brazil would finally shed its role as eternal country of the future and become a developed nation. Everything pointed in this direction. The national soccer team won the World Cup for the first time in 1958, a source of great pride to a soccer-crazed country. Renowned architect Oscar Niemeyer was creating his most famous buildings, including those in Brasília. The movie industry's Cinema Novo movement was emerging. In every field—painting, theater, literature— the late 1950s and early 1960s were a time of effervescence. It was the perfect environment for the advent of this fresh new form of music called bossa nova.

Bossa's lyrics reflected all of this. Most of the words were down-to-earth and depicted daily-life situations, using a casual tone to talk about the urban environment in which the authors lived. In "Desafinado" Newton Mendonça mentions a Rolliflex camera as naturally as if he were talking about his guitar. As most bossa musicians lived in Rio's Zona

Sul (South Zone)—the beach area—their themes, mainly in the beginning, were related to nature and love. They sang of waves, sailboats, flowers, blue skies, and, most of all, women. Music-making itself was also celebrated, as in Jobim's "Corcovado": "A cozy corner and a guitar/ This is a song to make the one you love happy."

Lyrics in bossa nova were used not only for their meanings, but also for their musical sounds. Ronaldo Bôscoli wrote the words for a Roberto Menescal song called "Rio" in which short words with similar sonorities are used to evoke Rio de Janeiro on a hot summer day: "É sal, é sol, é sul" (It's salt, it's sun, it's South). In many bossa songs, especially in the music of João Gilberto, such elemental lyrics and how they were sung were not meant to stand out. Rather, they were intended to blend into the music and serve as part of a whole. Harmony was essential, and few understood this as well as Antonio Carlos Jobim.

Jobim

Antonio Carlos (Tom) Jobim was born in Rio de Janeiro on January 25, 1927 in a neighborhood called Tijuca. When he was one year old, his family moved to his beloved Ipanema, where he grew up running in the dunes, swimming, playing soccer in the sandy, unpaved streets, and contemplating the birds, trees, dolphins, and other aspects of nature that were much more abundant in Rio in the 1930s. When Jobim was fourteen, his stepfather bought a piano for Tom's sister Helena; it wasn't long before Tom himself was playing it. His stepfather found him a piano teacher: Hans Joachim Koellreuter (born in 1915), a German who had come to Brazil escaping from World War II. Koellreuter had studied at the Berlin State Academy of Music and was an advocate of the twelve-tone system of Arnold Schoenberg. An excellent music professor, Koellreuter influenced a whole generation of avant-garde Brazilian pianists.

Tom also studied with music teachers Lúcia Branco and Tomas Teran, but his love for music became a passion when he discovered the works of the Brazilian composer Villa-Lobos, who had written masterpieces such as the "Bachianas Brasileiras," which merged baroque forms with Brazilian folk-music elements, and whose compositions still sound fresh and radical many decades later.

At the time, young Jobim didn't consider becoming a professional musician: he wanted to be an architect. He found a job in an architect's office but was soon disappointed with it. Tom had to go downtown every day

Antonio Carlos Jobim in the 1980s.

A SAMPLER OF JOBIM STANDARDS

TOM JOBIM: "Triste" (Sad); "Luiza"; "Ela É Carioca" (She's a Carioca); "Samba do Avião" (Samba of the Jet); "Corcovado" (English title: Quiet Nights of Quiet Stars); "Vivo Sonhando" (I Live Dreaming; English title: Dreamer); "Wave"; "Águas de Março" (Waters of March)

A re-release of a 1960s Jobim album. Arranger Nelson Riddle was just one of many prominent U.S. musicians with whom Jobim collaborated.

TOM AND VINÍCIUS: "Garota de Ipanema" (The Girl from Ipanema); "Por Toda Minha Vida" (For All My Life); "Água de Beber" (Water to Drink); "Só Danço Samba" (I Only Dance Samba); "Insensatez" (Foolishness; English title: How Insensitive); "O Grande Amor" (The Great Love); "Chega de Saudade (Enough of Saudade; English title: No More Blues); "A Felicidade" (Happiness)

TOM AND ALOYSIO DE OLIVEIRA: "Dindi"; "Inútil Paisagem" (Useless Landscape); "Demais" (Too Much)

TOM AND NEWTON MENDONÇA: "Desafinado" (Off-Key); "Samba de Uma Nota Só" (One Note Samba); "Meditação" (Meditation)

wearing a suit and a tie, and always came back home with the sensation of time lost.

Jobim decided to dedicate his life to music. He studied a lot—theory, harmony—but never forgot popular music. He recalled, "I could write a piece using the twelve-tone scale, but Brazil, with all its rhythms, was more important. I liked Pixinguinha, Donga, Vadico, Ary Barroso."

Tom started playing in nightclubs around 1950, but he was married already and money was really short. Things only started to get better when he found a job at the Continental record company in 1952, where he transcribed songs for composers who couldn't write music. The next year he landed a job as artistic director for the Odeon label (now owned by EMI). Meanwhile, he was writing songs with Newton Mendonça (1927-1960), an old beach friend and very good pianist. During the next several years, the two composed tunes like "Desafinado" and "Samba de Uma Nota Só" (One-Note Samba).

In 1954 Tom began his career as an arranger, and in the next few years arranged records by Dick Farney, Os Cariocas, and Elizeth Cardoso. He also started collaborating with another partner: Billy Blanco. The pair composed "Teresa da Praia" (Teresa of the Beach) and the symphonic ten-inch album *Sinfonia do Rio de Janeiro—Sinfonia Popular em Tempo de Samba*. The latter included vocals by the likes of Farney, Cardoso, Os Cariocas, Lúcio Alves, and others in tune with the nascent bossa style.

Tom was developing his own innovations with regard to Brazilian popular music, adding new twists to the venerable samba. He was not a great instrumentalist, like Bonfá or Powell, or a charismatic singer like

Lyra or Gilberto. But as a composer he was unique, and his songwriting would make him the most famous Brazilian musical figure of his time.

By the mid-1950s, Tom had garnered a great deal of prestige in the Brazilian music scene. He had a TV show in São Paulo called "Bom Tom" (a pun that means "nice Tom" and at the same time "good taste"). He was writing songs with Mendonça, Blanco, and—by this time—Bonfá, revitalizing the samba-canção. Then in 1956 Tom met a brilliant and fast-living poet who would be his most important songwriting partner.

Vinícius

Vinícius de Moraes (1913-80) was a link between great samba-canção lyricists epitomized by Noel Rosa and the young MPB wordsmiths— Chico Buarque, Aldir Blanc, and Caetano Veloso. His prodigious output included lyrics for more than 200 songs, most of which demonstrated a powerful sense of rhythm, sound, rhyme, economy, and metaphor. Vinícius' lyrics, like those of his bossa contemporaries, often centered on elemental themes, especially that of love, but with a subtlety and profundity that usually eludes translation.

Before becoming a famed bossa lyricist, Vinícius had already established a place for himself in Brazilian literature, having published several books of acclaimed poetry. His poems had evolved from an earlier formalism—his first book was published in 1933—to a very personal approach in which he brought the eternal, the cosmic, the inexplicable into the reality of daily life.

He wrote his first song lyrics in 1932 for a fox-trot called "Loura ou Morena" (Blonde or Brunette), composed with Haroldo Tapajós. But that didn't start a musical career. After penning two songs in 1933 that were recorded by RCA, Vinícius took a hiatus from lyric-writing until 1952.

During his nineteen-year sabbatical from music, he graduated from law school, studied English poetry at Oxford, and then became a diplomat. He was posted in Los Angeles between 1946 and 1950 and became vice-consul at the Brazilian consulate there. Once he returned to Rio, Vinícius plunged into night life again, and composed his first samba, "Quando Tu Passas por Mim" (When You Pass by Me).

But Vinícius was surviving mainly on the small amount of money he earned as a journalist, and asked for another diplomatic position abroad. He was lucky: he was assigned to Paris in 1953. There he met Sacha Gordine to whom he sold a story for a film: *Orfeu da Conceição*. Back in Brazil, Vinícius decided, while the French producer was having problems raising the money for the film, to stage the story as a play. So he started looking for a composer to write the music. Then he remembered a young musician he had seen perform once in a nightclub called Clube da Chave: Tom Jobim.

Vinícius de Moraes (left), Toquinho, a frequent singing/composing partner, on the stool (right). The photograph was taken in the 1970s.

Bossa nova was arguably born in 1956, the year that Jobim and Vinícius met and collaborated on music for the play *Orfeu da Conceição*," as well as the song "Chega de Saudade" (which in English picked up the title "No More Blues"). On the liner notes for the Paul Winter album *Rio*, Vinícius wrote about Jobim and those times: "I did not know I was giving this young composer from Ipanema a signal to begin a new movement in Brazilian music. About the same time, by a kind of telepathy, other young Brazilian composers like Carlos Lyra, Roberto Menescal, and Oscar Castro-Neves were beginning to compose in a similar style."

The play, with sets by Oscar Niemeyer, transplanted the Greek myth of Orpheus and Eurydice into the favelas and Carnaval of modern-day Rio. Staged in 1956, *Orfeu da Conceição* and its accompanying record (released the next year) were big hits, with Jobim-de Moraes songs that are now classics, like "Se Todos Fossem Iguais a Você" (If Everyone Were Like You) and "Eu e o Amor" (Me and Love).

In 1957, the French producer Sacha Gordine and director Marcel Camus finally came to Rio to make the *Orfeu da Conceição* movie. Gordine wanted original music for the French-Brazilian production, to be retitled *Orfeu Negro*. Jobim and Moraes penned new tunes, including the sweetly melancholy "A Felicidade" (Happiness): "Sadness has no end, but happiness does/ Happiness is like a feather the wind carries into the air/ It flies so lightly, yet has such a brief life."

Also contributing songs to the film was Luiz Bonfá, who added the two now-classic tunes "Samba de Orfeu" (Orpheus' Samba) and— with Antonio Maria—the lovely "Manhã de Carnaval" (Morning of the Carnaval). Such songs were, like Tom and Vinícius' contributions, essentially "early bossa nova," full of the warm intimacy and rich simplicity that would characterize the genre.

Then in 1958 the songs of Tom and Vinícius met the guitar and voice of João Gilberto, and the bossa nova style crystallized.

João Gilberto

Vocalist Elizeth Cardoso's 1958 LP *Canção do Amor Demais* (Song for an Excessive Love) featured Gilberto's new style of guitar-playing, Jobim-de Moraes' tunes, and Jobim's arrangements. Tom recalled, "We were developing our style. You can see it very clearly in this album."

Gilberto's arrival on the scene opened new perspectives with "the rhythm that he brought," according to Jobim in *Música Popular Brasileira*. The harmonic and melodic part of the bossa equation was already established, but "on the album of Elizeth Cardoso appeared for the first time the beat of bossa nova on the guitar played by João. That album constituted a boundary mark, a fission point, a break with the past."

Born in 1932 in Joazeiro, a small city in the interior of Bahia state, João Gilberto was known as the "pope" of bossa nova. Jobim wrote on the *Chega de Saudade* album that "bossa nova is serene, it has love and romance, but it is restless." These characteristics perfectly describe

João Gilberto's artistic personality. His singing and playing seem natural now that they've been incorporated into the repertoire of world music, but back in the fifties it was simply original, something new.

Gilberto's highly syncopated style of plucking acoustic guitar chords—nicknamed "violão gago" (stammering guitar) by some—introduced a type of rhythm that resembled a cooled and slowed samba, but was very difficult to play. "He was the only one who could do that beat at first," said Brazilian music critic Zuza Homem de Mello. "After time others could, too."

According to Oscar Castro-Neves, Gilberto's guitar style was "a decantation of the main elements of what samba was, which made bossa nova more palatable for foreigners and the rhythm more easily perceived. He imitated a whole (samba) ensemble, with his thumb doing the bass drum and his fingers doing the tambourines and ganzás and agogôs. The rhythm was right there with his voice and guitar alone. You didn't feel anything was missing."

João Gilberto at the Roxy in Los Angeles in 1977.

João's singing was new, too. Both voice and guitar were simultaneously melodic and highly rhythmic, as he syncopated sung notes against guitar motifs. "The way he phrases is incredible," said Castro-Neves. "The guitar would keep the tempo going and he would phrase in a way that was completely free, atop that pulsating rhythm. The way his phrases would fall—he would delay a chord here, put a note there—was very hypnotic.

"And he had a blend between the volume of his voice and the volume of the guitar. He could emphasize a note in the vocal and it would be like completing a chord on the guitar. Suddenly the voice really complemented the harmonic structure of the chord."

Gilberto sang quietly, subtly, with a low-pitched, smooth, precise voice without vibrato, as if whispering an extremely intimate secret only for the listener. (Miles Davis was quoted as saying that Gilberto "would sound good reading a newspaper.") In the book *Balanço da Bossa*, Augusto de Campos told how Tom Jobim took João Gilberto one day to a studio so that some recording industry bosses could hear him sing. After João finished singing...silence. Nobody knew what to say. After some time, one of the guys murmured to the one next to him, "Tom said he'd bring us a singer but ended up bringing a ventriloquist."

Gilberto's style was anti-show business, cozy and conversational, and the music business executives didn't understand it—yet.

THE BOSSA BOOM

Fortunately, Jobim had connections at the Odeon label, where he had once worked. The artistic director there, Aloysio de Oliveira, was the ex-leader of the Bando da Lua, which had backed Carmen Miranda in the United States in the 1940s. Through Oliveira's efforts, Odeon agreed to release Gilberto's first single, "Chega de Saudade" (the Jobim-de Moraes song written two years earlier), which most historians consider the first recorded bossa nova song. The arrangements were Tom's and the critical reaction was to a large extent highly negative. But the record sold well enough that Odeon decided to let João record an album.

In 1959 came the *Chega de Saudade* LP, arranged by Jobim and produced by de Oliveira. The record put the movement on track and is considered the first bossa nova album. Besides the title track, the LP included "Desafinado" and other tunes by Tom and Vinícius, two Ary Barroso classics, and three Carlos Lyra songs.

This radical and romantic new sound was a huge success, and during the next four years its beat took over the country. Bossa artists Lyra, Leão, Menescal, Sérgio Mendes, Baden Powell, and many others all came into the spotlight. After *Chega de Saudade*, Gilberto recorded two more very successful albums:

A still from the film *Black Orpheus*, with the stars Bruno Mello (Orpheus) and Marpessa Dawn (Eurydice).

O Amor, O Sorriso e a Flor (Love, Smile, and Flower) in 1960 and *João Gilberto* in 1961. These albums included both new bossa tunes and bossa interpretations of old standards by composers like Dorival Caymmi and the sambistas Bide and Marçal.

Also in 1959, the movie *Orfeu Negro* was released, putting bossa nova on the world musical map. Shot in Rio the previous year, mostly in the hills overlooking the city, it was beautifully photographed and filled with the vivid colors, sounds, and excitement of Rio and Carnaval. The extraordinary Jobim-de Moraes-Bonfá soundtrack featured vocals by Agostinho dos Santos and Elizeth Cardoso, guitar parts from Bonfá and Gilberto, and healthy doses of heavily percussive samba and macumba ritual music.

The movie won the grand prize at the Cannes Film Festival that year. Its theme song, Bonfá's "Manhã de Carnaval," was a worldwide smash hit, was covered by countless musicians, and sold (cumulatively) millions of copies. The film's music inspired critical adjectives such as "joyous," "rapturous," "unforgettable." Bonfá and Jobim became internationally famous.

Baden Powell

Another great Brazilian guitarist who became well known during the bossa nova era was Baden Powell de Aquino, called simply Baden Powell. Born in 1937 in Varre-e-Sai, a small town in Rio de Janeiro state, Baden demonstrated a technical mastery of the guitar and a singular capacity to mix Afro-Brazilian influences with jazz and classical elements. When he performs, Powell weaves a hypnotic spell with his guitar, with which he can produce sounds as soft and melodious as a mother singing a lullaby or as swinging and percussive as any drummer.

Commented Castro-Neves, "Baden is a monstrously influential guitar player, a marriage of a great performer and player. Very charismatic on stage. Baden was influenced by jazz, but filtered it through his Brazilian soul. His solos are very Brazilian, with definitely Brazilian phrasing. And he has fast fingers, the chops, to go with it. The way he does rhythm is personal, such as the way he plucks the strings in fast succession. He was extremely influential."

Baden entered the bossa nova scene at a young age. He was twenty-two when he co-wrote "Samba Triste" (Sad Samba) with Billy Blanco in 1959 and over the next two years appeared as a session guitarist on many bossa albums. In 1962, he began writing songs with Vinícius de Moraes. On many occasions, often for days on end, the two would hole up in Vinícius' apartment in Copacabana.

Baden and Vinícius composed more than fifty songs together. Some were bossas and some were afro-sambas (sambas enriched with other Afro-Brazilian elements). While Baden was mulatto, Vinícius was white but identified strongly with Afro-Brazilian culture. He was a son of Xangô in the candomblé religion and jokingly referred to himself as "the blackest white man in Brazil." The pair researched Afro-Brazilian music from Bahia, especially that played in candomblé sessions, and used it to create afro-sambas. "Berimbau," for example, was named after the musical bow used to accompany the capoeira ritual (Baden plays the berimbau's rhythmic part on the guitar). Another was "Canto de Ossanha," a song for the orixá Ossanha. It begins with a simple brooding bass-note riff on the guitar, that is accompanied by muted plucked guitar patterns and soft percussion, and builds steadily until the song explodes into a joyful upbeat guitar-percussion celebration. Many of their best numbers in this vein were gathered together for their 1966 album *Os Afro-Sambas*.

Baden-Vinícius tunes usually featured beautiful melodic themes which Powell would imaginatively elaborate on the acoustic guitar. Their song "Samba da Benção" (Blessing Samba) was included in the famous 1966 Claude Lelouch movie *Un Homme et Une Femme* (A Man and a Woman). Sang Vinícius in that tune: "To make a beautiful samba, you need a dose of sadness/ You need a dose of sadness, otherwise it's not a samba."

Baden Powell, from a photograph on his 1974 *Estudos* album jacket.

Once they split up, Vinícius went on to team with guitarist Toquinho, and Baden moved to Europe. In the 1970s and 1980s, Powell released many acclaimed albums there, as a solo artist and sometimes in the company of jazz artists such as violinist Stephane Grappelli.

Bossa Nova Criticism

Of course, musicians and singers that had nothing to do with the movement also wanted to sing or write bossa nova songs. The term "bossa nova" turned into an adjective for everything modern, surprising. There were bossa nova girls, a bossa nova president, as Kubitschek was called, and even bossa nova cars. There was also a lot of bossa nova criticism.

Many Brazilian music critics, including the respected José Ramos Tinhorão, blasted bossa nova as being little more than an imitation of American cool jazz. But Tom Jobim, for one, hotly retorted that "flat fives and sharp nines are not the exclusive domain of jazz composers, Bach also used them."

Indeed, both bossa and jazz songwriters drew from twentieth-century classical music: Claude Debussy and Maurice Ravel influenced musicians from Bix Beiderbecke to Django Reinhardt, and Bela Bartok and Igor Stravinsky had a strong effect on jazz improvisers in the 1940s and thereafter. Tracing harmonic lineage in either bossa or jazz is not an easy task, even though both drew from common sources. But bossa nova, putting many musical elements together in an original way, was something new, something definitely Brazilian, and soon had a powerful effect on American jazz and pop.

Added Jobim in *Música Popular Brasileira*, "Many people said that bossa nova was an Americanized phenomenon. I think this is entirely false. Much to the contrary, I think what influenced American music was the bossa nova. I received letters and telegrams from various illustrious composers . . . saying that bossa nova had been the biggest influence on American music in the last thirty years . . . . The bossa nova was an influence that is still happening today, influencing the music of the world."

THE NORTH AMERICAN INVASION

The seeds for the new genre's invasion of North America were being sown at the start of the 1960s, when American jazz musicians Charlie Byrd, Herbie Mann, Kenny Dorham, Roy Eldridge, Coleman Hawkins, Zoot Sims, Paul Winter, and others were touring Brazil (some in connection with a State Department-sponsored visit) and being exposed to the new sound. John Coltrane had previously cut a jazz-samba cover of Ary Barroso's "Bahia" (in 1958) and Capitol had released *Brazil's Brilliant João Gilberto* in 1961, but the American public was not yet ready to bite.

When Charlie Byrd returned from Brazil, he brought back with him a João Gilberto record and played it for his friend, the saxophonist Stan Getz. Charlie had a natural affinity for the style in part because "I had been studying the classical guitar for about ten years and playing with my fingers, which is the way the Brazilians play it. And it's the way you can play those rhythms much more authentically than you can with a pick." And at that time, recalled Byrd, "there were no jazz guitarists but me who played that way."

Byrd loved the melodies of bossa nova. In the ingredients of what became bossa, he noted, "you can't discount the strength of the tunes by Jobim, Gilberto, Menescal. It was very strong material, a key factor in making things happen. And I've said it before—I think Jobim is the most significant writer of popular music in the second half of the twentieth century. He is one hell of a songwriter, and he has written in all kinds of styles. His songs have beautiful lyrical lines and he has rhythmically and harmonically constructed them like a fine watchmaker."

When Getz listened to the Gilberto album, he was so impressed with it that he and Byrd decided to record an album together that would feature songs in the new style (by Jobim, Bonfá, Baden Powell, and Billy Blanco) as well as two standards by Ary Barroso. Creed Taylor, of later jazz fusion and CTI Records fame, produced. In April of 1962, Verve released Getz and Byrd's *Jazz Samba*, which included "Desafinado" and "Samba de Uma Nota Só."

"Desafinado" made the *Billboard* top 20 for pop singles and won a "best solo jazz performance" Grammy for Getz. The album did even better: it received a five-star review in *down beat* magazine and shot to the number one position on the *Billboard* pop chart. It sold hundreds of

BOSSA COMBOS

There were many talented groups that played bossa nova at the Beco das Garrafas clubs and at other Brazilian hotspots in the late 1950s and early 1960s. Among them were the Tamba Trio (Luis Eça, Bebeto, and Hélcio Milito), Zimbo Trio (which included Luis Chaves and Amilton Godoy), Sambalanço Trio (with César Camargo Mariano and Airto Moreira), Bossa Jazz Trio (with Amilson Godoy—younger brother of Amilton), Bossa Três (with Edson Machado), 3-D (with Antonio Adolfo), Jongo Trio, and the Sexteto Bossa Rio (led by young keyboardist Sérgio Mendes). A vocalist who often sang with the latter band was Leny Andrade; she went on to become one of Brazil's great singers, just as many of the above musicians continued to expand into other areas in succeeding decades.

September 1964 found saxophonist Paul Winter back in Rio, working out with Luiz Bonfá (guitar) and Luis Eça (at the piano).

thousands of copies, remarkable for a jazz record (especially an instrumental one), and stayed on the charts for seventy weeks. It was really jazz-bossa rather than bossa nova, but the new sound had struck a nerve. Byrd said, "I knew it was something that would have a lot of public appeal. I didn't know it would inspire bossa nova neckties."

Before the release of *Jazz Samba*, a young saxophonist named Paul Winter had also checked out a Gilberto album (played for him by critic-lyricist Gene Lees), loved it, and then toured Brazil and heard more of the new style. "It was such a breath of fresh air," recalled Winter. "We were hearing a very gentle voice that had the kind of soul and harmonic beauty that we loved in jazz. But as opposed to the hard-driving bebop that we were playing then, it was astounding to find a very quiet, gentle music that had an equal amount of magic. It was a whole new possibility for us.

"Guitar wasn't something that was part of our universe and here was someone doing all this subtle magic on the classical guitar. João Gilberto was sort of a new prophet. Following that tour, guitar became an integral part of my musical world." That year (1962), Winter and his sextet recorded *Jazz Meets the Bossa Nova* in Rio and New York, interpreting tunes by Jobim, Lyra, Menescal, and Dorival Caymmi. It also fell into the area of jazz-bossa, but was more "Brazilian" than *Jazz Samba* in that it included Brazilian percussionists who added afoxê, reco-reco, cuíca, and other instruments to the sound. It marked the beginning of Winter's long relationship with Brazilian music.

Also in 1962, flutist Herbie Mann released *Do the Bossa Nova with Herbie Mann*. About his trip to Brazil the previous year, Mann recalled, "I was so totally mesmerized by the country and the music that at that point I realized it was going to save my musical life. Up till that point my success had come from having an Afro-Cuban type jazz band with four percussionists. But Afro-Cuban music was so simplistic melody-wise that it really got boring. When I went to Brazil I saw that their music could be as rhythmically involved as other ethnic musics were but with it they had these melodic masterpieces. So as a jazz person, it was the best of both worlds—to have great melodies to improvise with combined with these rhythms."

Mann and trumpeter Kenny Dorham flew to Brazil in September of 1962 and recorded an album there with Sérgio Mendes' Sexteto Bossa Rio, which Mann describes at the time as "sort of like Horace Silver with a samba beat," and with Baden Powell, Jobim, and the Tamba Trio's Bebeto and Hélcio Milito. *Do the Bossa Nova* was an important meeting of American and Brazilian musicians, as was an album recorded in December of that year: *Cannonball's Bossa Nova*. That LP, released on Riverside Records in 1963, teamed the great jazz saxophonist

Cannonball Adderley with the Sexteto Bossa Rio, covering tunes by Jobim, Donato, and Ferreira-Einhorn. Mann and Adderley, like Byrd and Winter, would extensively record and play with Brazilians for years to come.

On November 21, 1962, at Carnegie Hall in New York, a now-legendary concert was staged by impresario Sidney Frey (owner of Audio Fidelity Records) that further publicized bossa nova. The show presented the Brazilian artists Gilberto, Bonfá, Castro-Neves, and others with American jazzmen (all enamored of the new style) such as Getz, Byrd, Gary Burton, Gary McFarland, and Lalo Schifrin. Despite inclement weather, it was a sellout, with some 2,800 spectators inside and more than a thousand turned away. The show was disorganized and the sound was terrible, but the concert got recording contracts for many Brazilian artists and marked the growing affinity of American jazz musicians for the bossa nova.

Bossa had conquered America, charming it with fresh sophistication and original charm, bridging "mass" popular music and "art" popular music (as John Storm Roberts phrased it in *The Latin Tinge*). Triggered mainly by the huge success of *Jazz Samba*, magazines and newspapers were full of articles about bossa nova, and dozens more jazz-bossa albums were released that year and next.

In the early 1960s, Ella Fitzgerald, Al Hirt, Zoot Sims, Curtis Fuller, Ray Charles, and Lalo Schifrin all recorded bossa-inspired tunes or albums. Pop imitations of bossa were present in abundance—music

SÉRGIO MENDES

Sérgio Mendes' *Fool on the Hill* LP was the pianist's best-selling record in the U.S., peaking at number three in 1968. The title cut made it to number six.

Sérgio Mendes (born in Niterói in 1941) was a fixture in the Beco das Garrafas, and recorded the albums *Sérgio Mendes & Bossa Rio*. He was also a participant on jazz-bossa albums with Cannonball Adderley, Herbie Mann, and Paul Winter. In 1964, he moved to the United States and cut an album for Capitol called *Sérgio Mendes and Brasil 1965*. His sound mixed bossa, American pop, and later, MPB, in a light, upbeat blend, usually with two female vocalists singing in unison, while a drummer—João Palma and Dom Um Romão were two—layed down a trademark crisp, catchy beat.

The Mendes formula was a huge success—his A&M album *Sérgio Mendes & Brasil '66* hit number seven on the pop charts in 1966. It went gold, as did his next three records—*Equinox*, *Look Around*, and *Fool on the Hill*. Mendes' band also scored two top 10 singles at that time, as well as a lesser hit with Jorge Ben's "Mas Que Nada," sung in Portuguese. Mendes reaped the most financial benefit from the bossa boom of any Brazilian, and demonstrated artistic versatility with albums such as the folkloric *Primal Roots* (1972) and *Arara* (1989).

critic John S. Wilson wrote of "bossa nova discs pouring in through windows and the cracks in the floor." Soon would come *Soul Bossa Nova* and *Boogie Woogie Bossa Nova*, not to mention Elvis Presley's *Bossa Nova Baby*, Horace Diaz's *Dixieland Bossa Nova* and Eydie Gourmet's *Blame It on the Bossa Nova*.

But there was still much to come. Getz and Byrd went their separate ways after their *Jazz Samba* success. Byrd would record many more Brazilian-flavored albums that decade and through to the end of the 1980s. Many of these releases were superb, as he delved deeply into the works of the venerable Brazilian composers Pixinguinha and Ernesto Nazaré, and worked with Laurindo Almeida and other talents.

Getz, Gilberto, and the Girl from Ipanema

Getz would grab the lion's share of fame from the bossa boom with his next few releases. His second jazz-bossa effort was *Big Band Bossa Nova*, which hit number 13 on the pop charts. He teamed with Bonfá for *Jazz Samba Encore* in 1963, and then—just as the bossa craze seemed to be dying out—joined Gilberto and Jobim for the album *Getz/Gilberto*, released in 1964. On it, João added guitar and vocals, Tom played piano, Milton Banana was on drums, and Tommy Williams on bass. In addition, two numbers featured João's wife Astrud, who had only come to the recording session to be with her husband. At Getz's insistence, she added English vocals to two songs, because João couldn't sing in English.

One of the tunes featuring Astrud's cool, light, and gentle vocals was Jobim-De Moraes' "The Girl from Ipanema," with English lyrics added by Norman Gimbel. With that song, Astrud became an instant international star, as she sang "Tall and tan and young and lovely/ The girl from Ipanema goes walking" and "When she walks she's like a samba/ That swings so cool and sways so gently."

Antonio Carlos Jobim, Helô Pinheiro (the real life inspiration for "The Girl from Ipanema"), and Helô's daughter, in the late 1980s.

"The Girl from Ipanema" was a duet between João (in Portuguese) and Astrud (in English), and it bridged the language-gap with the American audience. The breezy song won a Grammy award for best song that year, went to number five on the *Billboard* singles chart, and opened the minds of many Americans to the richness of Brazilian music. Its smooth syncopation and graceful lyricism made it into a standard, one of the most recorded and performed songs of its time. Unfortunately, in the 1960s and 1970s it was so overplayed, and covered by so many musicians (some great, some good, many bad), that in the United States "The Girl from Ipanema" began to epitomize cocktail-lounge music. Happily, time has dissipated the excesses of its commercialization, and a replaying of the song's definitive version (with João, Astrud, Jobim, and Getz) is again a delight to hear: cool, seductive, and wistful.

The inspiration of the song had been a beautiful, tanned teenage girl named Heloísa "Helô" Eneida Pinto (last name now Pinheiro) who used to "sway so gently" past a bar called Veloso on her way to Ipanema beach. Two regulars at Veloso were Tom and Vinícius, who turned their appreciation of Helô's sexy gracefulness into a song, and an unknowing muse into a pop icon of youth and beauty. Written in 1962, "Garota da Ipanema" was recorded the next year by Jobim, the Tamba Trio, and singer Pery Ribeiro before it gained English words and became "The Girl from Ipanema." Today the Veloso bar is named Garota de Ipanema after the song; Rua Montenegro, which it faced, is now called Rua Vinícius de Moraes.

The former Veloso bar, now renamed for the song that made it famous. The street was renamed as well—notice the sign at the far right bearing tribute to lyricist Vinícius de Moraes.

The *Getz/Gilberto* record garnered three other Grammys (best album, best jazz performance, and best engineering), and went to number two on the pop charts (it didn't hit number one because the Beatles were making pop music history that year). The LP spent an extraordinary ninety-six weeks on the charts (fifty of those in the top 40). Interestingly, just a few years later, the Beatles and bossa nova would both be strong influences on the next important Brazilian musical movement: Tropicália.

Perhaps the best of all the North American jazz-bossa albums was *The Sound of Ipanema*, a Paul Winter and Carlos Lyra collaboration released in 1964. Recorded in Rio, the album featured Lyra's compositions and musicians Sérgio Mendes (piano), Sebastião Neto (bass), and Milton Banana (drums). Winter was the only American on it, and he fit very well with the bossa spirit because of his lyrical and open-minded musical sensibility. The album was a smooth and engaging American-Brazilian fusion. Winter then cut the also superb *Rio* in 1965, featuring Luiz Bonfá, Roberto Menescal, and Luis Eça.

AFTER THE BOSSA BOOM

While bossa nova was enjoying its heyday in North America (roughly from 1962 through 1964), in Brazil, the bright, optimistic era that had begun with Kubitschek and helped create bossa nova was fading. In 1961, Jânio Quadros, the president elected after Kubitschek, resigned for reasons that are still obscure. His cryptic letter of resignation mentioned "foreign" and "terrible" forces that had forced him out. The vice president, Jango Goulart, took over. He had a more leftist orientation and faced great opposition from the conservative sectors of society. Artists in general supported the new president, who courted Cuba, re-established relations with Eastern Europe, condemned foreign economic imperialism, and promised to carry out basic reforms. He also increased the limits on

Bossa nova songstress Nara Leão, one of the original participants in the groundbreaking protest musical *Opinião*, standing next to the virtuoso accordionist Sivuca.

profits that foreign corporations could send out of Brazil (multinational firms controlled a large percentage of the country's economy).

Politically, Brazil was torn into two. This also generated a division in bossa nova. Some artists were engaged in politics, and consequently were writing more socially oriented lyrics. Many bossa nova artists—Carlos Lyra, Nara Leão, Sérgio Ricardo, Marcos Valle, and Paulo Sérgio Valle—protested poverty and social injustice in Brazil.

In 1964, a military coup toppled the Brazilian government, and replaced it with an authoritarian, repressive regime. This accelerated the movement of bossa nova's songwriters into different directions. *Opinião* (Opinion) was a protest musical in 1964 that matched singer Leão with sambista Zé Keti and northeastern bard João do Vale. A TV show called "O Fino da Bossa" (The Best of Bossa) often featured the more socially-oriented bossa tunes, which the government was not yet censoring to any great degree.

In 1965 began the era of the great Brazilian musical festivals, which would launch the new, eclectic Brazilian singers and songwriters who would comprise a new category—MPB (música popular brasileira). Many bossa figures would be absorbed by MPB, a few continued the bossa line, others moved into jazz and instrumental music, and some traveled to the U.S. and Europe to establish careers there.

Guitarist Luiz Bonfá moved to the U.S. in the 1960s and has frequently performed there and in Europe ever since. In 1989, Bonfá released *Non-Stop to Brazil*, his first recording in more than fifteen years. Musicians have been covering his classic "Manhã de Carnaval" for three decades now.

Carlos Lyra was perhaps the most musically complete bossa star, in that he was both an accomplished songwriter and vocalist. About him, Paul Winter commented, "His melodies are gorgeous, and his music so sensual and alluring. I remember many nights when Carlos would just melt the clothes off every lady in the room. That guy had a magic that probably surpasses that of any other performer I've ever known."

After leading bossa into its activist phase, adding social commentary and northeastern folk elements to albums such as "Pobre Menina Rica" (Poor Little Rich Girl), Lyra left for Mexico. He lived there between 1966 and 1971, writing music for film and the theater. Meanwhile, the Brazilian dictatorship in 1968 began its heaviest phase of censorship and repression. When Lyra returned to his homeland, he found a different country from the one he had left. He made a record in 1973 but only two of its songs passed the government censors; it was released with old material substituted instead. The following year he left Brazil again, this time for the U.S., where he stayed until 1977. Since then, back in Rio, he has taught astrology and performed concerts of his numerous bossa classics.

As for Vinícius, his final important collaborator was Antonio Petti Filho, known as Toquinho, whom he met in 1970. Toquinho (born in São Paulo in 1946) is a singer-songwriter and accomplished guitarist who mixes classical-guitar technique with the João Gilberto beat and Brazilian swing, and who absorbed influences from Baden Powell, Paulinho Nogueira, and Oscar Castro-Neves.

With Toquinho, Vinícius rediscovered the joy of making music. They worked a lot together, co-writing dozens of memorable tunes in the bossa nova and afro-samba veins, with Toquinho providing the strong melodies and the Vinícius adding his inimitable poetic flair. Sharing vocals and often singing in unison, Toquinho and Vinícius performed in concert and recorded sixteen albums together (some in Italy and Argentina). They were remarkably popular as a duo. Such Toquinho-de Moraes tunes as "As Cores de Abril" (The Colors of April) and "Como É Duro Trabalhar" (How It's Hard to Work) have become standards, heard wherever Brazilians pick up acoustic guitars to sing songs together. Another of their standards is "Aquarela" (Watercolor), in which they sing, "And the future is a spaceship/ That we try to pilot/ It doesn't have time or pity/ Nor an hour of arrival."

Their collaboration lasted until Vinícius' death in 1980. Since then, Toquinho has traveled the solo road and has maintained his knack for writing melodious ballads and further improved his formidable guitar technique. His album *A Luz do Solo* in 1985 was an excellent retrospective of his career up to that point, featuring songs he had written with Vinícius as well as with MPB artists Chico Buarque and Jorge Ben.

João Gilberto lived in the United States from 1966 until 1980, when he moved back to Rio. After *Getz/Gilberto*, João made only a handful of albums over the next twenty-five years. In 1990, he recorded his first studio album in ten years. It's not easy to see one of his shows or even find an interview with him in a magazine: João is shy and extremely reclusive. But he continues to be an inspiration for guitarists and singers around the world, and many are the Brazilian musicians who remember the very day, hour, and place where they first heard that strange new song, "Chega de Saudade," coming over the radio.

The Vinícius piano bar in Rio.

João and Astrud divorced soon after their success, and he was married for a time afterwards to the singer Miúcha, the sister of MPB star Chico Buarque. Astrud Gilberto (born in Bahia in 1940) continued the career which grew out of her serendipitous appearance on "The

João Gilberto in the late 1980s.

Frank Sinatra and Antonio Carlos Jobim collaborated on this 1967 album; it hit the top 40 in the spring of that year.

Girl from Ipanema," and was an active and popular solo artist through the 1970s and 1980s. João and Astrud's daughter Bebel has now established a career as a singer in Brazil.

After the success of *Getz/Gilberto* and "The Girl from Ipanema," Jobim became a famous name in North America. He appeared on American TV specials, recorded the solo albums *Wave* (1967) and *Tide* (1970) in the United States, among others, and appeared on two LPs with Frank Sinatra, *Francis Albert Sinatra & Antonio Carlos Jobim* (Reprise, 1967) and *Sinatra and Company* (Reprise, 1973). Tom's music had a profound effect on fans all over the world.

Jobim didn't stop developing artistically during the heady days of the 1960s. One of his greatest songs was "Águas de Março" (Waters of March), first recorded in 1972. It incorporated samba and maracatu influences, as well as an incredible string of images in its lengthy, wonderfully crafted lyrics. In the English version Jobim sang:

> A stick, a stone, it's the end of the road
> It's the rest of a stump, it's a little alone
> It's a sliver of glass, it is life, it's the sun
> It is the night, it is death, it's a trap,
> > it's a gun
> And the riverbank talks of the waters
> > of March
> It's the promise of life, it's the joy in
> > your heart.

The images wind on and on, vivid and concrete, evoking the deep mystery of life. Recorded by many artists (including Tom and Elis Regina in a marvelous duet in 1974), the tune is a lively, melodic-rhythmic-poetic masterpiece.

In the 1970s and 1980s, Tom's lyrics often reflected his love of nature and concern for ecological problems. Songs like "Boto" (an Amazonian porpoise) and "Borzeguim" celebrated nature and/or the Brazilian Indians and called for their protection. In the latter, he sang, "Leave the jaguar alive in the forest/ Leave the fish in the water . . . / Leave the Indian alive/ Leave the Indian alone."

In general, his music defies classification. One of his greatest works, the lovely and aesthetically adventurous 1976 album *Urubu* (named for the Brazilian black vulture) is a meeting of MPB, bossa nova, Brazilian regional music (heard in the capoeira rhythm), sounds of nature (including simulated bird calls), and classical music. The instrumental compositions of side two (three by Tom and one by his son Paulo Jobim) are performed by an orchestra and are essentially modern impressionistic tone poems. Produced by Claus Ogerman, the LP featured Miúcha on vocals, João Palma on drums, Ray Armando on percussion, and Ron Carter on bass. The album's masterful compositions are part of a rich and still growing body of work that rivals, in sophistication and originality, the music of 20th-century composers such as George Gershwin and Jobim's idol, Heitor Villa-Lobos.

THE BOSSA LEGACY

As Jobim argued, bossa nova had a huge impact on American music. In fact, it would become a permanent sub-set of jazz, and countless jazz and pop composers would incorporate bossa melodies, harmonies, rhythms, and textures into their songs over the next few decades. And, the guitar would be reinvigorated as a jazz instrument in part because of the inspired playing of João Gilberto, Baden Powell, Luiz Bonfá, Bola Sete, and other Brazilians.

The importance of bossa nova in the evolution of Brazilian music itself was also immense. After its golden years—1958 to 1964—the bossa nova movement lost momentum, but every musician that came after it fed on its sophisticated harmonies. Young musicians that before bossa nova would look for novelties abroad, started looking for them inside Brazil, inside themselves.

A new generation of musicians blossomed, creating new styles of pop music without denying its heritage. This new music is commonly called MPB. If asked about the beginning of their serious interest in music, most MPB members will answer, "Well, it all started with bossa nova."

OSCAR CASTRO-NEVES

Composer-guitarist-arranger Oscar Castro-Neves, born in Rio in 1940, wrote the early bossa nova standards such as "Patinho Feio" (Ugly Duckling) and "Onde Está Você?" (Where Are You?). In the 1960s, Oscar settled

Oscar Castro-Neves in the late 1980s.

in Los Angeles and was the music director for Sérgio Mendes' band for ten years. He worked extensively with the Paul Winter Consort in the 1970s and 1980s as a songwriter, guitarist, and co-producer. Commented Winter, "Oscar is a kind of grand repository of the whole Brazilian tradition from Villa-Lobos on, from the classical to the popular. I don't know a musician who has a broader range. He's a completely effervescent humanist, a great musical catalyst, and enormously inventive."

Oscar has scored films and television shows, and he has worked as a guitarist, arranger, and/or producer for Jobim, Quincy Jones, Lee Ritenour, Flora Purim, Hubert Laws, and many others. *Oscar!*, his first solo album, was released in 1987 by Paul Winter's Living Music label.

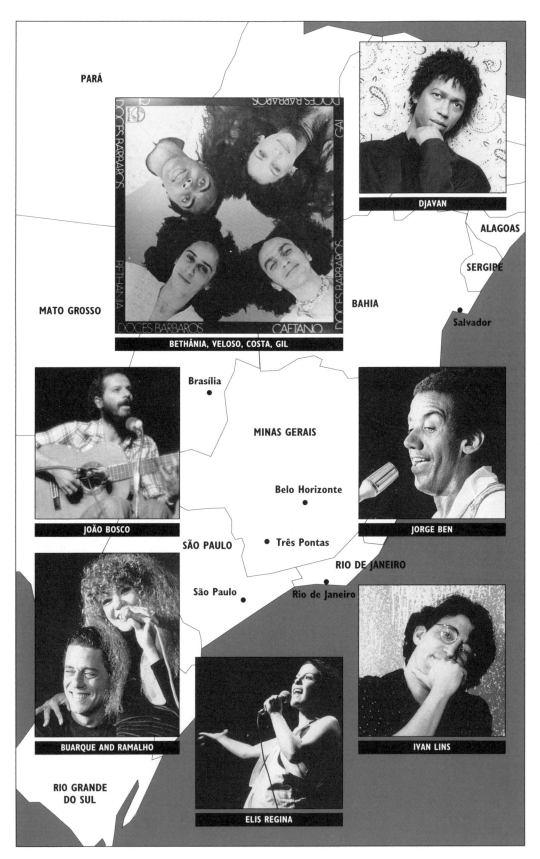

PARÁ

DJAVAN

ALAGOAS

SERGIPE

MATO GROSSO

BAHIA

Salvador

BETHÂNIA, VELOSO, COSTA, GIL

Brasília

MINAS GERAIS

Belo Horizonte

JOÃO BOSCO

JORGE BEN

SÃO PAULO

Três Pontas

RIO DE JANEIRO

São Paulo

Rio de Janeiro

BUARQUE AND RAMALHO

IVAN LINS

RIO GRANDE
DO SUL

ELIS REGINA

MPB: A MUSICAL RAINBOW

The Brazilian musical scene of the late 1960s and early 1970s saw the birth of a heterogeneous group of composers and musicians. Their music has since been dubbed *MPB*, an acronym that stands for "música popular brasileira" and refers to a generation of artists that includes Geraldo Azevedo, Maria Bethânia, João Bosco, Chico Buarque, Dori Caymmi, Gal Costa, Djavan, Gilberto Gil, Ivan Lins, Edu Lobo, Milton Nascimento, Elis Regina, Simone, Alceu Valença, and Caetano Veloso.

Their music defies easy categorization because it is intensely eclectic, varying greatly in style from artist to artist. The common thread among MPB songwriters is their keen ability to combine compelling melodies (a Brazilian tradition), rich harmonies (a legacy partly from bossa nova), varied rhythms (from Brazil, the U.S., and elsewhere), and poetic lyrics (another Brazilian trademark).

Simone, one of MPB's foremost vocal interpreters.

The MPB generation blossomed and gained national fame in a series of music festivals that began in 1965. These concerts had nothing to do with happenings like Woodstock or other rock spectacles. The Brazilian music festivals were competitive, nationally televised events with winners and losers, and the public participated actively, vociferously rooting for their favorites and booing the others. The festivals became a forum for discussion of Brazilian culture and politics, and performers were often cheered or jeered on the basis of their nationalism and political stance.

Not every Brazilian popular musician is MPB. If asked whether Martinho da Vila is an MPB musician, Brazilians almost certainly will answer in the negative, claiming he is a samba composer. Ask the same Brazilians about Lulu Santos and they'll respond that Lulu is a rock singer. Nevertheless both Martinho and Lulu are very popular Brazilian musicians.

What is MPB then? The movement grew out of the "general jelly" (an expression of poet Decio Pignatari) of Brazilian urban culture. MPB musicians absorbed influences from all parts of the country and the world, incorporating elements of bossa nova, jazz, bolero, sertaneja music, rock, northeastern music, reggae, and other genres into their compositions. They then mixed all these styles in such a way that the final product cannot be defined as any of the elements that compose it. It is a new whole: MPB.

Alceu Valença serenading a stadium full of concertgoers.

THE DARK TIMES

The up-and-coming MPB artists were also shaped by the political tumult of the era, which stifled some artists and inspired others to greater feats. Most MPB stars hit their strides during a time of heavy government repression, and many were exiled, jailed, censored, or otherwise harassed during this time. Theirs was an art sometimes created under great duress.

On March 31, 1964, the Brazilian military overthrew the government of João (Jango) Goulart, a president who had the support of the Left and of the most progressive layers of Brazilian society. He had been in that post since 1961, when the democratically elected Jânio Quadros had resigned from the presidency, and Goulart, his running mate, assumed the office. The generals who commanded the takeover in 1964 stated that they would only stay in charge for a year, while they "reorganized the country," and then they would hold new elections for president. In the meantime, they appointed General Humberto Castelo Branco to head the country, and he was the first of a succession of general-presidents. The military ended up holding power for twenty-one years, until they allowed the Brazilian Congress to elect a civilian president in 1985.

For a few years after the coup there was still some peaceful resistance. However, because the political rights of most union leaders and opposing politicians had been cancelled, artists, students, and journalists became the spearheads of resistance and protest. In the streets, students held demonstrations, first demanding better universities, then democracy and elections. The biggest one took place in Rio in 1968 and had over 100,000 participants. Such protests generated a strong and violent reaction from the military.

By the end of 1968, the political scene was radicalized to its limit. Fights between rightist and leftist students were frequent. Right-wing terrorist groups like MAC (the Anti-Communist Movement) and CCC (the Communist Hunter Command) had appeared as a counterpoint to leftist demonstrators. In 1968 in São Paulo, CCC members invaded a theater, attacking and beating actors, musicians, and technicians working on singer-songwriter Chico Buarque's play *Roda Viva*.

In Brasília, congressman Márcio Moreira Alves gave a speech before the chamber of deputies, proposing a boycott against the September 7th Independence Day celebrations. The senior officers of the military considered his words offensive to the armed forces and wanted to put him in jail. Congress, however, denied permission for Alves to be tried. That was the excuse the government needed for a second and deeper coup. On December 13, 1968, the military implemented Institutional Act No. 5, and Brazil was plunged into the most repressive dictatorship of its history. Congress was closed, all civil rights were banned (anybody could be kept in jail without a trial), and all forms of press and the arts had to be censored before they reached the public. Acting president General Costa e Silva wielded dictatorial powers.

An early album from Chico Buarque, the green-eyed young singer/songwriter who was idolized by Brazilians in the mid-sixties, fell out of favor, then firmly established himself as one of Brazil's most accomplished lyricists.

Politicians, students, artists, and intellectuals were arrested and tortured. Many dissidents "disappeared" and were never found; hundreds or even thousands of citizens were killed—nobody knows the total. Others were forced to leave the country. Many small guerrilla groups rose up to fight the government, but they weren't successful. By 1972 the military had the country firmly in its hands.

Act No. 5 was not revoked until 1978. The following year political prisoners were granted amnesty, marking the beginning of the Brazilian glasnost that would only be complete ten years later, with direct elections for president in 1989.

THE FESTIVALS BEGIN: VOICES OF PROTEST

Amidst the climate of growing fear and repression, the televised music festivals were a vital cultural outlet for many Brazilians. Not only did many musical careers begin there, but for a time (until Act No. 5 in 1968) they were a forum for political dissent—as expressed in song.

Elis Regina performing in 1978. She was one of the first of the MPB stars to gain fame through the TV music festivals.

The festival era opened in 1965. The first important one was sponsored by the TV Excelsior channel and took place in Guarujá, a beach town in São Paulo state. Generally, at these and later festivals, the TV station organized a jury formed of musicians, journalists, and music industry people. They sorted through tapes sent by applicants and classified those songs that would compete. With the television cameras transmitting, the nominees then performed live before large audiences at arenas or theaters, and the juries picked the winners. The musicians were rewarded with trophies, money, and national exposure. First prize at the TV Excelsior festival went to Edu Lobo and Vinícius de Moraes' "Arrastão" (Fishing Net), interpreted by an extremely talented young singer by the name of Elis Regina (whom we shall discuss later).

Edu Lobo

"Arrastão" co-author, Edu Lobo, was a songwriter, guitarist, and singer. He wrote beautiful, stirring songs that combined Brazilian folk music with bossa nova harmonies and whose lyrics protested the injustice and misery of Brazil's Northeast, an area that suffered more than the rest of the country from poverty and neo-feudalism.

Lobo's song "Borandá" (Let's Go), written in 1964 and released on his first album in 1965, was a bossa with a slight northeastern accent and poignant lyrics decrying the terrible droughts in the region. The 1967 Lobo-Capinam tune "Ponteio" (Strumming) had northeastern-style guitar work and its lyrics were a subtle, disguised protest against the political repression of the time: "Running in the middle of the world/ I never leave my guitar/ I'll see a new day/ And a new place to sing."

Born in Rio in 1943, Lobo was proficient in both samba-canção and bossa nova when he met Carlos Lyra in the mid-sixties. Lobo was impressed by Lyra's new bossa style which used northeastern musical elements and socially conscious lyrics. Edu would follow a similar line and, together with Regina and the composers Geraldo Vandré and Sérgio Ricardo, among others, he would expand bossa nova's intimate sound into extroverted, epic protest songs that the new military government didn't like one bit.

At this time, bossa nova split between the old guard and the new protest singers (who would help create "MPB"); the Brazilian audience became sharply divided in its preferences as well. Nationalistic music with a clearly Brazilian flavor was set against "foreign" music, such as the rock songs heard on the "Jovem Guarda" (Young Guard) TV show in the mid-1960s.

Lobo composed many standards: with moviemaker and lyricist Ruy Guerra, Edu wrote "Canção da Terra" (Song of the Land) and "Reza e Aleluia" (Pray and Say Hallelujah), and with Gianfranceso Guarnieri he composed "Upa Neguinho." His aforementioned "Borandá," which took first place in the 1967 TV Record Festival, was the last protest song to win a festival. From then on, censorship and the general hopelessness of the country dramatically reduced the number of protest songs performed. The situation made Edu decide to leave. In 1969 he moved to the U.S. where he played guitar on Paul Desmond's album *From the Hot Afternoon*, which included four Lobo songs. He returned to Brazil in 1971 and since then has concentrated on writing music for plays, movies, and ballets. Shy and quiet, Lobo is rarely seen on a stage anymore.

Geraldo Vandré

Singer-songwriter Geraldo Vandré was, as mentioned above, another musician who was shaking and stirring the bossa in a radical way. (Interestingly, Vandré's first guitar teacher was none other than the pope of bossa nova, João Gilberto.) Geraldo (born in 1935 in João Pessoa, Paraíba) incorporated many folkloric genres into his music, among them toada, frevo, moda, baião, and aboio. He said he interpreted them in a "more ideological than formal way," meaning that they served to create protest songs that had strong, angry lyrics.

Vandré's "ideological" adaptations had a distinctly progressive edge in part because of the creative virtuosity of his backup bands. In 1966 and 1967, he worked with Quarteto Novo, a now-legendary group that included Hermeto Pascoal on flute, Heraldo do Monte and Théo de Barros on guitars, and Airto Moreira on drums and percussion. Then in 1968, he was backed by Quarteto Livre, which included percussionist Naná Vasconcelos and guitarist Geraldo Azevedo. Most of the musicians in Vandré's groups went on to become stars in their own right.

Vandré's songs, performed by others, took first place in two festivals in 1966: "Porta-Estandarte" (Standard-Bearer) won the TV Excelsior event, and "Disparada" (Stampede) tied for first place in the TV Record contest. "Disparada" was a toada which told the story of a northeastern *vaqueiro* (cowboy) who is enraged that he and the other vaqueiros are treated like cattle. One day he rebels against the rancher.

For his fiery protest songs Vandré became a national hero, more famous even than Lobo. Armed only with his guitar, he was perceived as a serious threat by the military government.

Vandré's masterpiece would be "Prá Não Dizer Que Não Falei de Flores" (Not to Say I Didn't Speak of Flowers), a song also known by the shorter name of "Caminhando" (Walking). Brazilian journalist Millôr Fernandes considered it a "Brazilian Marseillaise, the true national anthem."

"Caminhando" took second in Rio's third International Song Festival (FIC) in 1968 (an event begun by TV Globo, Brazil's largest network, in 1966). The song was subsequently banned by the censors for ten years. General Luis de Franca Oliveira presented his reasons for the prohibition of "Caminhando"in the *Correio da Manhã* newspaper's October 10, 1968 edition, citing its "subversive lyrics, its offensiveness to the armed forces, and the fact that it would serve as a slogan for students' demonstrations."

He was right. Even after it was banned, it never ceased to be sung wherever people who resisted the dictatorship gathered. It was still present at protests at the end of the 1970s, when Brazilian society started to challenge the government, demanding a return to democracy.

After Act No. 5 was invoked, Geraldo had to leave Brazil in order to ensure his personal safety. From 1969 to 1973, he wandered through Chile, Algeria, Greece, Austria, Bulgaria, and finally France—where he made his only record during this time, *Das Terras do Benvira*. When he returned to Brazil in 1973, he was arrested as soon as he arrived. A month later he appeared on a national news program saying, among other things, that he hoped he could integrate his latest songs with the new Brazilian reality and that the connection made between his music and certain political groups had been made against his will.

This public statement was probably the price he had to pay to be allowed to remain in the country. After that, no more new songs by Geraldo were recorded, and he got rid of his stage name, Vandré. After seven albums, Geraldo's short but incandescent career was over. Eventually, there was only Geraldo Dias, the lawyer. But he'll always be remembered as the author of protest songs that make Brazilians want to stand and fight for what they think is right.

Chico Buarque and Elba Ramalho.

Chico Buarque the Poet

The 1966 TV Record festival ended in a tie for first-place between Geraldo Vandré and another newcomer, singer-songwriter Chico Buarque de Hollanda. With his melancholy, nasal voice Chico sang beautifully crafted, extremely literate sambas and marchas. He soon became very popular and would ultimately be considered one of the greatest lyricists of all time in Brazilian popular music.

Born in Rio in 1944 but raised in São Paulo and Italy, Buarque achieved national acclaim when he released his first three albums in the mid-1960s. He was hailed as the new heir apparent to the great samba-canção composers of the 1930s like Noel Rosa, and his popularity was the only thing that almost all of polarized Brazil agreed about: every woman wanted to marry him and every man admired him. To many he seemed the true defender of traditional Brazilian music against the furious attack of protest songs, the aesthetic revolution proposed by Tropicália (the musical movement led by Gilberto Gil and Caetano Veloso), and the alien electric guitars of Jovem Guarda rockers such as Roberto Carlos and Erasmo Carlos.

Chico found his path composing sambas in a traditional vein like "A Rita," "Olê Olá," "Pedro Pedreiro" (Pedro the Bricklayer), and marchas like his festival winner "A Banda" (The Band). Chico's early lyrics were subtle yet powerful, and often strongly nostalgic. Short excerpts do them little justice because they were intricately constructed, building themes and ideas over many verses. They almost always told about good things that had already gone by. Maybe that explained his enormous success: the present was so insecure that listening to a talented young musician who praised the past and reverently revived old Brazilian musical genres gave people some hope that soon things would return to the good old days. Such songs were very popular. Old or young, rich or poor, communists or capitalists, everybody loved Chico, the nice green-eyed young singer…until around 1968.

Chico didn't like being idolized. He felt used and abused, and his answer to his fans' blind devotion came in 1968 in the form of a play: *Roda Viva* (an expression that means "commotion"). The drama tells the story of a young pop star who is literally devoured by the public. During the performance of the play, actors offered "pieces" of the star's "liver" to the audience. That caused a scandal and an extreme backlash from conservatives. In São Paulo the theater was invaded by right-wing extremists and the actors were beaten; in Porto Alegre, after the opening night performance, the actors were told to leave the city or they'd be killed. The government censors immediately prohibited any further performances. *Roda Viva* marked the death of "nice guy" Chico Buarque.

While the government was censoring his play, Gilberto Gil and Caetano Veloso were attacking Buarque for the formal conservativism of his music. Chico was not the national choice anymore.

After the *Roda Viva* debacle, Chico went to Italy, stayed there for over a year, and played on European stages with such disparate performers as Josephine Baker and Toquinho. In 1970, Chico was the first of the exiled MPB musicians to return to Brazil. Although he wasn't arrested, he became a favorite target for censors. In 1971, only one out of every three songs he wrote was approved by them. Some passed only to be censored later. For example, "Apesar de Você" (In Spite of You) was only banned after it became a hit. The censors must have missed the irony in the lyrics; in hindsight the words obviously are directed towards the government:

> In spite of you
> Tomorrow is going to be another day
> I ask you where you are going
> To hide from the immense euphoria.

In 1971, Chico recorded his fifth album, *Construção* (Construction). It was a dramatic record that represented a break in his career. Nostalgic subjects gave way to an almost hallucinatory treatment of the disappointments and tragedies of everyday life. Buarque vividly evoked the dehumanization caused by work, marriage, routine, the system.

With blaring, edgy horns building tension and the percussion keeping a steady, ominous "tick-tock" beat, the album's title song described the ironic last day of a bricklayer who dies in the middle of the road after falling from a window:

> He sat down to rest as if he were a prince
> Ate beans with rice as if it were the greatest dish
> Drank and wept as if he were a machine
> Danced and laughed as if he were his fellow man
> Tripped over the sky as if he heard music
> Floated in the air as if it might be Saturday
> Ended up on the ground like a timid bundle
> Agonized shipwrecked in the middle of the sidewalk.

When they returned from exile in the early seventies, Caetano Veloso and Gilberto Gil patched up their friendship with Buarque, which had been badly shaken for a time because of aesthetic differences. Chico recorded a live album with Veloso, and then in 1973 wrote "Cálice" (Chalice) with Gil. When they first attempted to perform it in public, the police came on stage as they were singing and turned off the microphones. The song was banned, but it became yet another anthem against the dictatorship. Using powerful religious imagery, it was a metaphorical comment on repressive times and the silencing of an entire nation. Its clever and ironic title ("Cálice") was a homophone of the phrase "Cale-se," which means "Shut up." Sang Chico and Gilberto:

> How to drink this bitter drink
> Gulp down the pain, swallow the drudgery
> Though my mouth is quiet, my breast remains
> No one hears the silence in the city
> ...Father, take this cup away from me.

Gilbert Gil (pictured here) criticized Buarque for his musical conservatism in the mid sixties, but in the seventies, the two were once again friends and collaborating on songs such as "Cálice."

The censors continued to hound Buarque for the next several years; in 1974 and 1975 practically none of the songs that he wrote met with their approval and made it on record. Brazilians came to see Chico as a symbol of cultural resistance, even though little of his work actually reached the public. Buarque apparently gave up trying to get his own material through and instead recorded only covers on his 1974 album "Sinal Fechado" (Red Light). The record included the title song by Paulinho da Viola (which actually was a clever, coded protest) and tunes by Veloso, Gil, Noel Rosa, Toquinho, and an unknown newcomer: Julinho da Adelaide. The press material for the album included a biography for Julinho and described him as a sambista from the morro. Trouble was, Julinho didn't exist—he was an alter ego for Chico—and the truth was soon discovered. From then on, any composer sending a song to the censors had to include a copy of his or her identification card.

In the 1980s, the government censors became more lenient. Buarque began including formerly banned songs along with new ones on his albums. By this time, Chico had turned into an eclectic composer, writing marchas, fados, waltzes, and even rock tunes, but his main style was still samba. Throughout the decade his songwriting partners varied greatly; he worked with Francis Hime, Gil, Sivuca, Nascimento, Toquinho, and Jobim, among others. Buarque's lyrics continued to contrast dreams with reality, use subtle irony and evocative imagery, and artfully blend the comic with the tragic, often reflecting on existential and romantic matters. Vinícius de Moraes, one of Buarque's greatest fans, said that Chico "is a phenomenon who accomplished the perfect union of both cultivated and popular culture."

Elis Regina in 1974, talking to Tom Jobim, whose compositions she often covered in her career.

Elis Regina

Not all of the artists who gained prominence at the music festivals were highly politicized singer-songwriters. Many were simply talented musicians, who delved into controversial material only on occasion, or never at all. An example of the latter was Elis Regina, the young female singer who won the 1965 TV Excelsior event with the Edu Lobo/Vinícius de Moraes tune "Arrastão."

Born in 1945 in Carvalho da Costa, Rio Grande do Sul, Elis was only twenty years old when she took first place at that festival. Yet by this time she had already gained some recognition for her appearances on various TV programs, where her impassioned singing style was the opposite of subdued bossa nova

Elis' European following was bolstered by appearances such as this one at the Montreux Jazz festival in Switzerland.

behavior. The TV Excelsior victory helped propel her to the top, and her contagious energy and strongly emotional interpretations soon made Elis a big star in Brazil. By the 1970s, she was well known in Europe as well.

She recorded bossa, samba, and the new eclectic styles of the emerging MPB composers. She co-hosted the TV show "O Fino da Bossa" (The Best of Bossa) with singer Jair Rodrigues from 1965 to 1967 and the MPB show "Som Livre Exportação" (Free Sound Exportation) with Lins in 1970 and 1971. She also staged ingenious live shows that harmoniously blended music and theater.

Elis had a remarkable ability to find talented new composers. She was the first to record songs by Milton Nascimento, Ivan Lins, João Bosco, and Belchior, all of whom would later achieve renown. During her successful twenty-year career, some of Regina's hits included Lins'

"Madalena," Lobo's "Upa Neguinho" (Hey Black Boy), Belchior's "Como Nossos Pais" (Like Our Parents), and Tom Jobim's "Águas de Março" (Waters of March).

But the charismatic singer's life was cut tragically short by an accidental cocaine overdose in 1982. Her artistic abilities were in full flower, she was highly popular in both Brazil and abroad, and she was about to record a collaborative album with the jazz saxophonist Wayne Shorter. Most critics and MPB fans in Brazil considered her the most important Brazilian singer of her time. For many years after her death, one could find graffiti on the walls of Brazilian cities that read "Elis Vive" (Elis Lives).

Nana Caymmi.

Dori Caymmi.

Nana Caymmi and Dori Caymmi

The 1966 International Song Festival (FIC) in Rio was won by Nana Caymmi, the daughter of the legendary Bahian composer Dorival Caymmi. She triumphed with the tune "Saveiros" (Fishing Boats), written by Nelson Motta and Nana's younger brother Dori Caymmi. Neither she nor Dori were known as political firebrands; they just made great music.

Nana is a sophisticated, jazz-influenced singer who has never achieved the popular acclaim in Brazil that she has deserved. Nevertheless she is internationally known, especially in Europe where she has played the Montreux Jazz Festival—her acclaimed 1989 appearance there with pianist Wagner Tiso was made into a live album.

A favorite singer of Brazilian musicians, Nana has a deep, soulful voice; a good example of her vocal expressiveness is "Velho Piano" (Old Piano) on the album *Dori Caymmi*, in which she marvelously captures the shifting tensions, complex modulations, and intricate rhythms in her brother's composition. Among the cognoscenti of Rio and São Paulo, Nana has been a cult favorite for three decades.

The youngest of the Caymmi siblings, Danilo is a gifted composer and flutist.

Her brother Dori Caymmi, a Carioca born in 1943, has only three records under his name in Brazil but is one of the most accomplished arrangers, composers, and guitarists of his generation. American composer-producer Don Grusin, who often collaborated with Brazilian musicians in the 1980s, said "his melodies are my favorite melodies in the world and some of his chords are too. I think he's very unique." Grusin noted that, on his guitar, Dori often "tunes the top E down to a B, so that he has a double B. Then he makes these cluster chords by putting one finger on the top string and the second finger just one fret off, and he gets minor-second clusters." Grusin observed that such tonal effects were also favored by Ravel and Debussy: "It's a way to make the harmonic basis a lot more interesting."

Caymmi's musical accomplishments in the late 1960s reveal his many talents: he arranged the debut albums of Caetano Veloso and Gilberto Gil; had songs recorded by Nana, Milton Nascimento, Tom Jobim, Djavan, Elis Regina, and Maria Bethânia; and wrote music scores for movies and plays. Mixing Brazilian rhythms with influences from the likes of Bill Evans, Villa-Lobos, Debussy, and Ravel, Dori's music is a collection of impressionistic images. "I'm pretty much the guy who looks at nature and makes my portraits. I'm a painter, I use my music like that," he said in 1987.

His international career started in 1965 with a tour with Paul Winter in a short-lived group called the Paul Winter Brazilian Consort. In 1987, he arranged jazz singer Sarah Vaughan's album *Brazilian Romance*. It featured five of Dori's compositions and was nominated for a Grammy award.

With the 1988 release of *Dori Caymmi*, his first album in the United States, Dori joined the ranks of his fellow countrymen earning a wider audience outside Brazil. It was an album of vocal and instrumental music, on which Dori sang and played guitar. Paulo César Pinheiro added lyrics, and Don Grusin (keyboards), Jimmy Johnson (bass), and Laudir de Oliveira (percussion) accompanied. The work is intensely lyrical and richly textured, perfectly expressing Dori's unique style.

TROPICÁLIA

As the music festivals entered their third year, they continued to launch new artists. In 1967, it was the time of Gilberto Gil and Caetano Veloso, who used this forum to kick off a radical new musical movement: Tropicália.

By this time, the music festivals had become a national craze. The streets of Brazil would be deserted on festival nights because everybody would be home watching them on TV. Audience behavior at the festivals was similar to that of soccer fans at stadiums such as Maracanã. Those attending the festivals would go to the theater to support their favorites with flags and applause, and try to disturb the "enemies."

When Veloso performed his Tropicália anthem "Alegria Alegria" (Joy, Joy) at the TV Record festival, he was booed. Much of the audience was intensely nationalistic. They revered "authentically" Brazilian music and detested

Caetano Veloso performing to an appreciative crowd at Rio's Canecão arena in 1989.

what symbolized American colonialism. These fans considered "Alegria, Alegria" Americanized because it was a rock song and Veloso was backed by a rock group, Os Beat Boys. Many also didn't respond to its strange, fragmented imagery:

Walking against the wind

Without handkerchief, without documents

In the almost December sun, I go

The sun scatters into spaceships, guerrillas

. . . teeth, legs, flags, the bomb and Brigitte Bardot.

Gil's entry, "Domingo no Parque" (Sunday in the Park), received a much warmer response, in part because it wasn't rock and roll. But it was something markedly different. It included the Bahian capoeira rhythm, electric instrumentation, and cinematic lyrics. The song was arranged by conductor Rogério Duprat, a Paulista who had a solid background in both classical and experimental electronic music. He was willing to add his experience as an avant-garde musician to the popular music being made by the Tropicalistas.

Gilberto Gil.

The arrangement was influenced by the Beatles' "A Day in the Life," from their 1967 *Sgt. Pepper's* album. When Gil wrote "Domingo," he was listening over and over to the Beatles' song, which he says was "my myth of the time." Gil then created an equally fascinating song, in which Bahia met George Martin, who met Rogério Duprat.

When Gil and Veloso, both from Bahia, moved to São Paulo in 1965 and were exposed to the burgeoning, heady arts scene there and in Rio de Janeiro, they developed the idea of creating an iconoclastic mixture of music in which everything would have its space. Luiz Gonzaga, the Beatles, Chuck Berry, Jean-Luc Godard, João Gilberto: everything would be cannibalized and put into the stew. Their lyrics would be sometimes poignant, other times surreal, always provocative.

In Tropicália, anything went: rock and samba, folk music and urban music, the erudite and the kitsch, berimbaus and electronic instruments, noise and shouts. There had been rock and roll in Brazil since the late-1950s, but this was the first time it was being mixed with native styles (among other things).

Tropicália was not only a musical movement. It was an entire arts movement, which lasted roughly from 1967 to 1969. It manifested itself in music, film, theater, poetry, and the plastic arts. (The word "Tropicália" came from the title of a 1967 ambient-art piece by Hélio Oiticica.)

Some of the Tropicalistas' ideas had precedents in the works of the *Paulista* poet Oswald de Andrade, who four decades earlier had created the concept of artistic cannibalism, which he discussed in his "Cannibalistic Manifesto" of 1928. Gil and Veloso took Andrade's ideas to heart, devouring everything—national music and themes and imported cultural elements—and then re-elaborating it all "with autonomy" as Andrade had urged.

Others participated in the movement, including Tom Zé, Gal Costa, bossa muse Nara Leão, Torquato Neto, Os Mutantes, Capinam and Júlio Medaglia (another classical conductor). Together with Gil and Veloso, these artists released *Tropicália* in 1968, an album that was a collective manifesto.

Musically and lyrically, Tropicalista songs were often intelligent, provocative, and ironic montages. One of its most representative songs was Gil and Neto's "Geléia Geral" (General Jelly), which mixed *bumba-meu-boi*, a northeastern folk genre, with electric rock instrumentation. In the song's lyrics, the traditional was juxtaposed with the modern.

Rogério Duprat's arrangements accented the contemporary and traditional references. For example, he added tamborim percussion when the samba school Portela was mentioned. To further add to the mix, the word "bumba-meu-boi" is juxtaposed ironically with "*iê-iê-iê*" (yeah-yeah-yeah), the pejorative name given by Brazilian critics to 1960s rock and roll.

Not all the public understood what Gil and Veloso were doing. Many of them hated it. They didn't like the rock and roll part of it, they didn't like the electric guitars. When Veloso presented his latest outrage in 1968 in São Paulo, during the International Song Festival, he was booed even more loudly than he had been for "Alegria, Alegria." He appeared with the rock group Os Mutantes (who were dressed in plastic clothes) and performed "É Proibido Proibir" (Forbidding Is Forbidden). He didn't get to finish the song, but he did give a famous extemporaneous speech castigating his intolerant audience. It would take them a few years to get the point. Tropicália temporarily opened a gap between the political avant-garde and the cultural avant-garde, but by the early 1970s its ideas would be quite acceptable.

Tropicália songs were aesthetically daring and sporadically brilliant, and included a few masterpieces such as "Domingo no Parque." Ironically, the most controversial Tropicália tunes—the ones with the strongest rock and roll influence—were generally the weakest of the bunch. The movement had a brief life (it was over by 1969), but greatly accelerated MPB's musical experimentation and hybridization, and gave all musicians who came after it a greater sense of freedom.

THE MPB GENERATION

The creativity of Caetano Veloso and Gilberto Gil by no means ended once the Tropicália years were over. As the 1990s began, both artists remained at the forefront of their generation of Brazilian popular musicians, breaking new musical ground time and time again.

Gilberto Gil in 1989.

Maria Bethânia, Caetano Veloso, Gal Costa, and Gilberto Gil's 1976 album *Doces Bárbaros*.

Gilberto Gil

Gilberto Gil has continued to experiment with new musical styles, blending together international pop music (rock, funk, reggae) with Brazilian urban and folkloric music in his own singular extroverted, upbeat style.

Born in 1942 in Salvador, Gil spent his childhood and adolescence in the small town of Ituaçu, in the interior of Bahia state. There he absorbed a wide variety of influences: Luiz Gonzaga, classical music, polka, Italian music, fado, Celia Cruz, mambo, samba, bolero, Yma Sumac, Duke Ellington, Miles Davis, and Chet Baker. (Having such a rich musical diet at a young age may be one reason why Brazilian musicians so often excel at being original and eclectic songwriters). Gil's first instrument was the accordion, then later he switched to guitar after hearing a startling new song on the radio: João Gilberto's groundbreaking bossa tune "Chega de Saudade."

After studying business administration at the federal university in Salvador (where he met Veloso and Bethânia), and a brief stint working for a multinational corporation in São Paulo, Gil became a fulltime professional musician. His recording career kicked off in 1965 with a single containing the folkish protest tunes "Roda" (Wheel) and "Procissão" (Procession). In 1966, Elis Regina and Jair Rodrigues recorded the Gil-Torquato Neto tune "Louvação" (Praise), and it was a big success; Gil began to appear regularly on the "O Fino da Bossa" TV show.

Meanwhile, Gil and his close friend Caetano Veloso were absorbing new influences from the Beatles, psychedelia, and the hippies. In 1968 Gil's first two albums were released, *Louvação* and *Gilberto Gil*. The Tropicalistas succeeded in irritating the military dictatorship, who feared that the movement might sway Brazilian youth toward an alternative lifestyle that included drugs, chaos, and hippiedom. Gil was jailed in 1969 but never charged with a specific crime. "Just for being different," recalled Gil, "unexpected, daring, bold, adventurous, unknown, and dangerous." He laughed: "I never considered my lyrics and everything as really heavy. Never. My attitude—okay. But my words...."

In prison, Gil took up yoga, meditation, and a macrobiotic diet. Once out, he left for England, as did Veloso, and lived there in a self-imposed exile until 1972. When he returned to Brazil, both the government and nationalist-minded Brazilians were no longer so critical of Gil and his Tropicalista peers. Their rock-and-roll-flavored music was no longer seen as subversive by the Right or culturally imperialist by the Left. It was instead viewed as healthy experimentation and a necessary critique of Brazil and the modern world.

From this point on, Gil began to delve heavily into his Afro-Brazilian roots and to incorporate them into global pop fusions. In 1976 he paraded during Carnaval with the Filhos de Gandhi afoxé group and in 1977 attended an arts festival in Lagos, Nigeria; both experiences would profoundly affect his work in years to come. In Lagos, Gil met Fela Kuti, Stevie Wonder, and other African descendants from all over the world. "That caused something shaking, emotional, very intuitive, telluric. Like being replanted in the soil of Africa and then being able to flourish as a new tree," remembered Gil.

He expanded his exploration of African culture; the 1977 album *Refavela* included "Baba Alapalá" (an homage to the candomblé god Xangô), the marvelous afoxé "Patuscada de Gandhi," the use of Yoruba words in several songs, and the marked influence of Nigerian musical styles like highlife and ju-ju. Gil's self-immersion in his African roots paralleled the rise in Salvador of *blocos afro* (Afro-Brazilian Carnaval groups). Gil's participation in Bahia's "re-Africanization" helped propel the whole process.

From the late 1970s through the 1980s, Gil's albums continued to explore new territory with a variety of song styles: the funk-afoxé of "Toda Menina Baiana" (Every Bahian Girl) in 1978, the reggae "Vamos Fugir" (Let's Escape), recorded with the Wailers in 1984, and numerous songs exploring rock and technopop. His acute lyrics critiqued society; his lilting voice sang ballads; and his rhythmic blends evoked "a dance of the whole planet" as he sang in "Banda Um" (Band One). In the late eighties Gil became involved in politics, taking two years off from music to serve as the secretary of culture for the city of Salvador and to campaign and win a city-council office.

Caetano Veloso

Caetano Veloso (full name: Caetano Emanuel Vianna Telles Veloso), was born in 1942 in Santo Amaro da Purificação, Bahia. He was heavily influenced as a singer by his idol João Gilberto. As a composer, Caetano has an extraordinary ability to weave words and melody together in such a way that it is difficult to imagine them separately. A former philosophy

Caetano Veloso.

Caetano onstage with Elba Ramalho.

student and film critic in Salvador, Caetano is a restless intellectual. A severe critic of Brazilian music and himself, he is always ready to try new paths later followed by his MPB peers. To those who opposed Tropicália's mix of Brazilian music with foreign elements, Caetano retorted, "To say that samba can only be made with a tamborim, a frigideira, and a guitar without sevens and nines is not a solution."

In his own way, Caetano is quite nationalistic with regard to music. Veloso is famous for his knowledge of old Brazilian songs and was responsible for the comebacks of venerable figures like Luiz Gonzaga, the king of baião, who had been forgotten during the sixties.

Throughout that decade and the next, Caetano would embrace old styles and create new ones. In 1969, he recorded "Atrás do Trio Elétrico," which captured the sound of the musicians who play kinetic frevo atop sound trucks called "trios elétricos" during Carnaval in Salvador. He cut romantic, lyrical songs. And he also released experimental albums. For example, 1973's *Araçá Azul* combined static, folkloric music and incidental noise. It was perhaps the worst-selling album of all time by a big-name MPB artist. Yet his 1977 album *Bicho* (Animal) was very accessible, and featured many danceable tunes.

Each Veloso album was a quest for self-renovation and expanded possibilities. The song "O Que Queres" (What You Want) from 1984 was quintessential Caetano:

Where you want the act, I am spirit . . .
Where you want romance, (I am) rock and roll
Where you want the moon, I am the sun
Where you want pure nature, (I am) insecticide.

Like Gil, Caetano disturbed the authorities with his Tropicalista "chaos." He was imprisoned by the regime for four months in 1969, before a two-year exile in London. When he came home, leftists who had neither understood nor liked Veloso during Tropicália tried to adopt him as a symbol of resistance to the government, as they had with Chico Buarque. Veloso destroyed this idea in his first show by dancing on stage like Carmen Miranda, shocking both the Left and the Right. Brazil was not ready for androgynous behavior.

An iconoclast, Caetano has continued to startle followers ever since. "My role is to change people's minds," he has said, and his lyrics are often provocative and discursive, as in "Ele Me Deu um Beijo na Boca" (He Gave Me a Kiss on the Mouth), a 1982 song with many verses that

Caetano conceived as an imaginary dialogue with a friend, covering life, politics, music, art, spirituality:

> He gave me a kiss on the mouth and told me
> Life is empty like the bonnet of a headless baby
> …like the burrow of a drunken fox
> And I said enough of this talk, this bottomless well.

Musically, Caetano has explored samba, rock, bossa, afoxé, frevo, reggae, and most everything else, each style beautifully counterpointing his delicate, João Gilberto-influenced vocals and inquisitive words. Mass popular acceptance came in the 1980s, when Caetano went from cult figure to full-fledged star. He co-hosted a TV musical show with Chico Buarque ("Chico & Caetano"), had his songs covered extensively by other artists, and released two albums: 1987's *Caetano* and 1989's *Estrangeiro* (Foreigner) that found him still on his searching, wondering, contrary path. In "Branquinha" (Little White Girl), he sang "I am only an old Bahian/ A John Doe, a Caetano, any guy/ I go against the way, sing against the melody."

Gal Costa

Another participant in Tropicália was the singer Gal Costa, who was the movement's primary female representative. Her real name was Maria da Graça Costa Penna Burgos, and she was born in 1945 in Salvador. Wearing beads, necklaces, and colorful blouses, Gal's artistic career and lifestyle were symbols, in a way, of the openness and freedom that Tropicália sought: she was hippie, sophisticated torchsinger, Carnaval celebrant, and audacious sex symbol.

From the Tropicália days through the 1980s, Gal would work in close collaboration on many albums with Gil and Veloso, her friends from Bahia. Her recording career kicked off in 1967, when she cut *Domingo* (Sunday) with Caetano; then in 1968 she appeared on the *Tropicália* collective album and also released her first solo LP, *Gal Costa*.

While Gil and Veloso were living in exile, Gal was their spokesperson and would record their songs in Brazil. She also interpreted tunes by Roberto Carlos and Erasmo Carlos, Luis Melodia, and Jorge Ben. In the early years of her career, Gal's naturally beautiful voice could sometimes be raucous and uncontrolled,

Gal Costa.

especially on the more rock or blues-based numbers. But she began working hard to improve her technique. By the 1980s, her singing was superbly modulated, and her voice could be sweet or aggressive, poignant or seductive, gentle or piercing.

In that decade, she recorded in a variety of song styles (as befits an ex-Tropicalista), including samba, baião, frevo, blues, and rock. Her commercial success steadily grew, climaxing with her version of the Moraes Moreira-Abel Silva frevo "Festa do Interior" (Party in the Interior), the huge hit of the 1982 Carnaval season and part of the double-platinum album *Fantasia*. By 1984, her international fame was such that her album *Profana* (Profane) was released in Argentina, Japan, Venezuela, Spain, Italy, Israel, Portugal, Chile, Uruguay, Peru, and the United States.

Maria Bethânia

It should not be surprising that, like Costa, vocalist Maria Bethânia has also been closely involved with Gilberto Gil and Caetano Veloso throughout her career since she is Veloso's sister. Maria (real name Maria Vianna Telles Veloso) was the first of the foursome to gain fame. With her eloquent, sensuous voice, she quickly attracted attention as a singer, and hers would soon be the background music of choice for many a

Maria Bethânia.

Brazilian romantic rendezvous. In 1965, she recorded João do Vale's hard-hitting protest song "Carcará" and became nationally known as an intense, passionate vocal interpreter. That same year she replaced Nara Leão in the famous protest play *Opinião*.

Bethânia, born in 1946 in the town of Santo Amaro da Purificação, was until 1978—like Caetano—largely a cult figure. A small but faithful group of fans would attend her shows, in which she would perform barefoot, walking and running around the stage, reciting poetry and singing theatrically, capturing the hearts and minds of the audience with her personal magnetism. She did not seem to want stardom and did not even take part in Tropicália. Keeping away from groups, she was nicknamed "Rio's Greta Garbo." But Maria's 1978 album *Alibi* marked a turning point in her career. Her interpretations of romantic ballads by Chico Buarque, Gonzaguinha, and others so pleased the public that the LP eventually sold more than one million copies, the first time a female recording artist had done that in Brazil.

The album's success started a trend wherein female singers became the biggest record sellers: Bethânia, Costa, Simone, Clara Nunes, Beth Carvalho, and others sold millions of records in the late 1970s and early 1980s. Since then, Maria has become the female counterpoint to Roberto Carlos; she is the queen and he is the king of Brazilian romantic music. An artist who once sang for small, elite audiences, Maria now sings broken-heart songs for a huge legion of fans. She is also recognized internationally, and has performed in Argentina, France, and the United States, among many other countries.

Jorge Ben: Rhythm and Samba

Jorge Ben is another Brazilian artist who has helped bring cultural walls tumbling down, although without being shocking like the Tropicalistas or overtly political like Edu Lobo and Geraldo Vandré. Ben has simply fused the styles of different countries in his music in a very smooth, non-abrasive way that few listeners can resist. One of Brazil's most rhythmically creative musicians, Ben's tunes have a contagious swing, a transcontinental Afro-groove. The singer-guitarist-composer has been mixing rhythmic elements from North America, Brazil, and Africa since the 1960s, and some have termed his music "rhythm and samba."

Jorge Ben, who changed his name to Jorge Benjor in the late eighties.

Jorge (real name Jorge Duílio Menezes) was born in Rio in 1940. He started his career during the bossa boom years but would hit his stride during the MPB era. His career was helped by appearances in the festivals, notably the 1969 International Song Festival (FIC) in Rio.

Critics that give more importance to harmony and melody than to rhythm have accused Ben's music of being repetitive. But it is in rhythm that Jorge has let his creativity run free. Ben's songs fuse elements of rock, samba, maracatu, and baião, to which he adds his own very personal musical signature, which seems to trace straight back to some lost "fountain of swing" in Africa.

Jorge's best concerts are like tribal celebrations in which the entire audience dances almost to the point of a trance, propelled by Ben's funky, infectious rhythm-guitar strumming and the dense rhythms of his band Zé Pretinho. The latter often features two bass players, two drum sets, and three or more percussionists. Colorful, energetic, highly syncopated, Ben's music creates a celebratory atmosphere.

Like many musicians from his generation, Jorge Ben only started to take his guitar playing seriously after he heard João Gilberto, but "bossa nova harmonies were too complicated and I couldn't imitate them." So he developed his own style, playing only with the thumb and the forefinger. He used "mostly the bass strings of the guitar, resolving the song in the minor tones. That made bass and guitar clash all the time," bassist Roberto Colossi told *Nova História da MPB*. (Colossi sometimes accompanied Jorge Ben when he was playing bossa nova in the early 1960s.)

Back then it was so hard for bassists to play with Jorge that, on some cuts of his first album, the producer decided not to have a bass, leaving it all for Jorge's guitar. He also found a way of placing lyrics in his songs that many conservative musicians thought was wrong, ignoring the normal relation of syllables to notes. Often his words were longer than the musical phrases, which made him stretch the melody to fit his verses. And those verses often pursued unusual themes, such as alchemy, soccer, spaceships, and bandits, as well as love and daily life.

Jorge scored his first big hit in 1963 with the kinetic, irresistible "Mas, Que Nada" (Oh, Come On), a light pop mix of bossa and samba that dropped references to macumba and had a soaring chorus. The latter element would be well exploited by Sérgio Mendes, who scored a hit in the United States with "Mas, Que Nada" in 1966, with Lani Hall and Karen Philip singing the tune in Portuguese. Mendes rerecorded the tune in 1989 for his *Arara* album. Herb Alpert, Dizzy Gillespie, and José Feliciano would also record Ben's tunes.

In Brazil, Jorge enjoyed more successes. Since political themes never were part of Jorge's songs, he had no problems staying in the country after the 1968 crackdown. But by the time the 1970 FIC was staged, Act No. 5 was in full swing and many musicians had already left. The festivals began to lose their vitality, with many stars absent and the shadow of the dictatorship looming ominously. At that year's event, government censors prohibited twenty-five of the thirty-six finalists from performing their songs. Many musicians, such as Tom Jobim and Chico Buarque, signed a petition against censorship. They were arrested.

Ben's song "Eu Tambem Quero Mocotó" did go on stage and was performed by the singer Erlon Chaves and three female backup vocalists. They were arrested too, because censors decided the song and the dancing of the women were too lascivious.

When Ben won the 1972 FIC with "Fio Maravilha," it was the end of an era. There would be other, smaller musical festivals held later in the decade, but this would be the last major event of its kind.

Ben's career was solidly established thanks to his many hits between 1969 and 1972. In the seventies and eighties, he successfully toured Europe, and expanded his sonic range further. On his 1989 album *Benjor*, he jammed with his guest artists Nigeria's King

MARISA MONTE

One of the most promising young artists to appear at the end of the 1980s was Marisa Monte, who was born in Rio in 1967. She launched her eponymous first album in 1989 and achieved immediate success. She has a strong, versatile voice that can move from a deep, bluesy growl to a sweet, vulnerable vibrato. She is comfortable interpreting everything from Carmen Miranda to samba to rock to Luiz Gonzaga to Kurt Weill to a reggae version of "I Heard It Through the Grapevine."

Marisa Monte.

Sunny Ade and the Brazilian rock-ska-reggae band the Paralamas do Sucesso.

Also in 1989, Jorge's 1976 tune "Ponta de Lança Africano (Umbabarauma)" was included on David Byrne's *Beleza Tropical* anthology. The tune sounded contemporary and fresh. As the 1990s began, Ben's universal groove was still ahead of its time.

Ivan Lins and Vítor Martins

During the prime of the big televised festivals like the FIC and TV Record events, many young musicians felt shut out of these commercialized contests. In 1968, the Universitário Festival became an alternative. It was directed toward college students and sponsored initially by

Ivan Lins.

Rio's TV Tupi channel. One of those who attracted a lot of attention at the Universitário events was a singer-songwriter who played the piano: Ivan Lins.

American jazz flutist Herbie Mann stated that Lins "is the genius of lyrical music in Brazil, a magician with harmony. I've recorded fifteen to twenty of his songs and for me he's on the same par as Gershwin, Kern, Rogers and Hart, as well as Ravel and Debussy." Pianist George Duke said, "He reminds me of a modern-day Michel Legrand, the way his chords move, the way the circle of fifths move around. His chords are complicated, but the melody is so strong it's undeniable."

Born in Rio in 1945, Lins grew up in the Tijuca neighborhood. He started playing piano as a teenager, influenced by Luis Eça and João Donato. Later, he performed in a jazz-bossa trio while studying chemical engineering at college. Lins also loved the singing of David Clayton-Thomas, the lead vocalist for the American jazz-rock band Blood, Sweat and Tears, and in trying to sing like him developed a hoarse, soulful vocal style. It didn't really sound like Clayton-Thomas, but it intrigued TV Globo executives, who were looking for artists to fill the shoes of the many exiled musicians in the sixties. Globo created a show, "Som Livre Exportação," and invited Lins and others from the university festivals to host and perform on it. The program was a great success, and Ivan became a major star. Unfortunately, he also was massively overexposed, and when the network cancelled the show, the young artist went through hard times.

For Ivan, success returned in 1977 with his record *Somos Todos Iguais Nesta Noite* (We Are All the Same Tonight). By then he was already working with his most important lyricist, Vítor Martins, and had developed his instrumental skills after studying with Wilma Graça, who had also taught Lobo, Nascimento, Francis Hime (Buarque's songwriting partner), and Gonzaguinha (the son of Luiz Gonzaga).

Ivan's harmonies had begun to incorporate difficult chords and the frequent use of minor seconds. "There was a lot of jazz influence, bossa

GONZAGUINHA

Singer-songwriter Gonzaguinha, aka Luiz Gonzaga, Jr. (he is the son of the singer-accordionist Gonzaga, the famed northeastern musician) is another performer who gained visibility through the university music festivals. From 1973 on, with aggressive and ironic lyrics sung atop a mixture of urban and rural Brazilian music, he protested the country's situation and battled government censors (they blacklisted fifteen songs from his debut album). In time, after censorship waned, Gonzaguinha's romantic and good-humored side came to the fore with songs like "Feijão Maravilha" (Marvelous Beans). But he never forgot his desire for a more just society. His album *É* (Is) was released in North America in 1990.

Gonzaguinha, left, in concert with fellow MPB star Fagner, right. In many ways, Gonzaguinha helped fill the vacuum created by Geraldo Vandré's departure in the 1970s.

nova, Milton Nascimento, Dori Caymmi, Debussy, Ravel," Ivan says. He adds that such influences are not always obvious in his music, but "it is like when you try to fly Ravel's plane with your own engines." Ivan's singing also became more natural, less strained, more himself. He scored hits like "Nos Dias de Hoje" (In the Days of Today), "Começar de Novo" (Start Again), known as "The Island" in its English-language version, "Vitoriosa" (Victorious), and "Dinorah, Dinorah," achieving commercial success and critical acclaim.

Vítor Martins' eloquent lyrics contributed greatly to Ivan's comeback, and after 1978 Martins could be more outspoken in his verses as censorship loosened. For example, his words to "Antes Que Seja Tarde" (Before It Is Too Late) included these lines:

> We must liberate the dreams of our
>   youth before it is too late
> Men must be changed
> Before the call is extinguished
> Before faith dies out
> Before it is too late.

This is not to say Martins only writes anthems; he also writes some of the best romantic verses in Brazilian song.

At the end of the seventies Lins began to be discovered in the United States. Paul Winter recorded Lins and Ronaldo Monteiro's "Velho Sertão" in 1978, giving it a new name in English and using it as the title track for his album *Common Ground*. Lins gained further attention when Quincy Jones took notice of his music. Jones was about to produce a new album by jazz guitarist and vocalist George Benson, *Give Me the Night*. When the LP was released in 1980 it contained Lins' "Love Dance," with English lyrics by Paul Williams, and "Dinorah, Dinorah." Then Jones himself recorded "Velas" (Sails) on his 1981 album *The Dude*. The song won a Grammy for best jazz instrumental performance.

The doors were open for Lins and some of America's greatest jazz artists scrambled to record his compositions, coveted for their strong melodies, Brazilian rhythms, and interesting chords. Patti Austin, Herbie Mann, Joe Pass, Sarah Vaughan, and Ella Fitzgerald covered his compositions. Diane Schuur recorded "Love Dance" on her 1985 LP

Schuur Thing. And in 1986, Ivan sang two of his tunes on Dave Grusin and Lee Ritenour's Grammy Award-winning *Harlequin* album. But it didn't stop there.

In 1987, jazz singer Mark Murphy released *Night Mood,* an entire album of Lins tunes. The Manhattan Transfer vocal quartet recorded versions of "Antes Que Seja Tarde" and "Arlequim Desconhecido" (Unknown Harlequin) on their Grammy Award-winning *Brasil* album in 1987. The next year, Ivan sang two of his songs on the Crusaders' LP *Life in the Modern World.* And in 1989 he released his U.S. debut, *Love Dance.* After Tom Jobim and Milton Nascimento, Ivan Lins has become the most-recorded Brazilian composer outside Brazil in recent times.

João Bosco

João Bosco is one of MPB's most eclectic and imaginative musicians, and like Lins, garnered attention after successful university song festival appearances. Bosco often performs solo in concert, with just an acoustic guitar to accompany his singing. That's more than enough: he is the most self-sufficient of musicians, a band unto himself. He sits on a stool in an arena such as Rio's Canecão, wearing a red bow tie and a white silk shirt, easily inspiring the audience to sing along to a beautiful melody. Then he is apt to throw out a funny improvised line to make them laugh uproariously. Plucking the guitar strings with an infectious samba swing or in intricate flamenco patterns, Bosco moves from samba to merengue to bop, from Jackson do Pandeiro to the jazz standard "Round Midnight" to Ary Barroso. He'll add a few bars of Gershwin to a performance or scat a rendition of Ravel's "Bolero." He is like a postmodern troubadour, alternating the sublime with the ironic in flowing songs that incorporate radical modulations of key and idiom and tone.

Born in 1946 in Ponte Nova, Minas Gerais, Bosco recorded many successful albums in the seventies and had his songs covered by Elis Regina and many others. Until the mid-eighties, almost all of João's compositions were written with Aldir Blanc, a psychiatrist who gave up his profession to pen lyrics for Bosco's sambas and boleros.

Bosco in concert.

Blanc (born in Rio in 1946) writes stanzas that can be serious, ironic, surreal, ludicrous, simple, and full of multiple meanings—all in the same song. They are packed with Brazilian cultural references and comment about social manners and life among the working class. In "Bandalhismo" (Good-for-Nothing-Ism) in 1980, Blanc wittily updated a 1902 poem by Augusto dos Anjos ("Vandalismo"), bringing it into the sad underclass here and now: "My heart has squalid taverns/...Where trembling vagabond hands beat out samba-enredos on a matchbox."

João Bosco.

In more playful lyrics, Blanc may use Portuguese, Yoruba, Tupi, French, English, Spanish words, and polylingual combinations thereof, as well as vocalese, extensive slang, and imaginative puns.

Working together, Blanc and Bosco have created some of MPB's greatest standards, including some modern sambas that are an important contribution to the genre. Their 1984 album *Gagabirô* was a creative tour-de-force that fused Brazilian, African, and Cuban styles and showed off their multifaceted, virtuosic talents.

Americans heard Bosco for the first time on guitarist Lee Ritenour's *Festival* LP, on which João contributed vocals to his compositions "Latin Lovers" and "Odilê, Odilá." By the end of the eighties, he and Blanc were no longer writing songs together and had gone their separate ways.

Luis Melodia

In 1975 the TV Globo network tried to revive the by-then nearly defunct festivals. It promoted an event called "Abertura" (Opening) that as a whole wasn't successful but had the merit of giving larger exposure to a musician who was a cult artist at the time: Luis Melodia.

Samba, rock, blues, funk, baião: Melodia's musical language uses all these vocabularies. Bluesamba might be a good label for his work. His inventive tunes, full of original rhythmic divisions, are intricate and oblique. His lyrics are

Luis Melodia in concert in 1988.

surprising, often surrealistic, sung in an anguished, very personal voice. But Luis Melodia is not a big name in Brazil. He's more of a cult figure.

Luis Carlos dos Santos, his real name, is from the Estácio neighborhood in Rio, the cradle of samba. Born in 1951, he had his first taste of popularity at the age of twenty, when famed MPB vocalists Gal Costa and Maria Bethânia recorded his songs. Costa sang "Pérola Negra" (Black Pearl), and it became an instant classic. In the song, soothing trombone, piano, and bass guitar notes build a bluesy atmosphere in which the instruments tenderly work as a counterpoint to Melodia's calm voice tinged with anguish. The melody is slow, recitative, almost trance-inducing.

Melodia's first album was released in 1973, featuring a rhythmic mix of soul music, choro, rock, samba-canção. The record didn't sell much, but it had a great impact on the media. In 1975 Luis appeared at the Abertura festival and recorded his biggest hit single "Juventude Transviada" (Youth Led Astray), in which he sang: "Each face represents a lie/ Birth, life, and death/ Who would ever say." In 1976 he released a second album, *Maravilhas Contemporâneas* (Contemporary Marvels), then left his native Rio to live on Itaparica, an island near Salvador. He spent two years there, fishing, playing the guitar, and writing new songs. When he thought he was ready, he came back to make a new record. Such periodic cycles of stardom and withdrawal have formed the routine of his career. Through 1989, Melodia had released only six albums, bought by a loyal following that includes many of Brazil's top MPB and rock musicians.

Djavan

The song "Fato Consumado" (Consummated Fact) by Djavan took second place at the same 1975 Abertura Festival where Melodia performed his big hit. Djavan (pronounced Dee-jah-von) was the last big MPB star to be introduced by the dwindling festival system.

One of Brazil's most popular musicians in the eighties, Djavan Caetano Viana is also one of its best known performers outside the country. His songs, with their radiant melodies and funky, jazzy Brazilian swing, have been covered by many international artists. He is also known for his bright, clear, highly expressive voice, heard by many North Americans on his U.S. albums *Bird of Paradise* and *Puzzle of Hearts*, as well as on albums by Lee Ritenour, the Manhattan Transfer, and Don Grusin.

Born in 1949 in Maceió, the capital of the northeastern state of Alagoas, Djavan came to Rio at sixteen to try to establish a musical career. He brought with him a guitar and a bag of mixed influences, including Bahian and northeastern music, bossa nova, and jazz. Comparing himself to his famous peers from the Northeast such as Fagner, Alceu Valença, and Geraldo Azevedo, Djavan said, "They make music that is more regional, mine is more cosmopolitan." With these musical elements, Djavan forged a sophisticated, rhythmically vibrant, pan-American style that is his alone.

Djavan has viewed his music as a demonstration of affection towards people. "When I started my career Brazil was a different country already. I don't write protest songs like those that appeared after 1964. I write love songs, and expressing love is a way of protesting against this violent world." Djavan's lyrics might be called minimalist-symbolist. He sparingly uses exact words to convey his messages—sometimes clear, sometimes cryptic—as he explores love, emotion, nature, and mysticism. His lyrics to "Faltando um Pedaço" (Missing a Piece) are a good example: "Love is a big lasso, a step into a trap/ A wolf running in circles, to feed the pack."

Djavan.

Success in Brazil came for Djavan with his third album, *Djavan*, after which famous singers like Nana Caymmi, Gal Costa, Caetano Veloso, and Maria Bethânia recorded his songs. In the 1980s, his most successful albums in Brazil were *Luz* and *Lilás*. The former was recorded in the United States in 1982 with Djavan's band Sururu de Capote and guests Stevie Wonder, Hubert Laws, and Ernie Watts. Almost all the songs on *Luz* (Light) were hits in Brazil and it made Djavan a superstar. Small theaters were not big enough for his concerts anymore: he filled arenas all over the country.

Released in 1984, *Lilás* (Lilac) was also recorded in the U.S. and had a jazzy Américan accent in the arrangements and instrumentation. Djavan then went back to his roots on *Meu Lado* (My Side), recorded in Rio with the talents of drummer Téo Lima, bassist Sizão Machado, and keyboardists Hugo Fattoruso and Jota Moraes. It fused various Brazilian and Hispanic-American rhythms, and included a song in Zulu, Enoch Sontonga's "Hymn of the African National Congress." Then as now, Djavan has aptly balanced the sounds of three continents in his music.

Simone.

Simone

There were some great MPB artists who were not introduced by the festivals, as was the case with the singer Simone. About her, Don Grusin commented, "She has a kind of phrasing that I think no one else has. She really is a master of phraseology, as they used to say about Sinatra. When she lays out just a few notes and words, and comes to the end of it and her voice turns just a little, it kills me."

Tall, lean, and striking, Simone Bittencourt was born in Salvador in 1949 and was a member of the Brazilian national basketball team before becoming a professional singer. She recorded her first album *Simone* in 1973 and toured Europe as part of a "Panorama Brasileiro" multi-artist spectacular. The French audiences loved her, and a newspaper there described Simone as "a great singer with the smile of a madonna, feline to the nails, with a fragile sensuality in each of her interpretations."

Her deep, mellifluous voice has a special quality: it can seduce like a mistress, comfort like a mother, beckon like a siren. Simone also has a stage presence that is elegant, sexy, commanding. Both factors caused her to have tremendous success in both Europe and Brazil in the seventies and eighties.

Brazilians also expected her to be outspoken and to include politicized anthems on occasion. In 1979 she gave a now-legendary concert at which she performed Geraldo Vandré's most famous protest song, "Caminhando"

(Walking). This was a courageous act, since the Abertura had only recently curtailed their censorship and the military was still solidly in charge of Brazil. A great rustling and excitement could be heard in the audience when Simone began singing the song's first verses, "Walking and singing, following the tune."

Simone became one of Brazil's most popular vocalists, and she has performed to more than 100,000 fans twice—in 1981 at São Paulo's Morumbi

Stadium and in 1982 in Rio's Quinta da Boa Vista park. Like Costa and Bethânia, Simone has interpreted a wide variety of MPB material on her albums, including songs by Bosco and Blanc, Nascimento, Buarque, Tunai (João Bosco's brother), Francis Hime, Moraes Moreira, and Sueli Costa. From samba to MPB to romantic ballads, Simone is one of Brazil's top singers of her time.

MPB'S LEGACY

What if the military dictatorship and censorship had not affected the evolution of MPB? Singer-songwriter Geraldo Azevedo, who was imprisoned twice by the regime, felt the repression "interrupted a Brazilian cultural cycle." André Midani, president of WEA Brazil, disagreed. "It didn't kill a thing. On the contrary, I think it was a kind of catalyst. You had your big enemy, you wrote against him, and tried to pass your message along in spite of him. But when censorship disappeared, many MPB composers lost their compass; suddenly you could say whatever you wanted."

In any event, under pressure and in the thick of difficult times, MPB's composers and interpreters were a vital part of Brazil's cultural life from the late sixties to the end of the eighties. They came of age under brutal repression as their country suffered through the dark years of a military dictatorship, and in many ways they spoke for those voices who had been silenced by the government. MPB singers and songwriters took Western popular music to new heights, and touched both Brazil and the world.

PARÁ

TONINHO HORTA

MILTON

BAHIA

GOIÁS

MINAS GERAIS

MATO
GROSSO
DO SUL

Belo Horizonte
●

ESPÍRITO
SANTO

Três Pontas
●

SÃO PAULO

RIO DE JANEIRO

São Paulo
●

Rio de Janeiro
●

BETO GUEDES

SANTA
CATARINA

RIO GRANDE
DO SUL

WAGNER TISO, MILTON NASCIMENTO, TIM HAUSER

MILTON AND MINAS

CHAPTER 5

The rolling green hills of Minas Gerais hid
these are material, like the impressive dep
discovered in the eighteenth century in this B
literally means "General Mines." These treasu
Ouro Preto and São João del Rey, masterpiece,
they also helped bankroll the industrial revolut
Mineiro gold to pay for English manufactured

The region also holds secrets of a different ki
Political conspiracies have been plotted here: the
independence movement led by the dentist Tira
1789 by the colonial government. Mineiros
know how to keep quiet about their plans
and real feelings. They have a reputation in
Brazil for being quiet, complex, and mystical.
Such a temperament befits their environment:
Minas is mountainous, landlocked, and
located on a high plateau to the north of Rio
de Janeiro and São Paulo. It has a cooler
climate than the sultry, humid Atlantic coast.
Accordingly, Mineiros are much less expansive
than the extroverted Brazilians one finds in
Rio and Bahia.

The music of Milton Nascimento reflects
this difference; in it one can hear the more
reflective, pastoral, and spiritual nature of the
Mineiro. Nascimento is arguably the single
most important figure from the MPB
generation and one of the most accomplished
singers and composers that Brazilian popular
music has ever produced. Many of his
musical collaborators from Minas Gerais—

A church in Ouro Preto,
one of the oldest cities in
Minas Gerais state.

Wagner Tiso, Toninho Horta, Lô Borges, Márcio Borges, Beto Guedes,
Tavinho Moura, and Fernando Brant—have also made important
contributions to Brazilian music. Collectively nicknamed the *clube da
esquina* (the corner club) by the Brazilian press, many of these musicians

Milton Nascimento.

grew up in the same towns and first played together in cities like Três Pontas and Belo Horizonte, later establishing their musical careers on the larger stages of Rio and São Paulo.

The music of Nascimento and his Mineiro colleagues is full of elaborate harmonies, a rich variety of styles, and a strong lyricism expressive of a yearning imagination. It carries influences from a wide variety of sources: the choir music sung in the baroque churches of Minas, the folk *toadas* heard in the countryside, and the upbeat melodic pop-rock of the Beatles.

MILTON NASCIMENTO

Nascimento's music can evoke the deep voices of monks echoing in a centuries-old church, the song of a fisherman alone by a river, or a longing falsetto that could be from any culture, from any time. His music reflects Minas Gerais, yet it is not easy to define the various elements within his songs because they display such a remarkable formal liberty and diversity of influence. Nascimento's tunes seamlessly weave together threads of Mineiro toada, bossa nova, Gregorian chants, nueva cancion, fado from Portugal, Spanish guitar, Andean flute music, as well as jazz, rock, and classical music.

While Milton sometimes writes his own lyrics, more often they are penned by his longtime partners Beto Guedes, Márcio Borges, Fernando Brant, or Ronaldo Bastos (who is a Fluminense, a native of Rio de Janeiro state). Whether Milton uses their lyrics or his own, the songs are usually messages of compassion and friendship, expressions of loneliness and the need to love, or statements against oppression.

As a singer, Nascimento has a voice that is rich in timbre and infused with emotional power. He has a wide vocal range that swings from a deep masculine sound to a high feminine falsetto, employing beautiful enunciation and soaring flights of wordless singing to interpret his compositions.

"I think he's the best singer in the world now and one of the most original composers," stated Zuza Homem de Mello, a critic of Brazilian music for four decades. "Milton writes music that is apparently simple but in actuality is very difficult. It leaves musicians trying to decipher the secrets of the music when they attempt to play it. He has changes in rhythm in the middle of a song without your being able to perceive it."

In Homem de Mello's book *Música Popular Brasileira*, he quoted keyboardist-arranger Eumir Deodato as saying that—although Milton does sometimes incorporate elements of jazz and bossa nova in his music—"the general context of his music is all based on classical music, adapted, evidently, to totally unknown rhythms. To date I have not managed to discover the rhythmic impulse he gives to his songs. It is something new, mysterious, intriguing, and challenging... few people have a deep understanding of what Milton Nascimento is."

In another book, *A Canção Brasiliera*, Milton told author Vasco Mariz that "I use different divisions in my music: for example a 6/8 within a 4/4. I compose on the guitar and afterwards record. I always have difficulties writing my songs down on paper, because of rhythmic breaks, because of the design of the guitar."

Nascimento has drawn critical praise for his albums and concerts in South America, Europe, Japan, and North America. Jazz musicians revere his compositions for their beautiful melodies and challenging chords

Milton.

and rhythms, while jazz fans have been among Nascimento's biggest admirers because his tunes are often too melancholy or complex for the average pop music listener to enjoy at first listening.

Nascimento also told writer Mariz that the type of music he makes is a toada—a short, stanza-and-refrain song usually with a sentimental or melancholy melody and narrative lyrics: "The toada is different according to the region. That of Dorival Caymmi is maritime. Mine has a connection with the region of Três Pontas. But I don't consider mine regional, as neither my harmonies nor melodies are regional. I was greatly influenced by having grown up in Minas, but I think jazz is also important in my music."

From Três Pontas to Rio

Nascimento was born in 1942 in Rio de Janeiro, the son of Maria do Carmo Nascimento, who worked in the household of Lilia Silva Campos and her husband Josino Brito de Campos. Maria died when Milton was an infant and the Campos family adopted him. When Milton was three, they moved to the small rural Minas Gerais town of Três Pontas. Surrounded by mountains, Três Pontas (Three Peaks) has narrow streets and one-story houses whose doors open straight out to the sidewalk. Life is slow-paced here: in the late afternoon families put chairs outside their front doors and have a chat before dinner.

Senhor and Senhora Campos adopted two more children (Elizabeth and Luis Fernando) and had one daughter of their own (Joceline), but Milton was the only black member of the family, which caused malicious gossip. Though he felt mistreated and suffocated by the intolerant Três Pontas mentality of that era, at home he was totally accepted as a true son. "I'm fascinated by my family," Milton told us. "I think I couldn't have had more love, education, and freedom with any other family in the world. They shaped my life."

His adoptive father Josino was a professor of mathematics at high schools in Três Pontas, and also a bank clerk, a director of the local radio station, and an amateur astronomer. He spent many nights exploring Ursa Major, the Southern Cross, and the moons of Jupiter through his telescope with his eldest son at his side. Milton came to know the heavens "like the palm of my hand."

Milton was singing and playing instruments since he could remember. "My first instrument was a harmonica my godmother gave me. Then she gave me a button accordion, and when I got it my musical life started." In his backyard, in the shade of mango, guava, and black-currant trees, Milton began conceiving musical theater entertainments for a growing band of neighborhood pals. "It was very easy for me to make up stories, like Walt Disney ones, but my own. I would imitate voices, create songs, dialogues, everything on the spot. This was around age five or six." His happiness with his friends and family contrasted sharply with the discrimination he felt elsewhere in town.

Milton with his boyhood friend and noted Brazilian keyboardist/arranger Wagner Tiso (left) and Manhattan Transfer member Tim Hauser (right) at the Som Livre Studios in Rio, working on Milton's "Viola Violar" for the Transfer's 1987 Atlantic album *Brasil*.

When he was fourteen, Nascimento played his first guitar, a steel-stringed instrument. "It was then that I started looking for sounds, discovering chords, all by ear. This was a very fertile time here in Brazil. We used to listen to everything: samba, mambo, rock, bolero, rumba, foxtrots, classical music, influences from all over the world." Milton's favorite vocal artists included the Peruvian singer Yma Sumac, Brazilian chanteuse Ângela Maria, and the United States' Ray Charles. At the same time, Milton was absorbing the various regional sounds of his state: its toadas, its church music, and the songs of the *Folia de Reis* folkloric groups that performed their dramatic dances in the post-Christmas season.

Musically, a youth spent in Minas contrasted markedly with a youth spent in Rio. Milton would later tell writer Ricardo Gontijo that "in Minas, the majority of the composers make music based in 3/4 time. Because of this, the waltz represents to us what the samba represents to the Carioca."

When he was a teenager, Milton met Wagner Tiso, who lived on the same street, and the two became close friends. They formed a rock group that had many different names, including Luar de Prata (Silver Moonlight). Milton recalled, "We played rock, ballads, foxtrots, Little Richard, every kind of music we knew. We didn't have any musical prejudices, because in small towns we liked what we liked and nobody cared what it was or where it came from. I only discovered that there was such a thing as prejudice in music when I moved to the big city." Tiso would later serve as Nascimento's arranger and eventually became a brilliant keyboardist-composer in his own right.

In 1958 Milton heard the João Gilberto single "Chega de Saudade." "I went nuts," he remembered. "This shock with bossa nova opened our minds. We started searching for bossa nova on the radio, changing stations all the time. We didn't have a TV set, and the radio broadcast we received was terrible, with lots of static. So we would listen to a song one day and only listen to it again two weeks or a month later.

"So we had an agreement. Two of us would pick out the melody—usually Wagner and I—and somebody else would get the words. We'd invent our own harmony. Without perceiving it, we created our own style for accompanying those songs. Then when we got to the big city and heard how they (other musicians) played those same songs, we said to ourselves, 'Oh, we did it all wrong!' We decided to change everything, but people convinced us not to. They said nobody did it that way and that it was really great. So this was a great stimulus for our creativity."

Milton and Wagner and their band—now called the "W's Boys"—began to play dances and travel throughout Minas Gerais, playing rock and bossa. Milton also worked as a disk jockey for the Três Pontas radio station managed by his father, and was known for excessively spinning disks by Gilberto and Henry Mancini.

In 1963, Nascimento decided to move to the state capital, Belo Horizonte, to take an accounting job in an office and, as he said, "to see what would happen." Once there, Milton met several other like-minded musicians and wrote a letter to Wagner, urging him to come. The two began playing nightclubs like the Japanese bar Fujiama with new friends that included drummer Paulinho Braga and flutist/saxophonist Nivaldo Ornellas. Milton also met his important future collaborators, the brothers Lô and Márcio Borges.

In Belo Horizonte, Milton had his first prolonged exposure to bossa and jazz musicians. The experience was overwhelming: "My first contact with jazz left me speechless. I had never seen anyone play drums that way. I had never seen anyone play bass that way. I simply felt sick. (Afterwards) I couldn't sleep well, I couldn't eat. I said to myself, 'What's that? I'll never do anything like these people.'" But soon he found out that Belo Horizonte's jazz musicians felt the same way about his music. Thus started Milton's interest in jazz, and he listened intently to records by Miles Davis, John Coltrane, Charles Mingus, and Thelonious Monk, among others.

Milton started out interpreting other people's songs. That all changed one day when he and his friend Márcio Borges went to the movie theater to see François Truffaut's *Jules and Jim*. The film's intense imagery and vivid characters had a strong effect on the two young musicians. They arrived in the afternoon and only left late that night after the last show was over. Recalled Milton, "Maybe we saw it four times in a row—I and Márcio Borges, who on that very same day became my first songwriting partner. When I left the movie theater I said to myself that I had to create something. So we went to Márcio's place and started writing songs. All my songs are like a movie—they're all very cinematographic."

Milton and Márcio continued to play together, sometimes performing in the latter's group Evolussamba. Milton also met Fernando Brant (he and Márcio would eventually become Milton's most frequent songwriting partners), and he struck up a friendship with Márcio's little brother Lô. It was with Lô that Milton discovered the Beatles, who deeply impressed him. As Milton said, "In my youth my father had a lot of classical music and opera, so I was very given to classical music. And suddenly, with the development of the Beatles, I saw the fusion that George Martin had done with certain (classical) things and what had come with that generation."

Nascimento's singing and composing skills grew rapidly. In 1964 Milton appeared on a record with composer Pacífico Mascarenhas' quartet Sambacana, and in 1965 he was invited by TV Excelsior in São Paulo to participate in its first Festival of Popular Music. Milton took fourth place, with his interpretation of Baden Powell and Luis Fernando Freire's "Cidade Vazia" (Empty City), but more importantly he met a singer by the name of Elis Regina, who—as mentioned earlier—won the event with Edu Lobo's "Arrastão." Elis would later become a key interpreter of Milton's songs.

Milton then moved to the metropolis, seeking to establish a career. He recalled, "I spent two years in São Paulo, but they were worth twenty. Some people liked me, like Elis and the Zimbo Trio, but it was very hard to get into the music scene. I played in night clubs when I had the chance but competition was fierce. There were fifty unemployed musicians for every opening." In 1966 Regina recorded Nascimento's "Canção do Sal" (Salt Song), but his struggles continued and at times he returned to playing clubs in Belo Horizonte.

Milton Discovered

Milton had a stroke of good fortune in 1967. He wasn't inclined to enter his songs in the second International Song Festival in Rio because he had hated the intense competition of the 1965 TV Excelsior event. But singer Agostinho dos Santos, who sang on the *Black Orpheus* soundtrack, had taken the shy young musician under his wing, and submitted three of Milton's songs—"Travessia" (Cross), "Morro Velho" (Old Hill), and "Maria, Minha Fé" (Maria, My Faith)—to the festival without Nascimento's knowledge. All three were accepted, a remarkable achievement that focused great attention on the reticent Milton.

Arranger Eumir Deodato, who helped convince Milton to perform at the second International Song Festival in 1967.

However, Nascimento still didn't want to perform his tunes at the festival. Enter Eumir Deodato, whom Milton had recently met and who was going to arrange the songs for the occasion. Deodato insisted, recalled Milton, "that he'd only write the arrangements if I sang at least two. So I sang 'Travessia' and 'Morro Velho,' and Agostinho sang 'Maria, Minha Fé.'"

Milton walked out onto the stage, absolutely terrified, but by the end of the event he had won the festival's best performer award. "Travessia" was picked as the festival's second-best song and became an instant classic, with its sad acoustic guitar chords and Milton's deep melodious voice that soars powerfully in the song's chorus. The melancholy and simple "Morro Velho" took seventh place, and "Maria, Minha Fé" also placed among the fifteen finalists.

Nascimento's songs astonished the Brazilian public as well as foreign visitors to the festival: Quincy Jones would long remember "Morro Velho," and would participate in its rerecording twenty years later on Nascimento's album *Yauaretê*.

All three songs from the festival were included that year on Milton's first album, *Milton Nascimento*, arranged by famed bossa nova pianist Luis Eça (the record has since been rereleased by Sigla with the title *Travessia*). His festival performance and newly issued album drew international attention: in 1968, Milton was invited to perform in Mexico and the United States, and he recorded the album *Courage* for American label A&M. Included were six songs from *Travessia*. Creed Taylor produced the LP, and musicians Deodato (organ), Herbie Hancock (piano), and Airto Moreira (percussion) participated.

Quincy Jones and Milton Nascimento in the recording studio working on a remake of "Morro Velho" for the *Yauaretê* album released by CBS in 1987.

Over the next twenty years Nascimento recorded more than two dozen albums of remarkable compositional originality and vocal creativity. In 1969 Milton returned to the studio to cut two albums for EMI Brazil (*Milton Nascimento* and *Milton*) and wrote songs for director Ruy Guerra's film *Os Deuses e Os Mortos* (The Gods and the Dead). Five of his tunes were included on jazz saxophonist Paul Desmond's 1969 LP *From the Summer Afternoon*. And the next year, Milton had a successful one-year run with his musical show *Milton Nascimento e O Som Imaginário*. One of Brazil's best progressive fusion (jazz-rock-Brazilian) groups ever, O Som Imaginário (The Imaginary Sound), would both back Milton on later albums and record three LPs as a solo entity. Som Imaginário had a changing lineup that at different times included Tiso (piano), Zé Rodrix (organ and flutes), Tavito (guitar), Fredera (guitar), Robertinho Silva (drums), Laudir de Oliveira (percussion), Toninho Horta (guitar), Luis Alves (bass), and Naná Vasconcelos (percussion).

Guitarist Beto Guedes, one of the prime members of the Clube da Esquina.

Clube de Esquina

In 1971 Milton and his inseparable pals from Minas rented a house in Piratininga, a beach in Niterói, north of Rio. They stayed there for six months and composed the majority of the songs for the double album. The LP was orchestrated by Tiso and Deodato and featured songs written by Milton, Lô Borges, Márcio Borges, Beto Guedes, Ronaldo Bastos, and Fernando Brant. The record was released in 1972, with guitarist-singer-songwriter Lô taking second billing.

The record label EMI considered *Clube da Esquina* (Corner Club) reckless at best and only released it reluctantly, but the album proved to be an inspiring melding of Brazilian pop and Anglo-American rock influences. Lô contributed the dreamy "Mineiro rock" tunes "O Trem Azul" (The Blue Train), "Nuvem Cigana" (Gypsy Cloud), and "Tudo Que Você Podia Ser" (All You Could Be), all with strong hints of groups like the Beatles and Procol Harum.

Milton's songs on the album were often more Iberian and South American in flavor, as on "San Vicente" in which academic Charles Perrone noted elements of the Chilean *tonada* style (in the guitar accompaniment) and Paraguayan *guarania* (in the bass lines). It also included surreal lyrics by Brant:

American heart, I woke from a strange dream
A taste of glass and cut
A flavor of chocolate
In the body and in the city
A taste of life and death.

There were many memorable songs on the album, including the uptempo "Cravo e Canela" (Clove and Cinnamon) and the lively "Nada Será Como Antes" (Nothing Will Be Like Before). The album sold surprisingly well, and with it Milton became commercially viable as a recording artist, as did Beto Guedes, Lô Borges, Novelli, Danilo Caymmi, Toninho Horta, and Naná Vasconcelos, among others.

With this success behind them, they all recorded albums individually or together. The name "corner club" was used long afterwards by the press to describe Milton and his collaborators, even if they weren't from Minas Gerais.

On the 1973 album *Milagre dos Peixes* (Miracle of the Fishes) Milton and the Som Imaginário delved into even more experimental territory, casting Milton's lonely voice against dense instrumental soundscapes, as the other musicians went all out with their electric, percussive, and vocal effects. They had to—the government censors had banned almost all the lyrics on the album.

Musical Journeys

Minas in 1975 included Nascimento's two personal favorite songs: "Saudade dos Aviões da Panair" (Saudades for the Panair Planes) and the haunting "Ponta de Areia" (Sand Point). Also that year, Milton was the featured guest on the album *Native Dancer* by American jazz saxophonist Wayne Shorter, who had previously covered Milton's "Vera Cruz" on the album *Moto Grosso Feio* (sic) in 1970. *Native Dancer* achieved a smooth blend of Nascimento and Shorter's compositional

styles, of the expressiveness of Milton's voice and Wayne's saxophone. Furthermore, it introduced Nascimento to a wide North American jazz audience.

On his next album, *Geraes* in 1976, Milton journeyed far into his Brazilian roots and into Latin American folk styles. The album's title came from an archaic spelling of Gerais, and many of its songs drew from research Tavinho Moura had done in regional music—principally in the Jequitinhonha River valley that winds through northern Minas and southern Bahia. One example was "Calix Bento," which Moura had adapted from a traditional Folia de Reis song. Milton also expanded his explorations of music from other parts of South America: "Volver a Los 17" was composed by Chilean songwriter Violeta Parra, and Milton interpreted it in a duet with Argentinean singer Mercedes Sosa. Yet Milton did not forget Brazil's contemporary situation; he also included a politically charged song, "O Que Será (À Flor da Pele)," penned by Chico Buarque, with whom Milton sang the duet.

In 1978 Milton gathered together with the rest of the "clube" for a sequel. More of a pan-South American fusion, the album featured less rock and not as much Anglo-American influence. Again it was an ambitious double album and an aesthetic success.

Clube da Esquina 2 began with the "Credo," a song that opened and closed with beautiful a cappella singing and included spirited Andean-style guitar, flute, and vocals backing up Brant's political lyrics:

Let's go, walking hand-in-hand with the new soul
And live planting liberty in each heart
Have faith that our people will awake
Have faith that our people will be shocked.

Flávio Venturini's beautiful "Nascente" (River-Head), featured exquisite vocal harmonies between the songwriter and Nascimento. On "Paixão e Fé" (Passion and Faith), Milton's voice is accompanied by a Petrópolis (a city in Rio de Janeiro state) church choir conducted by Father José Luiz. The song sounds a little like the Beach Boys' Brian Wilson let loose in a baroque Brazilian church. "O Que Foi Feito de Vera" (What Happened to Vera) was a stirring Milton Nascimento-Elis

Regina duet, with a superb arrangement by César Camargo Mariano. Milton also adapted another *nueva cancion* tune by Chile's Parra, "Casamiento de Negros" (Blacks' Marriage). The album incorporated disparate folk genres, and a wide variety of traditional and modern instruments.

Sentinela in 1980 further mixed contemporary sounds with traditional Mineiro and Latin American influences, all filtered through Milton's own inimitable sensibility. In the transcendent title song, the narrator is standing vigil at the deathbed of a loved one and vows that he will not forget his friend or how he died: "Death, candle, I am a sentinel/ Of the body of my brother who's departing/ In this hour I see again all that happened." The dirge-like singing of Milton and guest vocalist Nana Caymmi is given further emotional power by a full choir of Benedictine monks that backs them. Tavinho Moura's "Peixinhos do Mar" (Little Fishes of the Sea) was an adaptation of a *marujada*, a dramatic processional dance with medieval roots. Also included was Cuban poet Silvio Rodriguez's composition "Sueño com Serpientes" (Dream with Serpents), on which Mercedes Sosa shared vocals with Milton. The last two songs featured the classically trained, avant-garde Mineiro musicians Uakti, who added richly resonant sound colors with their strange, invented instruments fashioned out of wood, glass, and PVC pipe.

Next came Nascimento's most unique concept album to date: 1982's *Missa dos Quilombos* (Mass of the Quilombos). The record is a choral work grounded both in Afro-Brazilian instruments and rhythms, and Catholic hymns and chants. Originally performed before a huge audience in Recife, Pernambuco, and recorded in a colonial church in Caraça, Minas Gerais, *Missa* is a cry against oppression and servitude, with lyrics written by poet Pedro Tierra and Catholic bishop and liberation theologist Pedro Casaldáliga. At the end of the musical mass, Hélder Câmara, the archbishop of Olinda and Recife, gives a rousing speech against hunger, injustice, racism, and economic exploitation of the poor. It was too unorthodox for the Vatican, which banned *Missa*.

In the 1980s, Milton turned out many more works, each venturing into a different area, welding elements of Brazilian folk and church music together with bossa, nueva cancion, jazz, and rock. On *Anima*, also in 1982, the percussion of Uakti and the jazz-rock guitar of Ricardo Silvera provided an interesting counterpoint to Nascimento's melodies and elaborate harmonies. On the other end of the spectrum was 1989's *Miltons*, a serene, spare work; on it, jazz pianist Herbie Hancock and percussionist Naná Vasconcelos provided the sole accompaniment to Nascimento's voice.

Many other renowned American musicians appeared on Milton's albums in the eighties, including Wayne Shorter, Paul Simon, Quincy Jones, Pat Metheny, and Hubert Laws. Conversely, his songs found their way onto the albums of dozens of musicians in other countries, all of whom had an appreciation for Milton's "world music," forged in Minas.

As a vocalist, he performed on albums like Paul Simon's *The Rhythm of the Saints*, the Manhattan Transfer's *Brasil*, and Sarah Vaughan's *Brazilian Romance*. By the close of the decade he had earned the respect of musicians around the globe.

MEMBERS OF THE "CLUBE"

Milton's songwriting style and overall sound have been inextricably linked to the music of his Mineiro friends and collaborators like Wagner Tiso, Beto Guedes, Toninho Horta, and Lô Borges. Although none have achieved the fame that Nascimento has, in or out of Brazil, they are all gifted, innovative composers and musicians.

Milton Nascimento and Paul Simon performing together. Their first collaboration occurred when Simon appeared on *Yauaretê*; Nascimento returned the favor on Simon's *The Rhythm of the Saints.*

Born in Três Pontas in 1945, Wagner Tiso has been an indispensable part of Milton Nascimento's success. "The two of us together make the cross," said Milton. Tiso played keyboards in the Som Imaginário group, arranged and orchestrated many Nascimento albums, and scored numerous Brazilian movies. Tiso's solo albums show off his sophisticated compositions as he alternates acoustic piano and electronic keyboards.

One of his key works is the 1988 release *Manú Çaruê, uma Aventura Holística*, a phantasmagoric pop symphony that mixes rock, baroque, and Brazilian influences. It fully demonstrates Tiso's composing, arranging, and playing skills.

Another "corner club" standout is Beto Guedes, known for his original songwriting, dexterity with various stringed instruments (guitar, mandolin, and others), and distinctively high, astringent voice. He was born in 1951 in Montes Claros in northern Minas Gerais. As a young musician, Beto forged his own style by mixing Anglo-American sixties' pop styles with his boyhood influences: *sertaneja* (country) music and the *choros* played by his father Godofredo (a saxophonist-clarinetist).

In the seventies and eighties, Beto would continue to contribute songs, vocals, and guitar playing to Nascimento's albums, while also releasing several excellent solo albums. About Guedes, New York Times critic Robert Palmer commented, "On the best of his albums, the remarkable *A Página do Relâmpago Elétrico*, he uses what sounds like four or five acoustic

Wagner Tiso.

guitars, each playing a different rhythmic pattern, to weave richly detailed sonic tapestries; the disk contrasts rural string-band styles and jazzy electric music. On 'Novena,' a song from his excellent album *Amor de Índio*, he cushions a ballad's sinuously brooding melody with chord voicings built around minor seconds, creating an astonishing lyricism of dissonances."

Another Mineiro talent who has been an essential part of Milton's albums over the years is Toninho Horta, born in Belo Horizonte in 1948. Toninho is a composer and guitarist who mixes influences from Minas Gerais *modinha*, religious music, the jazz of Wes Montgomery, and the bossa of João Gilberto.

The cover of Beto Guedes' 1985 album *Viagem das Mãos*.

Horta's harmonic ideas and instrumental technique, inspired by these diverse sources, have had a strong impact on many musicians outside of Brazil. "Toninho has emerged as one of the most harmonically sophisticated and melodically satisfying Brazilian composers of recent times," wrote jazz guitarist Pat Metheny in the liner notes of Horta's 1988 *Diamond Land* album. That record and *Moonstone* (1989) are both lyrical, imaginative, free-flying instrumental journeys. Metheny enthused that Horta "writes chord progressions that defy gravity, moving up when you think they're going down. As a guitarist, he's one of the world's great 'compers'.... He plays such great voicings with such a cool time feel."

Lô Borges, another of Milton's key collaborators, followed his *Clube da Esquina* success with the noted solo albums *Lô Borges* in 1972, *Via Láctea* (The Milky Way) in 1979, and *Nuvem Cigana* (Gypsy Cloud) in

Toninho Horta.

1981. Singer-guitarist-composer Tavinho Moura has continued to create progressive updates of Brazilian folkloric styles in albums such as 1980's *Tavinho Moura*. Other important Mineiro musicians include singer-songwriter Flávio Venturini, keyboardist Túlio Mourão, singer-songwriter Sueli Costa, and the sertaneja duo Pena Branca and Xavantinho.

Minas, with its strong cultural traditions, has given birth to many remarkable musicians who have kept their roots, even as they seek to transcend them. They have poured the mysticism and hidden emotion of the region into their music and fashioned a remarkably universal sound.

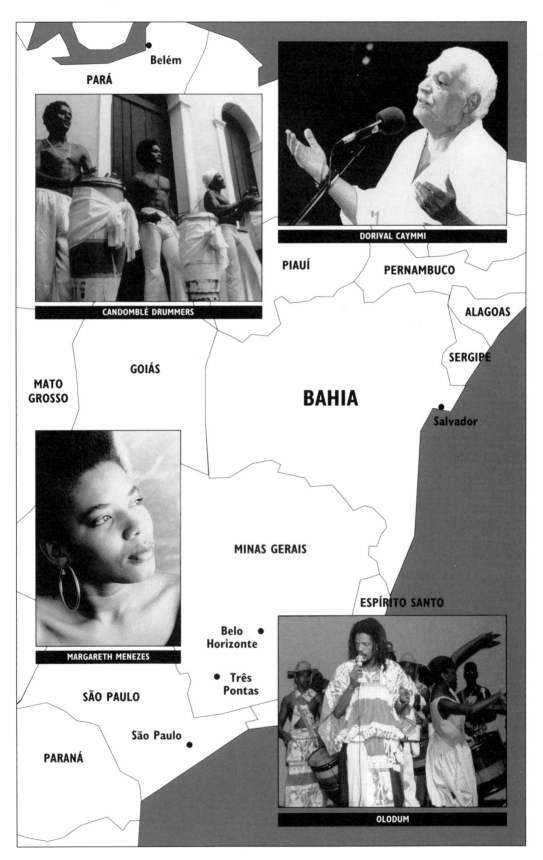

PARÁ

Belém

CANDOMBLÉ DRUMMERS

DORIVAL CAYMMI

PIAUÍ

PERNAMBUCO

ALAGOAS

SERGIPE

GOIÁS

MATO GROSSO

BAHIA

Salvador

MINAS GERAIS

MARGARETH MENEZES

ESPÍRITO SANTO

Belo Horizonte

Três Pontas

SÃO PAULO

São Paulo

PARANÁ

OLODUM

BAHIA OF ALL THE SAINTS

CHAPTER 6

Sun, sun, and rain
Drops of water and light
Yes, we are so many songs
Sambas, ballads, and blues
And the mixture of so many nations
Frevo, choro, and happiness
Reggae, maracatus, and baião
Pernambuco, Jamaica, and Bahia

—Moraes Moreira/Zeca Barreto
"Pernambuco, Jamaica e Bahia"

Salvador, the capital of Bahia state and until 1763 the capital of Brazil, is a port city that looks out across the Atlantic Ocean toward West Africa—to Ghana, Nigeria, Angola. Its culture is so different than that of the Northeast's mestizo-populated interior that at times Salvador, often called Bahia, seems situated on the outskirts of Luanda or Lagos.

Salvador, with its cobblestone streets, baroque churches ornamented with gold, and old houses decorated with blue Portuguese tile, is the most African of all Brazilian cities. It has the highest concentration of African descendants of any major metropolis in Brazil: an estimated eighty percent of its two million inhabitants are black or mulatto. Moreover, it has retained much of its African heritage, brought to Brazil by the slaves of past centuries. The white skirts and turbans worn by many Baianas (Bahian women) recall West Africa, as does the local cuisine, often cooked in coconut milk or palm oil, and spiced with red pepper.

Governor-general Tomé de Sousa established Portugal's colonial government for Brazil in Salvador in 1549. At that time, the city was called São Salvador da Bahia de Todos Os Santos—Savior Saint of the Bay of All the Saints. Over the next 300 years, plantations of sugar and cocoa were established along the Atlantic coast, and slavetraders sold hundreds of thousands of Africans to the Bahia plantation owners. Most of the Africans brought to Salvador were Yoruban, the predominant Afro-Brazilian culture in Bahia.

That culture is at the heart of Salvador today. For example, the presence of the candomblé is still felt everywhere, and it is the least Westernized of the various Afro-Brazilian religions. Candomblé deities, priests, and priestesses are celebrated in songs by many Bahian musicians.

A Bahian man in Pelourinho, one of the most important historic squares in Salvador. The wood-carved sculptures in the background of the photograph are evidence of the rich folk-art and cultural scene in the city.

♩ = 104

Berimbau		
Atabaque		

A rhythmic accompaniment to the capoeira dance. Additional instruments, such as pandeiro and agogô, are also used.

Two men practicing capoeira at a beach near Salvador at sunset. The man at left is accompanying their kicks with music from a berimbau.

Salvador's rich cultural heritage is also vividly on display in folkloric arts like *capoeira*, a spectacular, acrobatic martial-arts dance, brought to Brazil by Bantu slaves from Angola. In the streets of Bahia you will often find a ring of spectators watching two young men—barefoot, shirtless, and wearing white pants—who trade spinning kicks that just miss to a hypnotic rhythm played on the *berimbau*, a musical bow with one metal string and a gourd resonator. They whirl about on their hands and feet, going faster and faster as the tempo accelerates, coming closer and closer with their kicks, and it becomes obvious how capoeira—taken away from its musical context—is an effective fighting technique.

During the slavery era, the musical accompaniment enabled *capoeristas* to pretend that what they were practicing was only a harmless game. Eventually the authorities caught on and got worried. Out in the streets, capoeira fighters sometimes attached knives or razors to their feet or shoes, to deadly effect. In the nineteenth century, the police of Salvador expended great effort trying to suppress its practice but to little avail. Capoeira is now taught openly all over Brazil and in many other parts of the world.

Although the capoeira rhythm has even infiltrated Brazilian popular music—in songs like Gilberto Gil's "Domingo no Parque" and Baden Powell and Vinícius de Moraes's "Berimbau"— it is only one of many Afro-Brazilian musical styles that Bahian musicians have religiously preserved. They have also nurtured and perpetuated the various rhythms and songs of the candomblé ceremonies; and, for decades during Carnaval, large groups called *afoxés* have adapted these ritual rhythms for their street parades. Samba has also been devoutly maintained (some claim it came originally from Bahia).

Yet, the music of Bahia also reflects the miscegenation characteristic of all Brazil. Bahian musicians have absorbed the frevo of Pernambuco, the reggae of Jamaica, the funk of North America, the merengue of the Dominican Republic, and the lambada of Pará—adapting them, blending them in new Bahian musical recipes, and using them to keep Salvador's Carnaval ever innovative, playful, and hot.

The original name of Salvador referred to its being on a bay "of all the saints." The city has more than lived up to that appellation in its all-embracing openness toward music—for, musically, there are many saints watching over Bahia.

DORIVAL CAYMMI

Bahia has given Brazil many of its most important musicians, including the sambista Assis Valente, the "pope of bossa nova" João Gilberto, the guitar legend Pepeu Gomes, and the MPB stars Caetano Veloso, Gilberto Gil, Gal Costa, Maria Bethânia, and Simone. But when these contemporary musicians from Bahia speak of their influences, one name comes up time and time again: Dorival Caymmi.

Born in Salvador in 1914, Caymmi chronicled Bahia's wealth of musical forms and wrote popular songs based on many different regional styles. Dorival composed sambas, toadas, modinhas, *canções praieiras* (fishermen's songs), and *pontos de candomblé* (candomblé invocations). His melodies come straight from the heart and stay with the memory, and his picturesque lyrics indelibly capture Bahia's

Dorival Caymmi.

folklore and people. His tunes, whether upbeat or melancholy, musically capture life on the Bahian coast. Caymmi's songs create images of fishermen and their *jangadas* (sail-boats), the beauty and danger of the sea, the lush palm-lined shores, the church spires and candomblé temples. They exude the charm and sensuality of the Bahian woman, the easy-going tropical pace of Salvador.

All of Caymmi's compositions are beautifully crafted and have become a permanent part of Brazil's collective consciousness. In his samba

"Acontece Que Sou Baiano" (It Happens That I'm Bahian), Caymmi evokes his culture with references to a *pai-de santo*, a candomblé priest, and *requebrado*, a voluptuous movement of the hips:

> It happens that I'm Bahian
> …I already put a hen's foot in my doorway
> I already called a pai-de-santo
> To bless that woman, the one with the requebrado.

"É Doce Morrer no Mar" (It's Sweet to Die in the Sea) was written with Caymmi's good friend, the acclaimed novelist Jorge Amado, who also chronicles the region's culture. In this mournful toada, Caymmi tells of a fisherman who has died in the Atlantic, and will marry the candomblé goddess of the sea:

> In the green waves of the sea, my beloved
> He was drowned
> He made his bridegroom's bed
> In the lap of Yemanjá.

Another famous Caymmi song, "Oração de Mãe Menininha," was a tribute to the beloved *mãe-de-santo* of the Gantois candomblé temple in Salvador.

Dorival also composed songs in a more urban style that were perfect for radio play in the 1930s and 1940s. Caymmi was one of the major composers of the samba-canção era and supplied Carmen Miranda with many of her hits, including "O Que É Que a Baiana Tem?" (What Is It That the Baiana's Got?). Singers Gilberto, Veloso, Gil, Costa, Ângela Maria, Dick Farney, Chico Buarque, Fafá de Belém, and Elis Regina have covered Caymmi's songs. But perhaps the greatest interpretations have come from Dorival himself, who sings with a deep, smooth, often dolorous voice.

His songs were noteworthy for other reasons: their altered chords, the result of Caymmi's search for different harmonic sounds on his guitar; and their poetic use of colloquial Bahian language and natural simplicity in storytelling which had an important influence on Brazilian lyric-writing. Dorival continued recording and performing into the

---

DORIVAL CAYMMI STANDARDS

Some of Caymmi's most enduring songs include: "Samba da Minha Terra" (Samba of My Land), "Marina," "Nem Eu" (Me Neither), "Saudade de Itapoã," "Rosa Morena," "Saudade da Bahia," "João Valentão," "Requebre Que Eu Dou um Doce," and "Doralice."

Americans heard his music, probably without knowing it, when singer Andy Williams recorded Caymmi's waltz "Das Rosas" (Of the Roses) in the mid-1960s, with English lyrics supplied by Ray Gilbert. And Paul Winter covered "Promessa do Pescador" (Promise of a Fisherman) in an inspired rendition on his 1978 album *Common Ground*.

1980s, sometimes in conjunction with his three very talented musical children: Nana, Dori, and Danilo.

FREVO IN BAHIA

In the 1930s and 1940s, Dorival Caymmi was an esteemed musical ambassador from Bahia: his hit songs took local Bahian styles to the far corners of Brazil. In the next decade, Bahia was itself invaded by an electrified version of a musical genre from outside: *frevo*, a highly syncopated, fast-tempo marcha that had originated decades earlier in Recife.

Bahian music and its Carnaval were markedly changed in 1950 when two musicians, Dodô and Osmar, appeared during the pre-Lent festivities atop an old Ford pickup truck. They performed frevo from the bed of the truck, using an electric guitar, electrified cavaquinho, and portable amps. It caused a sensation. In 1951, they performed with a third instrumentalist and the name *trio elétrico* (electric trio) was born. From then on, trio elétrico trucks were a common sight in Salvador's Carnaval, winding through the city's old, narrow streets, inciting crowds to dance and sing.

The trios elétricos grew in size, popularity, and their ability to generate massive decibels. In the 1970s, the trucks would carry many musicians and tall, precarious banks of speakers. As they drove on, thousands of celebrants would trail behind, dancing and leaping deliriously.

Frevo became an important vehicle for instrumental improvisation. In Bahia, it became inextricably mixed with the trio-elétrico sound, which has come to mean frenetic guitar and cavaquinho soloing coupled with a voracious cannibalization of other styles. Trio-elétrico

Guitarist Pepeu Gomes, former member of Os Novos Baianos.

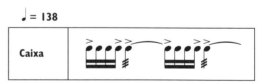

A caixa pattern from a frevo rhythm.

musicians would play hyperkinetic, amplified frevo, as well as overheated renditions of everything from rock to Rimsky-Korsakov's "Flight of the Bumblebee." Anything that made the listener move and dance was incorporated, and this would trigger the creation in Salvador of many new musical hybrid forms in the 1970s and 1980s.

One of the first groups to mix frevo with other styles was Os Novos Baianos (the New Bahians) in the late 1960s and early 1970s. One of the front members of the group was virtuoso guitarist Pepeu Gomes, who was quite adept at mixing frevo and rock on his instrument. He would continue to do so on many solo albums that decade and next. Farther north in Pernambuco, another talented guitarist working in this field was Robertinho de Recife, who threw in a little merengue with his rock and frevo on albums such as 1980's *E Agora Prá Vocês... (And Now For You...).*

The Novos Baianos were backed by the talents of Dadi, a Carioca bassist, and Armandinho, an excellent Bahian cavaquinho and mandolin player (he was also Osmar's son). After the band broke up in 1976, Dadi and Armandinho and the other backing players formed a seminal instrumental group called Cor de Som (Color of Sound), which played frevo, choro, and samba with jazz-fusion-like arrangements.

Moraes Moreira in concert.

Besides Gomes, another "front man" of the Novos Baianos was the singer-guitarist-composer Moraes Moreira, who also established a successful solo career. In the 1980s, he wrote several Carnaval smash hits, including the ecstatic frevo "Festa do Interior" (Party in the Interior), written with Abel Silva and recorded by Gal Costa in 1981. If that tune had been cut later in the decade, however, it probably wouldn't have been as big a hit, especially with the young blacks of Salvador. For by then Bahia's pop music and its Carnaval songs were being conquered by several new musical fusions, inspired by trio-elétrico cannibalization and by a wave of Afro-Brazilian awareness that swept through Salvador in the 1980s. Interestingly, Moraes was on top of both trends—in 1979 he and lyricist Antonio Risério composed "Assim Pintou Moçambique" (Thus Mozambique Came on the Scene), a song that fused the *ijexá* rhythm of the afoxé groups with the trio-elétrico sound.

SALVADOR, AFRICA

In the late 1960s and early 1970s many young black Brazilians were fascinated by the music of James Brown, the Jackson Five, and other African-Americans. The wave of black pride that hit the United States ("Black is beautiful") also echoed in Brazil in the favelas of Rio and other large cities. The popularity of American soul music inspired a cultural movement nicknamed "black-rio" in Rio de Janeiro, "black-sampa" in São Paulo, and "black-mineiro" in Minas Gerais. It was panned by many critics as more "cultural imperialism" and "alienation" caused by the United States. But among many blacks in Brazil, it inspired a renewed pride in African roots, as did the wave of independence movements in Africa in the 1970s. Angola and Mozambique, former Portuguese colonies, were among the many African nations that achieved self-rule in that decade. And in Bahia, Afro-Brazilian pride was further sparked by the popularity of reggae stars Bob Marley, Peter Tosh, and Jimmy Cliff, whose lyrics decried racism and government corruption, while praising Mother Africa.

All this led two young Bahians, named Vovô and Apolônio, to have the idea in 1974 of creating a new type of *bloco afro* (short for "bloco afro-brasileiro") to parade during Carnaval. Afoxé groups that played African-derived music had existed before in Salvador: the Pândegos da África (Revelers of Africa) had paraded in the 1890s. But in the early twentieth century, official repression and—later—a lack of interest took a toll on these groups and their legacy was faltering. By the time Vovô and Apolônio had their brainstorm, the only afoxé group around was the Filhos de Gandhi, and they were almost defunct.

In their Curuzu-Liberdade neighborhood in Salvador, Vovô and Apolônio created a new musical-cultural entity, the bloco afro Ilê Aiyê, designed to explore not only Afro-Brazilian music but all aspects of African life and culture. And whites could not be members. The sequence of events is described at length by the writer-lyricist Antonio Risério (who co-wrote the aforementioned "Assim Pintou Moçambique") in his book *Carnaval Ijexá*. Vovô told Risério that "in that era there was that business of black power and so we thought about making a bloco just for blacks, with African motives."

Ilê Aiyê (a Yoruban phrase that roughly translates as "house of life") quickly attracted many musicians and members, and made its Carnaval debut in 1975. Parading down to the beach, pounding out Afro-Brazilian rhythms on surdos, repiques, and other percussion instruments, it caused a lot of excitement in Salvador. Soon after, Paulinho Camafeu's song "Ilê Aiyê" would be recorded by Gilberto Gil on his *Refavela* album: "What bloco is this/ I want to know/ It's the black world/ That we have come to show you."

Ilê Aiyê would develop into a Carnaval parade group with more than two thousand marchers. Each year, they would explore a different aspect of their African heritage, with costumes researched and woven to match the theme. Ilê Aiyê struck a deep nerve, and triggered the formation of dozens more blocos afro in the late 1970s and 1980s. They would carry forward the evolution of Afro-based styles, performing *samba-reggae* (a kind of samba in which the repique drums play like the rhythm guitar in reggae). And, like the escolas de samba in Rio, all these blocos would serve as community and cultural institutions, albeit with more emphasis on educating young Bahians about their African ancestry.

Afoxés

Many of the blocos afro that would be formed were afoxés. These are blocos that primarily play the afoxé song form, which—as mentioned above—derives from candomblé ceremonial music. *Afoxê* is also the name of a musical instrument: a gourd with strung beads around it, otherwise known as the *xequerê*. *Ijexá* is a generic name used by many musicians for the slow, hypnotic rhythm or rhythms played by an afoxé.

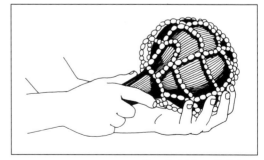

The afoxê (also called the xequerê) is played by moving the beads around the hollow gourd. The resulting rhythmic sound is a common accompaniment to Bahian music.

Candomblé drummers outside a temple in Salvador demonstrating the atabaque playing they use to summon the *orixás* (the gods of the candomblé religion).

Candomblé followers in Salvador.

The rhythm is beat out on atabaques of three sizes (the *rum*, *rumpi*, and *lê*), with lots of syncopation on the *onguê*, a deep-toned type of agogô. Other instruments sometimes used include the *ganzá* and the aforementioned afoxê.

Afoxés are the most authentic manifestation of Gegê-Nagô (Ewe-Yoruban) dances, rhythms, and liturgy outside of the candomblé temples. Earlier in the century, afoxé members were usually candomblé devotees, and their music and dances came straight out of that religion. Often they would perform a ritual in the temple, before heading out onto the street to parade during Carnaval.

By the mid-1970s, the last remnant of this tradition was the Filhos de Gandhi group. They had been founded in 1949 and were named for Mahatma Gandhi, who had helped lead India to independence, and who inspired them with his message of peace and nonviolent resistance. Most of the Filhos de Gandhi were candomblé devotees, and they remain the most traditional of all the currently existing afoxés.

The Filhos de Gandhi were invigorated by the surge of interest in African roots that swept through Salvador in the 1970s, and by the return to Salvador of one of its leading MPB stars, Gilberto Gil. After he came back from exile in London, Gil immersed himself in the process of rediscovering his roots. Eventually, he sought out the Filhos de Gandhi, hoping to join them and involve himself with their music and culture. He told Antonio Risério, "I found about twenty of them, with their drums on the ground, in a corner of the Praça da Sé. They didn't have resources, nor the will to take a place in the Bahian Carnaval." Gil joined and devoted himself to their musical and cultural discipline.

Gil's energy and celebrity helped revitalize the Filhos de Gandhi. In 1976's Carnaval, a year after Ilê Aiyê had made its debut, Gil paraded with his adopted afoxé, all of whom were dressed in costumes of white turbans, white sandals, blue socks, blue-and-white sashes, and strings of beads that evoke certain *orixás*. Their dances were rather serene and sane compared to the trio-elétrico freneticism, and paraders used venerable movements and steps from dances devoted to Oxum, the goddess of fresh water, and Oxalá, god of the sky and universe.

In 1977, Gil recorded the afoxé "Patuscada de Gandhi" (Revelry of Gandhi) on his *Refavela* album. By 1980 the bloco was thriving, with more than a thousand members (all men), and by the end of the decade that number soared over three thousand. And in 1981 the first all-female afoxé, the Filhas de Gandhi (Daughters of Gandhi), was founded.

Carnaval in Bahia

By 1980, Bahia's Carnaval had become thoroughly Africanized, evidenced by trio-elétrico founders Dodô and Osmar presenting "afroelétrico" music, as Risério called it, and by Moraes Moreira dressing in the costume of the afoxé Badauê (founded in 1978), and performing his frevo and reggae-ijexá. By the next year's Carnaval, an estimated 80,000 people were parading in blocos afro.

From 1979 to 1986 other afoxés were founded, including Olori and Oju-Obá, and blocos afro like Malê-Debalê, Afreketê, Muzenza, and Ara-Kêtu. They differ with regard to instrumentation and the emphasis they give to different countries or cultural events. The bloco Muzenza, for example, has a huge admiration for Bob Marley and Jimmy Cliff, and parades in the green, yellow, and black colors of the Jamaican flag. The afoxé Badauê is centered around members who trace their ancestry to Mali. Each bloco and afoxé usually has its own theme around which it organizes its Carnaval parade, as does each samba school in Rio.

Because of the boom in Afro-Brazilian consciousness and the proliferation of blocos afro, Bahian popular music in the eighties was suddenly full of Yoruban words, candomblé images, and references to Africa and Jamaica. The afoxés and blocos afro have also helped make Bahia's Carnaval one of the best in Brazil. While much of the merrymaking in Rio focuses on private clubs and on the samba school parades at the Sambódromo (where thousands of fans watch from the grandstands), the revelry in Bahia is mostly out on the street. Hundreds of thousands of celebrants come here from all over Brazil and the world to participate in the annual madness. They jam the historic squares and cobblestone streets to dance to the music of the blocos afro and the trios elétricos in a Carnaval that is chaotic, exhilarating, occasionally violent, and probably pretty close in spirit to the ancient seasonal festivities in Rome such as the Bacchanalia.

Olodum

It is night in the Pelourinho, the famed historical square in the heart of old Salvador. A sultry breeze washes over the large, free-spirited crowd gathered here under a hazy moon. Atop a makeshift stage, with their backs to the iron balconies, colorful facades and tile roofs of centuries-old colonial buildings, stand the members of the group Olodum. There are singers, percussionists, and dancers on stage, and nearby an unfurled banner reads "África—Olodum—Bahia."

The surdo players begin to generate a solid beat and the caixas add a constant pattern of higher-pitched sixteenth notes, accenting the back

Olodum, the recording group, performing live in Rio. It is composed of about thirty leading musicians representing the more than 2,000 members of the bloco afro of the same name.

Paul Simon performed in the streets of Salvador with members of Olodum for a music video of "The Obvious Child."

beats. The repique kicks in a reggae cadence as other instruments like the African kalimba (thumb-piano) with its dry, plucky notes join in, and rhythms build and interact. The music is mesmerizing, as samba meets afoxé and reggae. It creates a heavy, dense, ritualistic sound.

Women start to dance spontaneously in large groups and some athletic young men practice capoeira, throwing spinning kicks to the beat. The smell of marijuana permeates the salty air. Now the master percussionist appears behind his set of two timbales and adds sharp, rapid rhythmic bursts that contrast with the other instruments, leading and counterpointing them. The lead vocalist and the chorus begin to sing of Egypt or Mozambique or South Africa.

The thousands in the audience—mostly black or mulatto—feel their senses heightened and pride strengthened, and are carried off into a state of euphoria by the music, the marijuana, and the dancing. This concert is one more manifestation of the living, breathing renaissance of African culture in Bahia.

Olodum (the Yoruban word for "supreme divinity") is a bloco afro that was founded in 1979, and it is also the name of a pop group connected to that organization. The Olodum bloco has some 2,500 members and is headquartered in the Pelourinho square, where it sponsors courses, lectures, and debates for the awareness of Bahians of African descent. The Carnaval parade theme in 1989 for the Olodum bloco was "Núbia—Axum—Etiópia," which was also the name of the recording group Olodum's second album.

Olodum has recorded several acclaimed albums under the leadership of Mestre Neguinho do Samba (real name Antonio Luis Alves de Souza). He has been responsible for the group's many rhythmic innovations, and for shaping their sound, which consists almost exclusively of vocals and percussion. North Americans heard a bit of Olodum's sound, albeit in a muted and simplified form, on Paul Simon's song "The Obvious Child," from his *The Rhythm of the Saints* album.

BAHIA IN THE EIGHTIES

Olodum was one of the most important groups to come from Bahia in the 1980s and was part of the wide spectrum of new music being created there that decade. Many other new acts appeared, inspired by the revived Afro-consciousness and ready to mix together various Afro-American musics to invent a plethora of new musical hybrids.

It helped that many Brazilian and Caribbean forms—samba, frevo, ijexá, reggae, merengue, lambada, salsa—mesh quite well together rhythmically, and that trio-elétrico groups like to throw every musical reference they have into their sizzling, freewheeling presentations. The fast-paced creativity that went on in Salvador in the 1980s was also aided by an improvement in technology: cheaper and better synthesizers were now available, and Bahian artists in general had increased access to modern recording studios. In many cases they didn't wait for deals with the big labels, and instead put out their own independent records.

Another new hybrid was *fricote* (also called *deboche*), introduced by Luiz Caldas in his 1985 song "Fricote." Caldas fused the ijexá rhythm with reggae, juiced up the tempo, and had a huge hit song on his hands. He also mixed together reggae, ijexá, and maxixe in his 1986 song "Reggae do Camaleão" (Chameleon's Reggae).

Caldas was born in Feira de Santana, Bahia in 1963 and moved to Salvador at eighteen to join the Trio Elétrico Tapajós. He recorded three albums with them before financing his own singles. He found an independent label to release his 1985 debut album *Magia* (Magic) and talked PolyGram into picking up the distribution. That LP and *Flor Cigana* (Gypsy Flower) in 1986 both went platinum and he became Salvador's biggest selling musician at that time.

Other Bahian artists, also working along these lines and having great commercial success, included Banda Mel, Banda Reflexu's,

Glittery pop star Luiz Caldas has concocted many new rhythmic blends; fricote is one of the most notable.

Banda Reflexu's, a group that helped popularize samba-reggae, one of many new Bahian musical inventions from the last decade.

Margareth Menezes.

Chiclete com Banana, Abel Duere (Angola-born but a long-time Bahian resident), Gerônimo, Cid Guerreiro, Lazzo Matumbi, Roberto Mendes, Missinho, and Carlos Pita. Veteran artists incorporated the new sounds as well. Moraes Moreira released a string of excellent 1980s albums; *Mestiço É Isso* (Meztizo Is This) perhaps best showcased his musical miscegenation.

Margareth Menezes

A young Bahian musician who catapulted to international fame in that decade was the singer Margareth Menezes (born in Salvador in 1962), who caught the ear of American rock singer David Byrne on a Brazilian visit. He asked her to open for him on his North American tours in 1988 and 1989, and she subsequently released a solo album there, *Elegibô*, in 1990. On it, Menezes used her deep, powerful voice and sensual flair to interpret a variety of Bahian styles, notably afoxé and samba-reggae. The album's uplifting title song was a hymn to an ancient Yoruban city called Elegibô, and it is best described as *samba-reggae exaltação* (exaltation samba-reggae). The album spent over two months at the number one position on *Billboard*'s World Music chart that year.

David Byrne performing with Margareth.

On *Elegibô*, Margareth also included a song called "Abra a Boca e Feche Os Olhos" (Open Your Mouth and Shut Your Eyes), a tune cowritten by Gerônimo that had the suggestive, double-entendre lyrics and breath-stealing rhythm of a style that had a brief, global popularity in 1989: *lambada*.

The Lambada

While lambada did not originate in Bahia, it was there that it achieved its greatest exposure and was incorporated into the whirlwind of trio-elétrico jamming. Originally a mixture of merengue and the Afro-Brazilian folk style *carimbó*, lambada was born in Pará state and then traveled to Bahia in the late 1970s or early 1980s (see Chapter 7—"North by Northeast"). In Salvador, local musicians took the lambada and augmented it in the usual Bahian fashion, adding new Afro-Brazilian elements and Caribbean influences, creating complex rhythmic blends.

To complicate things further, once lambada became popular in Europe, every musical style from fricote to samba-reggae was also exported to the Continent under the brand-name "lambada."

In 1989 the daring, sexy lambada dance emerged in the nightclubs of Europe. In it, couples press tightly together, dipping and swirling sensually to the uptempo, high-energy rhythms of lambada songs. On the European continent that year, especially in France and Germany, lambada seemed the essence of tropical passion.

It was in the Bahian resort town of Porto Seguro in 1988 that French music entrepreneurs Jean Karakos and Olivier Lorsac (aka Olivier Lamotte d'Incamps) first heard and saw the exotic new style. They organized a multinational group called Kaoma (whose lead singer was Loalwa Braz, a Brazilian) to sing lambada songs in Europe. Kaoma's big hit was "Lambada," a cover of Márcia Ferreira's "Chorando Se Foi" (Crying She Went), which in turn was a Portuguese-language version of a Bolivian tune called "Llorando Se Fue," written by Gonzalo and Ulises Hermosa. "Lambada," which Karakos and Olivier registered under the pseudonym "Chico de Oliveira" in France, was a hybrid that mixed a Bolivian folk theme with lambada, and had a northeastern Brazilian accent as well. Heavily promoted, "Lambada" hit number one on the charts in fifteen countries, was number one on the *Music & Media* Pan-European pop chart for months, and sold more than five million units worldwide (the album sold two million copies).

By 1990, nightclubs in New York and Los Angeles offered "lambada" nights, Kaoma's album (called *World Beat* in the United States) went gold and hit number one on the *Billboard* Latin music chart, and some lamentable, low-budget exploitation movies attempted to cash in on the craze.

In Brazil, lambada pressed on, expanding beyond its regional success in the North, Northeast, and in the city of São Paulo to capture Rio de Janeiro and the national market. Many leading Brazilian pop artists added at least one lambada to their albums in 1989 and 1990.

Bahian-style lambada was just the latest rhythmically imaginative offering from Salvador, a remarkably musical city that receives influences from all continents, infusing all styles with its own special swing and playfulness, and then sending them back out to the world.

Dancers with the band Kaoma performing the sensuous lambada.

A basic carimbó rhythm.

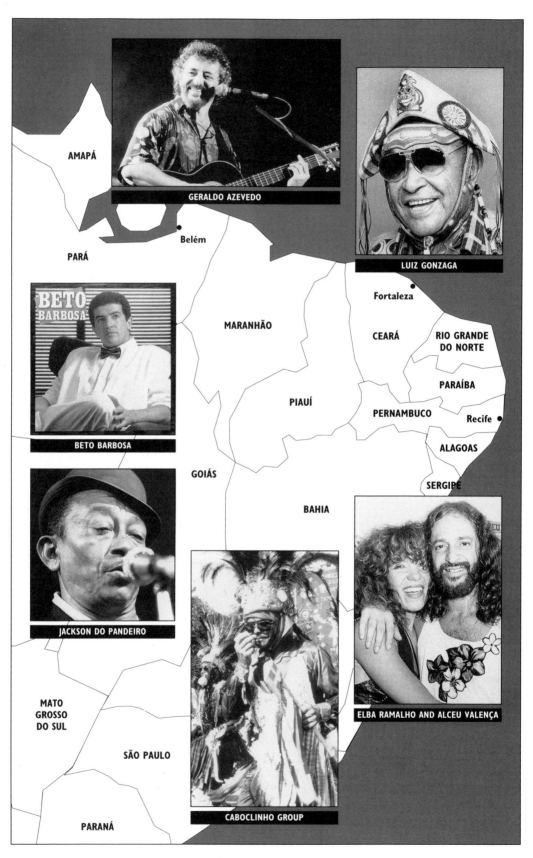

AMAPÁ

GERALDO AZEVEDO

LUIZ GONZAGA

PARÁ

• Belém

• Fortaleza

MARANHÃO

CEARÁ

RIO GRANDE
DO NORTE

BETO BARBOSA

PARAÍBA

PIAUÍ

PERNAMBUCO

Recife •

BETO BARBOSA

ALAGOAS

GOIÁS

SERGIPE

BAHIA

JACKSON DO PANDEIRO

MATO
GROSSO
DO SUL

ELBA RAMALHO AND ALCEU VALENÇA

SÃO PAULO

PARANÁ

CABOCLINHO GROUP

NORTH BY NORTHEAST

CHAPTER 7

Today, many miles away
In sad solitude
I wait for the rain to fall again
For me to return to my sertão
    —Luiz Gonzaga/Humberto Teixeira, "Asa Branca"

During the 1940s the most popular music in Brazil consisted largely of either samba-canção songs or imported genres—tangos, polkas, boleros, foxtrots, and waltzes. The accordionist Luiz Gonzaga changed all that when he scored huge commercial successes late in the decade with two singles that pulsed with boisterous northeastern rhythms and that were charged with a raw poignancy.

Gonzaga sang stories about Brazil's Northeast over accordion riffs that were long, drawn out, and melancholy on slow tunes or fast, festive, and tumbling over each other on dance numbers. His songs captured the imagination of the country. "Asa Branca" (quoted above) had a haunting melody and lyrics that described a disastrous drought striking the *sertão*, the vast, arid interior of northeastern Brazil. The song's title refers to a type of pigeon that, according to folklore, is the last bird to abandon the sertão during droughts. "Asa Branca" became an unofficial anthem of the Northeast and has been covered by dozens of artists, including Elis Regina, Caetano Veloso, Lulu Santos, Sivuca, Hermeto Pascoal, Baden Powell, Paul Winter, and Herbie Mann.

A statue of the legendary Catholic priest Padre Cícero, that overlooks the town of Juazeiro do Norte, deep in the sertão of Ceará state.

Gonzaga helped introduce Brazil to the sounds and culture of its Northeast—an area rich in folklore and musical tradition. It is a region that is quite different from the cosmopolitan urban centers of Rio and São Paulo to the south; in many ways the Northeast is like another country. The region has nearly thirty-five million inhabitants living in the cities of Salvador, Recife, and Fortaleza on the lush coast, or in towns and farms in the sertão.

Luiz Gonzaga.

Lampião and his gang. The bandit-hero was admired by the poor and feared by the rich in the sertão, which he roamed and looted in the 1920s and 1930s.

The sertão has a mostly poor, illiterate population who tend their own small plots of land or work for powerful landowners who rule their communities in a feudal manner. Much of the sertão is covered with thorny scrub called *caatinga*, which is a vivid green when it rains and a gray thicket during dry times. Cowherds (*vaqueiros*) must wear head-to-foot leather to protect themselves from the spines and barbs of the caatinga and often cover their horses' chests with cowhide as well. In the sertão, crops are picked by hand, day-to-day existence is hard, and life expectancy is short. The *sertanejos* (those who live in the sertão) are stoic, passionate, and given to mysticism. Machismo, as one might expect, is strong here, and blood feuds last for decades.

However, whether northeasterners live in a modern mansion in Fortaleza or a dirt-floored hovel in the backlands, they are famous in Brazil for their warmth and hospitality. It is almost impossible to visit a home there and not be asked to dinner or offered a place to sleep if the hour is late.

Many northeasterners are strongly religious, attending Catholic church, praying to a myriad of saints, and often practicing the Afro-Brazilian religion *umbanda* as well. But some sertanejos early in this century took to banditry rather than accept the humble misery that was their lot; they would raid towns and farms, then escape on horseback to hiding places in the dense tangles of caatinga in the rugged sertão.

One such *cangaceiro* (outlaw) was the legendary Lampião (1898-1934), famed for his courage, ruthlessness, generosity, and—of course—musical ability. He sang and played the accordion well, often danced all night at parties, and popularized the *xaxado*, a men's dance with a shuffling rhythm. Lampião is revered today by many sertanejos as a bandit-hero, and has been the subject of songs, movies, plays, and books.

Roughly every ten years, the usual January-to-May rains fail to refresh the parched sertão. When that happens, the caatinga shrivels in the tropical sun, rivers dry up, cattle drop dead, and hundreds of thousands of people go hungry. Many relocate to overcrowded refugee shanty-towns in the northeastern capitals. Countless others emigrate to Rio and São Paulo in search of food and work. There they work in factories and construction sites, as maids and as doormen, generally discriminated against because of their strong accents and lack of education. They stay in overcrowded favelas, either settling there for good or just waiting for rain to return to the sertão so they can go home. Northeasterners in the big southern cities often gather in weekly fairs to eat their own regional specialities, drink the sugar cane liquor *cachaça*, sell their wares, and dance to the galloping rhythms of earthy, accordion-driven *forró* (a generic term for dance-oriented northeastern styles).

LUIZ GONZAGA

Luiz Gonzaga (1912-89) served as a spokesman of sorts for the rural Northeast, its history, and its culture, as he sang tales and woes of the sertão to urban audiences in the industrialized, rapidly growing cities of Rio and São Paulo. Born on the Caiçara ranch just outside the small town of Exu in the Pernambuco sertão, Luiz Gonzaga do Nascimento was the son of a farmworker who was well-respected in the region for his accordion playing. Young Luiz began tilling the fields at age seven; not long after he was traveling with his father to various local dances, parties, and festivals, where he mastered the accordion and other instruments. As a boy, Gonzaga admired the freedom and audacity of the cangaceiros, and his idol was of course Lampião, then in the prime of his outlaw fame.

At age eighteen, Gonzaga left for Ceará to join the army. He remained an enlisted man until 1939, playing the cornet in the army band, and studying accordion with Domingos Ambrósio, who taught Luiz the popular music of the Southeast. Afterwards, he moved to Rio and survived by playing his accordion in clubs and houses of ill repute. He made some appearances on live radio shows, but didn't make much of an impression until one night a group of students from Ceará state asked him why he didn't play some music from the sertão. So on Ary Barroso's radio program, Gonzaga played the northeastern-flavored "Vira e Mexe," won first prize, and was asked to do an encore by an enthusiastic audience. That year he recorded two 78-RPM singles for RCA, and his career took off.

Gonzaga began to record some rhythms from the Northeast as well as the requisite waltzes, polkas, mazurkas, and chorinhos. Then in 1946 he recorded the revolutionary song "Baião," whose title became the name of the new genre. Written by Gonzaga and Humberto Teixeira, a lawyer-composer from Ceará, the tune exhorted listeners to try the new dance: "I'm going to show all of you/ How you dance a baião/ And whoever wants to learn/ Please pay attention."

Luiz Gonzaga.

Gonzaga and Teixeira's baião derived from an older, folkloric baião or *baiano*, a northeastern circle dance of African origin. In the interior of Pernambuco, this dance would be performed as

Gonzaga and Zé Ramalho.

♩ = 104–108

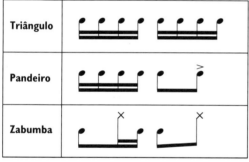

A simple baião rhythm ensemble.

a prelude to a desafio, a sung poetic contest, between two sertanejo singer-guitarists. The instrumental musical introduction that accompanied the dance came to be called baião or rojão.

Gonzaga and Teixeira urbanized the baião, taking its syncopated 2/4 rhythm and expanding it into an entire song form of its own. They added a steady beat from beginning to end (which made it easier to dance to), changed the instrumentation (most importantly replacing the guitar with an accordion and adding a triangle and *zabumba* bass drum), and introduced a melody that used a natural scale with a raised fourth and flattened seventh (sometimes mixing this with a minor scale).

The flat seventh is referred to by some as the *sétima nordestina* (northeastern seventh) and is usually attributed to African influences, as are the flattened third and/or flattened fifths or sevenths in the American blues. But other tonal peculiarities of the baião are thought by some scholars, such as conductor Júlio Medaglia, to resemble medieval modes utilized in Gregorian chant.

In any event, Gonzaga had created a vivid new dance music, whose accordion/bass drum/triangle instrumentation gave it a rocking, earthy sound, akin to American zydeco. Later the term *forró*, which originally meant and still means a party or place to play northeastern dance music, would be used as a generic tag for danceable northeastern styles such as *coco*, *xote*, *xaxado*, and the more festive varieties of baião. According to others, forró refers specifically to a faster, livelier type of baião, introduced by Gonzaga in tunes such as "O Forró de Mané Vito" and "O Forró de Zé Antão."

Gonzaga followed "Baião" with a string of hits—performed by himself as well as others—and by 1950 the baião style was heard as often as the samba on Brazilian radio. Cowriting tunes with Teixeira, and later with Zé Dantas, a doctor-composer from Pernambuco, Gonzaga's success continued through the decade. Besides the baião, Gonzaga and his cowriters popularized the *xaxado* (the style favored by Lampião) and *xote* (another 2/4, very danceable rhythm). For shows, Gonzaga dressed in the ornamented leather hat and jacket of a cangaceiro like his boyhood bandit hero.

A Gonzaga-Texeira hit in 1950 for several other artists was the lively "Paraíba" (Paraíba is a state in the Northeast), which paid tribute to the stoicism of the women left behind in the sertão when their men traveled south to seek work. In the song, the narrator is a lonely husband who describes his journey and conveys his saudades to this wife:

When the mud turned to stone and the mandacaru cactus dried up
When the dove became thirsty, beat its wings and left
It was then that I went away, carrying my pain
Today I send a hug to you, little one.

In the 1960s, Gonzaga's music fell out of favor with the critics and the urban public, but his career was revived in the seventies when he was championed by such MPB artists as Caetano Veloso, who startled his hip fans by proclaiming the out-of-style Gonzaga "a genius" and recording a cover of "Asa Branca" in 1971. His tunes were covered by MPB stars throughout the eighties. "Vem Morena" was recorded by Gilberto Gil in 1984 and by Gonzaga and Fagner in 1988.

Late in his life, Gonzaga became a musical legend in Brazil, and even more than that for the Northeast. One incident aptly illustrates his almost mythic stature in the region of his youth. In June 1978, a member of the Sampaio clan killed Zito Alencar, the mayor of Exu, reigniting a twenty-year-old war between the two families. Gonzaga, armed only with his accordion, decided to be a peacemaker. He returned to his native city for the first time in almost fifty years and succeeded in calming the tensions there between the Sampaios and the Alencars. It was something perhaps only Gonzaga could have done, for he had now become as famous in the sertão as the idol of his youth, the bandit Lampião.

JACKSON DO PANDEIRO

While Luiz Gonzaga brought the rural sounds of the Northeast to the attention of all Brazil, his contemporary Jackson do Pandeiro (his name could be translated as Tambourine Jackson) did much to popularize the Northeast's coastal and urban sounds, especially the *coco*. Pandeiro (1919-1982) is mentioned repeatedly by contemporary Brazilian recording artists as an important influence; like Gonzaga, Jackson became a musical father-figure to many of them.

Born in Alagoa Grande, Paraíba, the singer-percussionist (real name José Gomes Filho), played good-time music with an uncanny rhythmic sense. He was a master of the *coco*, the merry and lively Afro-Brazilian form that has a stanza-and-refrain structure and pulls the listener along with a fast tempo and irresistible syncopation. A circle dance, the coco was known to have been present on the northeastern littoral as far back as the eighteenth century. In the coco, singers and dancers form a circle, with solo dancers enclosed within the circle at times. The dance occasionally includes the *umbigada* movement.

Singer-songwriter Manezinho Araújo believes that the coco originated in the Palmares quilombo

JACKSON DO PANDEIRO'S HITS

"Sebastiana," "Forró em Limoeiro" (Forró in Limoeiro), "Chiclete com Banana" (Bubblegum with Banana), "Cantiga do Sapo" (Song of the Toad), "Um a Um" (One to One), "Vou Gargalhar" (I'm Going to Laugh), and "O Canto da Ema" (Song of the Rhea).

Jackson do Pandeiro performing in 1972.

Jackson do Pandeiro's album *Isso É Que É Forró!*, issued by Polygram in 1981.

in the backlands of Alagoas in the seventeenth century, from a work song sung by African-Brazilians breaking coconuts on rocks. Its rhythm is typically in 2/4 time and can be maintained by the clapping of hands, or by a ganzá, coconut shells, pandeiro, and atabaque.

Many of Jackson's biggest hits were recorded in the 1950s and 1960s. Some were cowritten by Jackson (and often registered under his wife's name, Almira Castilho) and others were his interpretations of tunes by Gordurinha, João do Vale, and others. Besides being a great musician, Jackson was a funny guy, and could make audiences laugh at his crazy dance steps and humorous facial expressions while he sang.

Jackson was also a master of another important northeastern song form, the *embolada*, which is structurally quite similar to the coco (indeed, many scholars consider it to be essentially a more sophisticated form of the coco). The embolada, typically accompanied by pandeiro and ganzá, has a rapid tempo, short note values, small musical intervals, and rolls on at a breathless pace. Whereas the coco usually tells a simple, intelligible story, the embolada often employs improvised, tongue-twisting lyrics. "The embolada is like the jam session of the coco, like jiving," comments filmmaker-folklorist Ivan Cordeiro, a native of Recife.

The embolada has set refrains that allow the singer to organize in his mind his next improvised stanza. Alliterative and hard-to-pronounce words are often used, and the lyrics may be comical, satirical, or descriptive. The tempo is gradually increased until the singer's words are pronounced so fast that they are almost unintelligible: they become emboladas (mixed together). Manezinho Araújo, born in Cabo, Pernambuco, in 1910, was one of the greatest performers of the genre, the "king of the embolada" from the 1930s to the 1950s.

DESAFIOS

An embolada can be sung by a soloist, or utilized by two vocalists for the poetic song duels called *desafios*. They share long improvisations, extended rhyming, and a spirit of bravado with American rap music, yet they are generally a much more complex and demanding poetic form. Such "song challenges" are also present in Venezuela (*porfías*), Argentina (*contrapunto*), Chile (*payas*), Spain, and Portugal, and have been around for centuries.

In public squares in the cities of the Northeast, crowds gather around embolada singers who are engaged in a desafio. One keeps the rhythm with a pandeiro, the other with a ganzá. The improvised vocals fly back and forth, as one singer offers a question, challenge, or insult and the other responds, trying to top his opponent, always in the same rigidly observed poetic form, spoken more than sung (the words are the thing). Sometimes riddles are posed; in *Dicionário do Folclore Brasileiro*, author Luis da Câmara Cascudo quotes a famous stanza sung by João Izidro to his desafio challenger (it rhymes in Portuguese):

> To say you were never imprisoned
> Is a well-known lie
> You spent nine months
> In an oppressed prison
> A prison with only one entrance.
> Where was the exit?

Gathered around the singers, the audience admires the verbal dexterity and laughs at the better jokes and insults hurled by the two. Afterwards a hat is passed to collect some coins.

Desafios are also performed with both singers playing guitar, and they can last hours or even entire nights. The participants are sometimes illiterate but demonstrate an astonishing capacity for wordplay and a remarkable grasp of regional culture. The stanzas are haikus of sorts, with the number of verses and/or syllables determined by the poetic form used (the *martelo* involves ten syllables per verse, while the *galope* is a martelo with six verses per stanza). Desafios may use the embolada song style as a structure or other musical forms.

The singers in the desafio are called *repentistas*, and they strive to come up with an improvised verse (a *repente*) that will break the concentration of their opponent and leave him unable to respond. The first repentista who is not able to invent and pronounce a fast response loses the desafio.

JOÃO DO VALE

While repentistas express themselves through the improvised performance, João do Vale has worked for decades crafting popular songs that have been brought to life in the recording studio by dozens of other artists. But for all the many famous tunes João has written, few people in the country know his name. For example, when Brazilians gather to play guitars and sing at the beach or in someone's house, they often sing a beautiful, mysterious tune called "Na Asa do Vento" (On the Wing of the Wind), which was recorded by Caetano Veloso in 1975. Those who sing the song seldom know who wrote it, although they might guess

João do Vale (left) in the recording studio with Gonzaguinha, who is the son of Luiz Gonzaga and a notable MPB musician.

that it was Caetano Veloso or maybe—if they're older—Dolores Duran, who sang the intriguing lyrics in 1956:

> Love is a bandit
> It can even cost you money
> It's a flower that has no scent
> That all the world wants to smell.

If you mention João do Vale's name, it will inevitably draw a blank stare. Yet it was João do Vale (born in 1933 in Pedreiras, Maranhão) who cowrote that song with Luis Vieira and composed hundreds of other recorded tunes, dozens of them standards. Although comparatively unknown, João had a huge impact through his prolific songwriting. He was an important popularizer of northeastern song styles, along with Gonzaga and Pandeiro, and indeed supplied the latter with a few hits, including "O Canto da Ema."

He was also a great lyricist, who told the story of his life and of the poor people of Maranhão in concise, poignant narratives that used vivid images and the vernacular of the sertão (a dialect sometimes difficult for urban Brazilians to fathom). He could indulge in earthy good humor—the lascivious "Peba na Pimenta" (Armadillo in the Pepper) is a playful tune full of lewd double-entendres—or meditate lyrically about love or nature, as in "Na Asa do Vento."

In the 1960s, João stepped into the limelight for a few years. Early in that decade, Zé Keti took him to a hip musician's hangout—the restaurant Zicartola, run by the sambista Cartola and his wife Zica. João began performing there and was invited to play a role in the 1964 musical theater piece *Opinião*, alongside Keti and bossa muse Nara Leão. The play was a success, and one of its songs, João's stirring anthem

"Carcará," launched Maria Bethânia (who replaced Leão) to fame the next year when she recorded it as a single. In that decade and the next, Veloso, Gilberto Gil, and many other famed Brazilian musicians recorded his tunes.

João didn't have a great voice and by the 1980s had fallen out of the public eye, but his peers never forgot him. In 1981, his many friends (like Tom Jobim, Chico Buarque, Leão and many more) gathered with João to record the album *João do Vale*, a star-studded retrospective of his greatest hits.

NORTHEASTERN FOLK TRADITIONS

The history and folklore of the Northeast is kept alive in its music, in the *literatura de cordel* (hand-bound booklets of folk stories and moral tales in rhymed verse), and in its many processional and dramatic dances. Its culture derives from the usual Brazilian roots of Portugal, different African nations, and the native Amerindians. But in the Northeast, this heritage mixed together for many centuries in a relative isolation, especially in the backlands. The cosmopolitan influences of Rio de Janeiro were far to the South. The Northeast created its own singular cultural traditions, some of which include archaic traits from Africa or Portugal that no longer exist in their places of origin.

Ancient Iberian musical elements often turn up in folk music from the Northeast. Both Arabic scales (the Moors occupied Portugal for centuries) and medieval modes and harmonies have been noted in many northeastern songs by scholars such as Antonio Jose Madureira, co-founder of the 1970s group Quinteto Armorial. That band explored northeastern roots in a meticulously elaborated context in the LPs *Do Romance ao Galope Nordestino* and *Aralume*.

In the 1980s, the northeastern troubadours Xangai, Elomar, and Vital Farias explored their medieval-Moorish-sertanejo heritage with the remarkable albums *Cantoria* and *Cantoria 2*.

Another unique northeastern tradition is the *maracatu*, an Afro-Brazilian processional dance performed during Carnaval in Recife and other cities in Pernambuco and Ceará. In maracatu, participants sing and dance to a heavy, slow, almost trance-inducing rhythm played usually on zabumbas, tambores, chocalhos, and gonguês. Performers dress up as a king, queen, baianas, and other characters, including the *dama de passo*. The latter is a woman who carries the mysterious, fetishistic *calunga* cloth doll, a figure of a black woman dressed in white. The maracatu doesn't have a dramatic theme, and little is known about its origins. But some scholars feel it may derive

Bumba-meu-boi, a processional dance that celebrates the death and resurrection of a mythical bull, performed in São Luis, the capital of Maranhão state.

♩ = 100

The agogô part from a maracatu rhythm.

from an early form of another Afro-Brazilian processional dance, one that is practiced nationally: the *congo* or *congada*.

Congos are found in the North and Northeast, while congadas are typical of central and southern Brazil. They derive from a mixture of African traditions and Portuguese and Spanish elements. Enacted during the Christmas season and at other times of the year, congos feature characters dressed as African royalty and their courts and ministers. Participants enact various scenarios of war and peace, singing their lines to an accompaniment of drums, chocalhos, pandeiros, and violas.

Caboclinho gróups are a specifically northeastern tradition that dates back at least to the late nineteenth century. Inspired by the legacy of the Brazilian Indian, caboclinhos parade during Carnaval in Pernambuco and several other northeastern states. Their performers dress as Indians and dance in the street to the sound of flutes, fifes, and arrows banging on bows. They assume positions of attack and defense, and perform dramatic dances, with assorted characters and a varied choreography that illustrates different stories about the native Indians during Brazil's colonization.

A caboclinho group parading in Botafogo, Pernambuco state.

All these folk traditions and musical styles provided the roots for contemporary musicians—Alceu Valença, Geraldo Azevedo, and Elba Ramalho, for example—who would mix their northeastern culture with modern influences and instruments to add a fresh new sound to Brazilian popular music.

THE NORTHEASTERN WAVE

At the beginning of the 1970s, a new and more cosmopolitan generation of singers and musicians swept down to Rio from Fortaleza, Recife, and other points close to the equator. Inspired by bossa, rock, and Tropicália, this generation of northeastern artists added keyboards, electric guitars, pop arrangements, and other influences to baião, xote, maracatu, and embolada. By doing so they created a new and vibrant musical language, with an inventiveness equal to that of the Tropicalistas in the late 1960s but with a stronger base in northeastern folkloric roots. Recalled singer-songwriter Geraldo Azevedo, "After bossa nova and Tropicália, there was a strong northeastern movement. It didn't have a name, but I think it was as important."

Four members of the Northeastern Wave (l. to r.): Xangai, Geraldo Azevedo, Vital Farias, Elomar.

Alceu Valença

One of the most original musicians of his time, singer-songwriter Alceu Valença led the northeastern musical invasion. One of his most kinetic styles is *forrock*, a driving, folksy mixture of forró music with electric guitar and drums. On stage, Alceu often takes on a trickster's persona and dresses as a court jester. His visceral, imaginative music has made him one of MPB's biggest stars, as well as an acclaimed performer in Europe and Japan. He was born in 1946 in São Bento do Una, a small village in Pernambuco located just inland from the sertão, to a middle-class family. His father was both a farmer and a lawyer.

Alceu Valença performing at Rio's Scala in 1988.

Valença was heavily influenced musically by Luiz Gonzaga and Jackson do Pandeiro; he absorbed Jackson's clownish spirit and would later record cocos in the Pandeiro style. As a youth, Alceu also soaked in all the unrecorded but vital music played by local troubadours. "My grandfather played guitar, he was more or less a repentista. He influenced me with the sonority of the region and passed this taste for popular music to me."

At age nine, Alceu and his family moved to Recife, the capital of Pernambuco, and he began to play guitar at age fourteen. "In the big city, Recife, a million folkloric things passed by on my street, Rua dos Palmares. But on the radio they didn't play that kind of music. What they played came from Rio, as well as international music." Two foreign singers made a deep impact on the young Valença: Ray Charles, singing both "I Can't Stop Loving You" and "Hit the Road, Jack," and Elvis Presley's early albums.

Alceu's career began in Recife, where he played everything that was out of style with his well-off peers: namely northeastern music. "The middle class was ashamed of the baião. They wanted what was imported, canned."

Valença attended college and obtained a law degree but was unenthusiastic about entering the legal profession. He made the obligatory pop musician's journey to Rio in 1970 and began to enter his songs in the music festivals. In 1972 he and Azevedo recorded an album together,

Alceu Valença performing with one of his musical mentors Jackson do Pandeiro in 1978.

Valença with fellow northeasterner Elba Ramalho.

with Rogério Duprat (who had often worked with the Tropicalistas) handling the orchestration. Then Alceu made his solo debut with "Molhado de Suor" (Wet with Sweat) in 1974, chosen by critics as one of the year's top three albums. Alceu's alchemical blend of blues, rock, and northeastern styles began to win great acclaim. His 1978 *rock-embolada* "Agalopado" conveyed his incendiary spirit:

> I sing the pain, the love, the disillusion
> And the infinite sadness of lovers
> Don Quixote free of Cervantes
> I discover that the windmills are real
> Between beasts, owls, jackals
> I turn to stone in the middle of the road
> I turn into a rose, path of spines
> I ignite these glacial times.

In 1982 came perhaps his finest work to date, the platinum-selling *Cavalo de Pau* (Stick Horse), and also an appearance at the Montreux Jazz Festival in Switzerland.

Mixing Luiz Gonzaga and Elvis Presley, maracatu with synthesizers, coco with electric guitar, Alceu concocts exhilarating musical blends. Atop them, he sings his idiosyncratic stories using "a hybrid language, urban and rural." In concert, Valença strives for an "almost operatic" climate in which he improvises a great deal and assumes many roles. He commented, "I have the clown side and the more cool side. I have various persons inside me, faces, masks, and my music is this—frevo to maracatu to something totally romantic."

Geraldo Azevedo

Another key figure in the northeastern wave was Alceu's partner on his first album: singer-songwriter Geraldo Azevedo. His lyrical songs center around his voice and guitar, the music light and clear, the lyrics evoking the northeastern coast, its beaches, jangadas, and coconut trees. Azevedo grounds his songs in styles such as toada, xote, and reggae, which he augments with bossa vocal influences and modern arrangements. The result is suave, carefully constructed music that is gentle, reflective, and romantic.

Born in 1945 in Petrolina, Pernambuco, on the banks of the São Francisco River, Geraldo grew up in a musical household where everyone played instruments or sang. "The folklore of the region—maracatu, coco, repentistas, it's in all of us without our perceiving it," remarked Azevedo. As a teenager, he listened to northeasterners Luis Gonzaga and Jackson do Pandeiro, as well as such diverse musicians as Spanish classical guitarist Andres Segovia, Brazilian guitarist Baden Powell, Johann Sebastian Bach, and romantic crooner Nelson Gonçalves. But it was the bossa singer João Gilberto who inspired Azevedo to become a professional musician: "He made me more serious about looking into harmony. We didn't have those [bossa nova] harmonies in Petrolina."

At eighteen he moved to Recife to attend college, and while there he performed with the members of Grupo Construção—Naná Vasconcelos, Teca Calazans, and Paulo Guimarães, among others. Five years later, in 1968, Geraldo moved to Rio and formed the group Quarteto Livre with Vasconcelos and others to back up singer-songwriter Geraldo Vandré. Azevedo made his recording debut in 1972 with the aforementioned *Alceu Valença e Geraldo Azevedo*, which included one of his most memorable songs, the haunting toada "Novena," in which he poetically evokes the intense Catholicism of his childhood:

> While the family prays
> Someone follows the novena into the
>   chasm
> Of owed prayers
> Of the whisper of an agony without end.

In 1976, he released his first solo LP, *Geraldo Azevedo*, which included the beautiful and melancholy Azevedo-Valença tune "Caravan."

A young Azevedo and Valença on the cover of their 1972 album.

Geraldo Azevedo.

Ramalho performing onstage with a dancer from her stage show.

Elba Ramalho.

In the song, Azevedo showed his gift for vivid imagery, singing:

> Life is a gypsy woman, it's a caravan
> It's a stone of ice in the sun
> Thaw your eyes
> They are alone in a sea of clear water.

Since then, Azevedo has recorded a number of excellent albums that show off his superb songwriting—*Bicho de Sete Cabeças* (Seven-Headed Animal), *A Luz do Solo* (Solo Light), *De Outra Maneira* (Another Way), and *Eterno Presente* (Eternal Present).

Elba Ramalho

Born in 1951 in Conceição do Piancó, Paraíba, Elba Ramalho is one of the foremost vocalists to come from the Northeast. She was a national-class handball player, a drummer in an all-girl rock band, and a sociology student before traveling to Rio as a singer for the northeastern group Quinteto Violado. Also an actress, she has appeared on stage and screen, in plays such as *Lampião no Inferno*, directed by Azevedo, and in the Ruy Guerra film *Ópera do Malandro*, based on Chico Buarque's theater piece.

Ramalho launched her first album on CBS in 1979, *Ave de Prata* (Silver Bird), and has since become a national and international star. With her ability to interpret a wide range of northeastern styles, her high-energy performing style, and her flamboyant, theatrical concerts, her popularity soared in the mid-1980s with the smash album *Do Jeito Que a Gente Gosta* (The Way We Like It). The LP featured infectious forrós, maracatus, and the biting, politicized repentista-style track "Nordeste Independente" (An Independent Northeast).

In the late eighties, Ramalho continued to expand her repertoire, adding Caribbean and other new rhythms to her song list. Elba and her backup group Banda Rojão have done much to expand the vocabulary of northeastern pop, mixing keyboards, wind instruments, and new vocal arrangements with forró and other northeastern styles.

Also from the Northeast

Along with Elba Ramalho and the late Gonzaga, Dominguinhos has been one of the top *forrozeiros* (forró-makers) of Brazil in recent years. Born in 1941 in Garanhuns, Pernambuco, Dominguinhos has written numerous standards, including "Só Quero um Xodó," cowritten with Anastácia. One of Brazil's greatest accordionists, he has appeared at the Free Jazz Festival and made numerous appearances on other artists' albums when the perfect northeastern-accordion touch was required.

Another hot forrozeiro is the joyful accordionist Baú dos 8 Baixos (Baú of the Eight Basses), real name Sebastião Moraes. Singer-songwriter Marcus Vinícius, whose music is a meeting of northeastern roots with modern classical music and other influences, was also part of the wave. Meanwhile, Zé Ramalho combined sertanejo-style guitar, Dylanesque stylings, and esoteric images into an unusual pop hybrid.

The so-called Pessoal do Ceará (People of Ceará) included Fagner, Ednardo, Belchior, and Amelinha, all of whom began their musical careers in Fortaleza, the capital of Ceará state. Fagner (born in 1950 in Orós, Ceará) has ventured far into pop-romantic-ballad territory at times but also has been an excellent interpreter of northeastern styles, especially on his albums in the seventies, and in later works like the 1988 RCA release *Gonzagão & Fagner*.

Luiz Gonzaga's musical heirs—Ramalho, Valença, Azevedo, and all the others—have continued the popularization and expansion of the northeastern folk genres, while keeping the music's roots and traditions alive. They have taken the verbal prestidigitations of the desafio and the rollicking good times of the forró around the globe, greatly adding to the richness of Brazilian popular music along the way.

The album cover of Luiz Gonzaga and Fagner's 1988 album, released by RCA-BMG.

CARIMBÓ, LAMBADA, AND THE NORTH

Like the Northeast, Brazil's North is a region of rich folklore and musical invention. It is a hot and humid area, covered mostly by tropical rain forest, and includes much of the Amazon Basin. One of its states is Pará, where lambada was created in the 1970s, in and around the capital city of Belém.

A record cover of a lambada compilation album issued by French label Carrere.

Betto Dougllas, as pictured on his 1988 BR/Continental album.

Belém is a bustling port city of nearly one million inhabitants, located just upstream from where the huge Tocantins River converges with the even mightier Amazon, as both rivers spill into the Atlantic Ocean. Marajó Island, around which the estuaries of the Tocantins and Amazon flow as they reach their ocean destination, is the size of Switzerland. Belém receives cultural influences from the Guyanas, located just a few hundred miles away, and from the Caribbean. In the 1970s the city's radio stations were heavily programming merengue, salsa, and rumba, as well as electrified versions of Pará's native Afro-Brazilian song/dance form, carimbó. According to a series of articles on lambada in the newspaper *Folha de São Paulo*, Belém disc jockey Haroldo Caraciolo of the Clube AM station began in 1974 to call all such music "lambada," which in Portuguese means "beating," "slap," or "shot of cachaça."

In 1976 the guitarist Joachim de Lima Vieira applied the name "lambada" to a musical hybrid that he had popularized: a fusion of merengue from the Dominican Republic, electric carimbó, and hints of other Caribbean motifs. Syncopated with a 2/4 time signature, it had a fast tempo and simple, insistent riffs on the electric guitar or sax, with drums and bass accompanying (congas came later). Those who later performed lambadas with vocals often sing flirtatious lyrics loaded with double-entendres. Vieira recorded *Lambada das Quebradas*, considered the first lambada album, that same year, although it wasn't released until 1978.

The lambada dance was also a new hybrid, mixing elements of the merengue, maxixe, samba, and forró dances. The lambada's popularity grew quickly. In Belém, the rhythm was spread through *festas de aparelhagem*—"sound parties" where DJs set up enormous sound systems for one-night dances—and then by radio. The new rhythm and dance spread to Manaus, the capital of Amazonas state, and Salvador, and eventually to Fortaleza, where it is said the dance grew more erotic. In the late 1980s it hit São Paulo, where numerous lambada dance clubs called *lambaterias* opened.

In the 1980s, some of the most successful lambada performers from Pará included saxophonist Manezinho do Sax and vocalists Beto Barbosa, Betto Dougllas, Carlos Santos, Alípio Martins, Márcia

Rodrigues, and Márcia Ferreira. The latter singer had a big hit with "Chorando Se Foi," which (as we have seen) would later gain global fame as "Lambada," performed by Kaoma.

Márcia Rodrigues was the most popular female lambada vocalist at the end of the decade. Often called the "muse of lambada," she melted audiences with her powerful voice and provocative style. When she performed for miners at the Amazonian gold-rush town of Laranjal do Jari in 1989, several rough-and-tumble fans approached her after the show. They pointed revolvers at the sixteen-year-old star and demanded she sleep with them. But Márcia was able to talk them out of it. "I beat them with my sweetness," she told a São Paulo newspaper. She escaped unharmed, ready to continue her lambada tour of the northern backlands.

Early on, lambada had a booster in Fafá de Belém, who was a sort of cultural ambassador from Brazil's North to the rest of the country during the 1970s and 1980s. Born in 1957, her real name is Maria de Fátima Palha de Figueiredo, and she has a strong, appealing voice that she uses to interpret a wide variety of popular songs, with a focus on romantic ballads. But her regionality has set her apart; she was probably the first major MPB star to record carimbó and lambada.

Fafá de Belém, one of the first pop musicians to include lambada tunes in her repertoire.

Adding to the complexity of lambada's musical identity is that big lambada stars, such as Beto Barbosa, often augment the genre with cumbia, salsa, and other Caribbean genres, as well as spicing it (especially in the late 1980s) with additions of Bahian sounds such as samba-reggae and fricote. Still, the sound of lambada from Pará generally retains a lighter, more upbeat sound than lambada from Bahia, which has more synthesizers and is more Afro-Brazilian.

Besides lambada and carimbó, the state of Pará has many other songs and dances, such as *siriá* (a folkloric style from the Cametá region, played in the marujada and boi-bumbá dramatic dances) and *sirimbó* (a mix of siriá and carimbó). But it took lambada to show the rest of Brazil in the eighties that the beat goes on in the North.

One of the most popular purveyors of lambada, Beto Barbosa, on the cover of his 1988 LP.

PARÁ

CEARÁ

PARAÍBA

PIAUÍ

PERNAMBUCO

Recife •

GOIÁS

ALAGOAS

SERGIPE

NANÁ VASCONCELOS

BAHIA

HERMETO PASCOAL

THE MONTHLY MAGAZINE DEVOTED TO THE INTERESTS

BMG BANJO MANDOLIN GUITAR

LAURINDO ALMEIDA

MINAS GERAIS

Belo Horizonte
•

UAKTI

LAURINDO ALMEIDA

• Três Pontas

SÃO PAULO

RIO DE JANEIRO

São Paulo
•

Rio de Janeiro

PARANÁ

PAULO MOURA

SANTA
CATARINA

AIRTO MOREIRA AND FLORA PURIM

EGBERTO GISMONTI

INSTRUMENTAL MUSIC AND JAZZ

CHAPTER 8

Instrumental music has always been a richly varied part of the Brazilian sound—from Pixinguinha's elegant choros to Uakti's primordial chamber music played on specially designed instruments. And part of the instrumental spectrum in Brazil is jazz, which its musicians have absorbed and expressed in their own way.

Conversely, many of America's top jazz and instrumental artists in the late twentieth century—musicians like George Duke, Herbie Mann, Lyle Mays, Pat Metheny, Lee Ritenour, and Paul Winter—have been heavily influenced by Brazilian music.

Before examining Brazil's prominent figures in the jazz and instrumental areas and how they and other pop artists (like Milton Nascimento) have influenced foreign musicians, it is necessary to take a side trip back 120 years to the origins of an idiom that would pave the way for modern explorations. It was called *choro*.

An American-Brazilian cross-cultural jam session (l. to r.): Herbie Hancock (keyboards), Ron Carter (bass), Milton Nascimento (guitar), an unidentified drummer, Pat Metheny (guitar), Randy Brecker (sax), Naná Vasconcelos (percussion).

CHORO: IMPROVISATION SOUTH OF NEW ORLEANS

Around 1870 in Rio a new musical style emerged that would become one of the most creative musical manifestations in Brazil. Choro was primarily an instrumental form, and to a North American ear it might sound a little like a small Dixieland jazz combo playing with strange rhythms, extreme melodic leaps, unexpected modulations, and occasional breakneck tempos. Interestingly, choro's development in Brazil slightly predated the rise of ragtime and jazz in North America. Choro and jazz were both characterized in part by their use of improvisation and African-derived musical elements.

There is much debate about the origin of the name. *Choro* also means "the act of weeping or sobbing" in Portuguese, and some experts suggest the music gained this appellation because of its sometimes melancholy sound (although it just as often sounds merry and playful). Others think the name derives from *xolo*, a word used long ago by some Afro-Brazilians for their parties or dances.

In its early days, choro was less a genre than a style, with Afro-Brazilian syncopation and a Brazilian flair added to the European genres—from waltzes and polkas to schottishes and mazurcas—that were fashionable at the end of the nineteenth century. Early choro groups generally included a flute, a guitar, and a cavaquinho. The guitar supplied the lowest tones with its bass strings, the cavaquinho handled the rhythm, and the flute acted as the soloist (other instruments would come later).

A simplified choro rhythm.

Choro musicians improvised upon European rhythms and melodies, developing a dialogue between the soloist and the accompanists in which the objective was the *derrubada* or "drop"—the moment in which the accompanying instruments could no longer follow the soloist's creative and unpredictable riffs. This "competitive" characteristic is reflected in many choro titles: Viriato Ferreira da Silva's "Caiu, Não Disse?" (Didn't I Tell You You Would Fall?), Ernesto Nazaré's "Apanhei-Te Cavaquinho" (I Got You Cavaquinho), and Pixinguinha-Lacerda's "Cuidado, Colega" (Careful, Pal) are three examples.

The first choro musicians were not professionals. They didn't mind playing for a whole night at parties as long as there was a lot of food and drink present. Between 1870 and 1919, there were hundreds of choro groups in Rio that spent nights moving from house to house, party to party.

By the first decade of the twentieth century choro had developed into an independent genre with its own basic characteristics, played in a binary rhythm with a medium to fast tempo. And, unlike jazz, only one instrumentalist in choro performs the solos.

Choro's Early Champions

An important figure in the development of choro was Joaquim Antonio da Silva Calado (1848-1880), whose pioneering ensemble group Choro Carioca was the most popular of its type in the 1870s. Calado was a virtuoso flutist, whose solos often featured spectacular octave leaps and mercurial key changes. Few of his compositions were published but those that were exerted a great influence on his musician peers.

Two others who also helped develop the fledgling genre were the pianists Chiquinha Gonzaga (1847-1935) and Ernesto Nazaré (1863-1934), both of whom were educated in classical music and wrote in many popular styles, including tangos, polkas, and waltzes. Chiquinha (Francisca Hedwiges Gonzaga) wrote the tremendously successful choro-polka "Atraente" (Attractive) in 1877, and later the choro "Forrobodó" (Noisy Party) in 1912. Ernesto Nazaré (the old spelling of his name is "Nazareth") will always be remembered for the choros "Odeon" (1909) and "Apanhei-te Cavaquinho" (1913). From then on, the genre began to achieve its musical individuality.

Another popular composer from this time was Zequinha de Abreu (1880-1935), who in 1917 wrote the classic "Tico-Tico no Fubá" (Tico-Tico Bird in the Cornmeal), which Carmen Miranda sang in the 1947 film *Copacabana*, and which was recorded later by Pepeu Gomes, jazz musician Paquito D'Rivera, and many others.

The legendary Pixinguinha was both a founding father of samba and a superb choro flutist-composer. Many, in fact, consider him the greatest choro musician of all time. He played Europe and South America and was a pioneer in the dissemination of Brazilian music overseas. And he was musically innovative: Pixinguinha and his group Os Oito Batutas formed an instrumental ensemble that was the first of its type to incorporate percussion instruments such as the ganzá, pandeiro, and reco-reco. In addition, he composed a number of notable works in the choro idiom, including "Sofre Porque Queres" (You Suffer Because You Want To) and "Carinhoso" (Affectionate).

When Pixinguinha and his band went to Paris in 1922 for a wildly successful six-month stay playing choro and maxixe, they in turn were influenced by the foxtrot orchestras they heard there. Pixinguinha and the Batutas returned home and added saxophone, clarinet, and trumpet to their instrumentation, and foxtrots, shimmies, and ragtime to their repertoire. "Salon Orchestras" or "jazz bands" (a misnomer as they played little jazz) became the rage in Rio in the 1920s and began taking the place of the choro groups. Foxtrots, tangos, maxixes, and sambas dominated; choros were relegated mainly to parties and bars.

In the 1940s, a new generation of choro musicians appeared. Flutists Benedito Lacerda and Altamiro Carrilho, mandolin virtuoso Jacó do Bandolim, clarinet and alto saxophonist Abel Ferreira, bandleader Severino Araújo, and cavaquinho master Valdir Azevedo were responsible for a short-lived but important choro revival. Most of the famous choros that young musicians play today were composed by this group, such as "Brasileirinho" (Little Brazilian) by Valdir Azevedo. This generation had a period of great popularity, but by the mid-1950s choro was forgotten again, by the public and the media. The next revival would occur in the 1970s, stimulated by musicians like Paulo Moura, Turíbio Santos, Arthur Moreira Lima, Paulinho da Viola, Hermeto Pascoal, and the Novos Baianos, all of whom included choros on their records.

An album of classic Pixinguinha songs released by Brazilian independent label Kuarup.

Although its mass appeal has gone up and down in cycles, choro has remained a vital part of the Brazilian musical landscape throughout the twentieth century. Choro is still a fundamental part of the musical vocabulary for most Brazilian instrumentalists.

PAULO MOURA

Paulo Moura is one of choro's greatest contemporary practitioners and serves as a good example of how late twentieth-century Brazilian musicians dexterously wove choro together with a variety of other styles. Moura is a virtuoso on both saxophone and clarinet, from which he can coax refined, raucous, or soulful sounds, depending on the occasion.

Paulo Moura.

He is a master of many other instumental idioms as well, including jazz, bossa, classical music, and *samba de gafieira*, an orchestrated style performed in dance halls.

Born in 1933, Moura began as a classical clarinetist with the Municipal Theatre Orchestra of Rio and later ventured into jazz-bossa with Sérgio Mendes' Sexteto Bossa Rio. From the late sixties on, Paulo remained a highly influential force in Brazilian popular music, teaching music theory to the likes of Wagner Tiso and Mauro Senise, arranging albums by Elis Regina, Fagner, and Milton Nascimento, and appearing as a sideman on many acclaimed recordings (including Marisa Monte's noteworthy debut album in 1989). But most importantly, he has recorded solo albums: the 1976 *Confusão Urbana, Suburbana e Rural* (Urban, Suburban and Rural Confusion) was a masterful tour through landscapes of modern and traditional Brazilian music.

Clara Sverner and Paulo Moura at the Mistura Up club in Rio.

That album made Paulo internationally famous, and it displays an incredible range. In the choro "Espinha de Bacalhau" (Cod Spine), Moura's capricious soprano sax leaps and winds spectacularly across the strumming of cavaquinho and guitar. The samba "Notícia" (News) swells with a big band sound. Paulo's sax follows the slower and more sentimental arrangements while an insistent cuíca yelps, calls, and whoops amidst the orchestration. "Bicho Papão" (Bogeyman) features a wild, fast beating of bass and hand drums, a rather unsettling jazzy sax solo, and an urban traffic jam of a horn section. "Tema do Zeca da Cuíca" (Cuíca Zeca's Theme) is a variegated montage of electric guitar riffs, cuíca gasps, wistful flute-playing, and intermittent Gil Evans-like strings, all coalescing into a rolling, breathless batucada. "Carimbó do Moura" balances Paulo's joyful clarinet playing with a rollicking carimbó rhythm from Pará. A dazzling fusion of multiple styles, *Confusão...* was arguably one of the most important Brazilian albums of the 1970s.

Moura continued to weave together jazz, choro, and samba in the eighties. He also recorded traditional works. In 1988 he and a pianist friend paid a beautiful homage to choro's greatest exponent with their album *Clara Sverner & Paulo Moura Interpretam Pixinguinha.*

LAURINDO ALMEIDA

Laurindo Almeida is from an older generation than Moura but has also displayed a great facility for meshing old and new instrumental styles. Born in 1917 in Santos, São Paulo, Almeida is a guitarist known for his harmonic mastery, subtle dynamics, rich embellishments, and adept improvisatory skills with a variety of song forms.

Almeida's career has spanned several generations. One of his first gigs was performing in a guitar duo with the legendary Garoto in the late 1930s, playing choros and sambas while adding chords that were harmonically advanced for the time. In 1947, Almeida journeyed to the United States to play with Stan Kenton's orchestra, in which he was a featured guitarist for three years.

Laurindo settled in Los Angeles and began a recording career. He teamed with saxophonist Bud Shank to cut *Laurindo Almeida Quartet Featuring Bud Shank* in 1954 for Pacific Jazz Records (the LP would be re-released in 1961 as *Brazilliance* by the World Pacific label). On that innovative album, Almeida and Shank wedded cool jazz with samba, baião, and choro.

Almeida and Shank's "jazz-samba" was not bossa nova, as some have claimed; it lacked the characteristic João Gilberto beat, the harmonic stamp of Jobim and others, and the economy of expression achieved by bossa. It also, quite simply, had a different mood and sound. But Almeida and Shank's hybrid forms were certainly valuable in their own right.

On subsequent albums, Almeida continued to fuse a variety of Brazilian idioms with jazz and classical forms. For example, he explored modinha, choro, maracatu, and boi-bumbá in *Duets with the Spanish Guitar* in 1957.

He was also an able interpreter of "classical" composers; he covered Villa-Lobos and Radamés Gnattali on *Impressões do Brasil,* and played guitar transcriptions of Debussy, Ravel, and Bach on the Grammy-winning *The Spanish Guitar of Laurindo Almeida* in 1960. Almeida continued his jazz-samba collaborations with Shank on *Holiday in Brazil* and *Latin Contrasts* (later re-issued as *Brazilliance, Vol. 2* and *Brazilliance, Vol. 3*).

Though Almeida was several thousand miles away from the burgeoning bossa nova movement in Rio in the late 1950s, he adapted that to his own style when it was carried to American shores by Getz, Byrd, and others. His 1962 album *Viva Bossa Nova!* was a commercial success: it hit

Laurindo Almeida.

the number nine spot on the charts. During this period, Almeida won ten Grammy awards, with most of them coming in the late 1950s and early 1960s. But his illustrious career was just getting underway.

Laurindo Almeida in 1951 on the cover of *BMG* magazine.

Bola Sete (guitar), Paulinho (drums), and Sebastião Neto (bass) on the cover of an album recorded for Fantasy in the 1960s.

In 1974, Almeida and Shank formed the L.A. Four with bassist Ray Brown and drummer Chuck Flores, and the group recorded nine albums together (Flores' place would be taken by Shelly Manne, then by Jeff Hamilton), performing a varied repertoire that included jazz, classical, and Brazilian-oriented material. Almeida also recorded with pianist George Shearing, singer Sammy Davis, Jr., and the Modern Jazz Quartet, and arranged, scored, and played on numerous film and TV scores (including *A Star Is Born*, "Bonanza," and "The Fugitive").

In the late 1980s, he recorded trio albums with guitarists Sharon Isbin and Larry Coryell, and with Charlie Byrd and Carlos Barbosa-Lima. Almeida has been a strong musical force now for five decades, a guitarist who has won great acclaim and collaborated with an astonishing range of artists.

Bola Sete

Another guitarist who was adept at mixing jazz and samba, and playing choro and bossa, was Bola Sete ("Seven Ball," real name Djalma Andrade, 1923-1987). Born in Rio, Sete studied classical music at the National School of Music and was influenced early in his career by Andres Segovia, Django Reinhardt, and Charlie Christian. He developed a versatile repertoire, playing in samba groups and composing choros ("Cosminho no Choro," for example).

In the 1950s he toured Europe and Latin America, and moved to the United States in 1959. He lived there for the rest of his life, developing his own jazz-samba fusion. Bola toured with Dizzy Gillespie and recorded several albums for Fantasy in the 1960s (one of the best was *Autêntico!* with bassist Sebastião Neto and drummer Paulinho). In North America, he received praise for his virtuoso guitarwork, more jazz-oriented than that of his bossa-nova peers. Sete's later albums were rescued from obscurity by pianist George Winston, a devoted fan who reissued them through the Windham Hill record company.

EGBERTO GISMONTI

Of Brazil's great instrumental musicians, few have followed as singular a path as Egberto Gismonti. The composer and multi-instrumentalist had his formal training in both the conservatory and the Amazon jungle.

Gismonti (born in 1947 in Carmo, a small city in Rio de Janeiro state) has been engaged in a lifelong search for new musical languages. He started by taking fifteen years of classical piano lessons in Rio and then studying orchestration and composition in Paris with the noted composer-teacher Nadia Boulanger (who also instructed Aaron Copland) and the serialist composer Jean Barraqué. But Egberto's interest in all kinds of popular music—jazz, samba, choro, baião, bossa—drew him out of the conservatory and into a new musical world of his own making. Along the way he would delve into African, Amerindian, and Asian rhythms and tonal systems.

Gismonti cannot be pegged as any one type of musician: his compositions have too much Brazilian rhythm to be classical; they are too impressionistic and contain too many Brazilian elements to be jazz; and their harmonies are too challenging for his music to fit anywhere else.

He can be intensely lyrical, sounding something like a highly rhythmic Ralph Towner on guitar or Keith Jarrett on piano, improvising atop baião and frevo patterns. Gismonti has also written beautiful melodies that have been covered by many musicians ("Sonho" was recorded by Henry Mancini, Paul Mauriat, and more than a dozen others). Then again, his music can be jarring, strange, and difficult.

Nevertheless, Egberto is an internationally popular instrumentalist. *Dança das Cabeças* (Dance of the Minds), recorded with percussionist Naná Vasconcelos, has been released in eighteen countries and has sold over 200,000 copies (a large sum for experimental non-vocal music). Egberto is quite popular in Europe, where his work has been released on the ECM label, and is well respected by jazz and classical

Egberto Gismonti.

musicians around the globe. He has collaborated on many albums with some noted international jazz-instrumental artists, like percussionists Vasconcelos and Collin Walcott, bassist Charlie Haden, saxophonist Jan Garbarek, flutist Paul Horn, and guitarist Ralph Towner.

Egberto plays acoustic and electric keyboards, eight and ten-string guitar, sitar, accordion, violoncello, all kinds of flutes, and numerous other instruments he has discovered in many trips around the world. And he is also a versatile composer. He has recorded acoustic solo albums (the beautiful, lyrical *Solo* in 1979 is one), and

Gismonti on the keyboards in a 1986 performance.

he has deftly combined pianos and synthesizers (one example is his 1985 album *Trem Caipira*). Gismonti has also formed fusion bands: Academia de Danças was an all-star group that featured Robertinho

Evidence of Gismonti's fluency on both guitar and keyboards.

Silva on drums, Nivaldo Ornellas on sax and flute, and Luis Alves on bass.

In another solo album, 1982's *Fantasia*, Gismonti used sound samplers to simulate an entire orchestra. The opening two cuts on that album—"Overture" and "Infância"—demonstrate the range Egberto may explore in just a few minutes: the overture begins with a foundation of sustained chords over which dissonant harmonic clusters are juxtaposed with nervous rhythmic patterns. This anxious mood then mellows as "Infância" begins; the main theme is introduced and worked through many variations. The composition ends with a rambunctious baião-like feeling that evokes images of children dancing and playing.

Keyboardist Lyle Mays said, "For me personally Egberto has been a kind of model in that he is willing to use a child singing one minute and then have a chamber orchestra the next, then a whole bank of synthesizers. He has a raw edge that sometimes puts people off, but to me the vision behind his music is just astounding."

Another adventurous Gismonti album, *Sol do Meio Dia* (Noonday Sun), released in 1978, was influenced by his friendship with Sapain, a shaman from the Yawalapiti tribe in the Amazon jungle near the Xingu River. Gismonti stayed with the Yawalapiti for several weeks in 1977 and learned much about the primitive tribe's music from Sapain. The experience with the Yawalapiti affected him in two ways: Gismonti's own music became more spontaneous, and he became concerned with finding a perfect integration between musician, music, and instrument.

Watching Gismonti play live is an unforgettable experience. On guitar he can play with blinding speed and superb precision, and produce a wide range of timbral effects. Sometimes he plays the guitar like a piano or percussion instrument, using his left hand to pluck and "hammer" the strings. His improvisations on guitar and on piano (on which he is equally proficient) are consistently surprising and imaginative. He also sings in a gentle voice, often with lyrics composed by poet Geraldo Carneiro. However, vocals in Egberto's music are primarily part of the sound, functioning like another instrument.

After recording twelve albums between 1968 and 1978, Gismonti created his own label, Carmo, which enabled him to make as many experimental albums as he wanted. At the same time he has continued to record for ECM, which now has a large catalog of much of his best work.

HERMETO PASCOAL

One of Brazil's most colorful multi-instrumentalists is Hermeto Pascoal, born in 1936 in Lagoa da Canoa, a neighborhood in the town of Arapiraca in Alagoas. When he performs, Pascoal cuts a striking figure: an albino with a flowing white beard and long, luminous white hair, he tends to dart from instrument to instrument on stage, full of energy and inspiration as he follows each musical impulse wherever it leads him. His music is not for those with a lazy ear: in one song he may shift from a merry frevo played by horns and guitars to a droning, dolorous toada on the accordion, then swing between xaxado and maxixe, plunge into a free-jazz piano interlude, and finish with a cuíca and saxophone giddily chasing each other all over the scales.

Like Gismonti, Pascoal has an uncanny ability to create new sounds. But while Egberto will often do that by playing conventional instruments in unusual ways, Hermeto will do it by making ordinary household objects into instruments. He can elicit interesting tones from pots, pans, jars, sewing machines—whatever is on hand.

On his 1984 composition "Tiruliruli" he took a phrase from a Brazilian soccer announcer's on-air play-by-play report and repeated it over and over, gradually adding more and more harmonium embellishments until he had created a quirky but strangely affecting short piece. In Hermeto's world, everything has musical possibilities. Percussionist/drummer Airto Moreira has called him "the most complete musician I ever met in my life. A genius."

Hermeto was a child musical prodigy. He started with the flute, and at the age of seven learned to play the accordion. By eleven he was already performing at dances and *forrós* in the region around Arapiraca. When he was fourteen, his family moved to Recife, and Hermeto began to earn money on radio programs there. He moved to Caruaru (also in Pernambuco), a city famous for its regional music, at age sixteen. There Hermeto played his accordion on local radio programs and at dances, returning to Recife only a few years later. For a brief time during this period, he joined with his brother José Neto and Sivuca (another musician who would later be well known) to form a curious trio: each was an albino and played the accordion. The short-lived group was humorously called O Mundo em Chamas (World on Fire).

Hermeto Pascoal in the late 1980s.

Although he was self-taught, Hermeto's musical development continued at a rapid pace: the piano came next, and then various wind and percussion instruments. Pascoal traveled south and struggled to make a living by playing any and all types of music in Rio and São Paulo in the late fifties and early sixties.

In 1964, he formed the Sambrasa Trio with Airto Moreira and bassist Humberto Claiber. "When I met him, he was subbing for other accordionists, and we started getting him work," reported Moreira. "We would often stay up all night talking about music." Later, Airto was

Hermeto Pascoal.

in a band called Trio Novo with guitarists Heraldo do Monte and Théo de Barros; Hermeto joined them and the group changed its name to Quarteto Novo. The quartet dedicated itself to a progressive re-invention of northeastern song styles. "We played baião, xaxado, other northeastern Brazilian rhythms, but the arrangements were very jazzy, in 4/4 time with modern harmonies," said Airto. Unfortunately, the band cut just one LP—1967's *Quarteto Novo*, long out of print.

After the group split up, Hermeto journeyed to the United States. He was invited to record by jazzman Miles Davis and played piano on Miles' *Live-Evil* LP (1970). Pascoal also cut the acclaimed solo album *Hermeto* on Buddha Records (also released in 1970). While in North America, the multi-instrumentalist drew raves both for his extraordinary improvisational abilities in concert and for his idiosyncratic and original compositions. His material was recorded by such diverse artists as Gil Evans and the Berlin Symphony.

Hermeto's songs explored choro, frevo, maxixe, baião, jazz, and many other forms, mixing them freely and in unusual combinations. Individual songs often had multiple rhythms.

He returned to Brazil in 1973, recorded *A Música Livre de Hermeto Pascoal*, before heading back north to the United States in 1976 to record *Slave's Mass*. That album featured one of Hermeto's most unusual instruments—piglets, whose little grunts he incorporated into the music—along with the human talents of Airto, Flora Purim, Laudir de Oliveira, Raul de Souza, David Amaro, Ron Carter, and Alphonso Johnson.

Hermeto also performed on albums by Airto, Purim, and Tom Jobim. Because of his eclecticism and radical experimentation, Pascoal became a cult figure and mentor to many musicians. Lyle Mays told us, "Hermeto is worth listening to just for his wild creativity. His music tends to show me that there are possibilities that I should try to open myself up to explore. He has a real devotion to the making of music and it comes across—let's go for it, let's do everything we can!"

His recordings are indeed free-wheeling and uninhibited, and they usually feature the backing of Pernambuco (percussion), Jovino Santos Neto (keyboards), Márcio Bahia (drums), Carlos Malta (flutes, saxophones), and Itiberê Zwarg (bass), all very talented musicians.

In concert, Hermeto is unpredictable. He may stalk off the stage in a rage if the sound is inadequate or if the audience is clinking their cocktail glasses and talking too loudly. But more than likely he will give a unique performance—unique because at each show the group picks different songs from their vast repertoire and enlivens them with improvisation, humorous between-song comments, and Hermeto's ability to make music with almost any animate or inanimate object on earth.

Hermeto recorded only eight albums between 1967 and 1980, a small number for someone of his artistic stature. His record sales were not large, especially in his native country. But in 1983 he connected with Som da Gente Records, a new, small, audiophile label that specialized in instrumental music. Founded by husband-and-wife songwriters Walter Santos and Tereza Souza, Som da Gente offered Hermeto the use of its recording studio, Nosso Estúdio, as a secure outlet for his uncompromising creativity. Hermeto recorded four albums for the label in the late eighties and continued to expand his sonic universe. As described by Howard Mandel in *down beat*, Pascoal is "as pan-global a leader as Sun Ra and as surefooted an individualist as Rahsaan Roland Kirk."

AIRTO MOREIRA

While Sérgio Mendes was the biggest Brazilian name in the United States in the late 1960s, husband-and-wife musicians Airto Moreira and Flora Purim were the most visible figures in the 1970s, adding their Brazilian spirit to the burgeoning jazz-fusion scene of those years. Airto spearheaded the Brazilian "percussion invasion" of the late 1960s and 1970s that infused American jazz with new rhythms, percussion textures, and tone colors. Although drummers Milton Banana and Hélcio Milito had recorded with Americans during the bossa era, and Dom Um Romão and João Palma had played with Mendes in the mid-1960s, Airto would have the greatest impact outside of Brazil of any Brazilian drummer-percussionist.

Airto was born in 1941 in Itaiópolis, Santa Catarina, and grew up in the city of Curitiba. After playing with the bossa group Sambalanço Trio in the early sixties, he was part of the aforementioned Sambrasa Trio and Quarteto Novo with Hermeto Pascoal. Airto was interested both in jazz and progressive interpretations of traditional Brazilian styles, and he was a multi-talented instrumentalist who didn't fit into any one niche. "At that time, percussionists in Brazil were usually specialists," he recalled. "One guy would play tambourine really well, another guy would be a cuíca player, another

SIVUCA

Sivuca, Hermeto's old bandmate from O Mundo Em Chamas, is an accordion virtuoso who also sings and plays the piano and guitar. Real name Severino D'Oliveira, Sivuca was born in 1930 in Itabaiana, Pernambuco. He plays a mixture of many styles (jazz, forró, choro, waltz, classical), all embellished with rich improvisation. He has been a fixture on the international jazz scene since the 1960s and has toured and recorded with Miriam Makeba, Harry Belafonte, Oscar Brown, Jr., Airto, and Toots Thielemans. Sivuca has also released solo albums—*Som Brasil* (Brazil Sound) is a prime example of his style that is both folksy and jazzy.

The cover of Sivuca's *Som Brasil* album.

would play surdo. But I mixed instruments and played everything."

In Rio, Airto had met and fallen in love with a young singer by the name of Flora Purim. In 1968, she decided to travel to the United States to pursue a jazz career, and Airto opted to follow her there, convinced he could eventually persuade her to return to Brazil with him. That was not to be, but he and Flora did stay together, marrying in 1972 and settling permanently in California.

When he first came to the United States, Airto had come prepared to work. "I brought all the hand percussion instruments I had, and the fact is that I came at the right time." Jazz was especially ready for him in the late 1960s: Miles Davis, Larry Coryell, Herbie Hancock, Tony Williams, Chick Corea, Weather Report, and other artists were creating new musical hybrids by mixing free jazz and bebop with funk, rock, Latin styles, and (especially after Airto and Flora) Brazilian music and instrumentation. Brazil offered an alternative to Cuban music, which had heavily influenced many jazz musicians in the forties and fifties with rumba, charanga, and mambo rhythms, and congas, maracas, timbales, and bongos. After Castro's revolution in 1959, the American-Cuban interchange slowed somewhat.

After arriving in the U.S., Airto spent several months studying with composer-arranger Moacir Santos, then began integrating himself into the American jazz scene, playing first with Paul Winter (one of the few Americans familiar with Brazilian hand percussion instruments) and

MOACIR SANTOS

Moacir Santos, who taught music theory to both Airto and Flora Purim, has been an influential music professor and mentor for many young Brazilian musicians since he moved to the United States in 1969. Before that, in Brazil, he was a talented saxophonist and an influential arranger and composer. He scored a big hit in Brazil with "Naná" in 1964, and in the U.S. recorded three LPs for Blue Note in the early 1970s (including *Maestro*, for which he received a Grammy nomination). He is known for his esoteric mixes of jazz and Brazilian idioms, and his complicated rhythms.

Moacir Santos, as pictured on the cover of one of his albums.

doing session work with Wayne Shorter, Cannonball Adderley, and others.

Airto astonished American musicians and producers with his vast array of percussion pieces—cuíca, berimbau, agogô, afoxê, pandeiro (his strongest solo instrument), rain stick, ganzá, and various other rattlers, shakers, and drums, as well as musical devices that he invented. Each instrument had different tones and textural possibilities, and their sum total—especially in Airto's dexterous hands—was all rather staggering for Americans who were seeing Airto perform for the first time.

Airto Moreira and wife Flora Purim in the 1980s.

When he would show up at a recording studio with all his gear in tow "the producers would go crazy," Airto told us. "They would go up to the pile of percussion instruments and say 'I like this one. Play this.'"

Airto played the berimbau on albums by Paul Desmond and others. He added cuíca to Paul Simon's "Me and Julio Down by the Schoolyard," a salsa-flavored hit single in 1972. Remembered Moreira, "He said he wanted something different, like a human voice. I had the cuíca and he said, 'That's it!'"

Airto caught the attention of Miles Davis, who used him on the albums *At Fillmore* and

International musical travelers (l. to r.): Airto, Ndugu Chancler, Raul de Souza, Miroslav Vituous, Flora Purim, George Duke, and Cannonball Adderley.

Live-Evil, both recorded in 1970. He also played with Weather Report on their groundbreaking eponymous first album in 1971 but couldn't join the group permanently because of his commitment with Miles. Airto recalled that Miles "really didn't want me to play rhythm all the time. He wanted me to play colors and sounds more than rhythm. I would play the cuíca to kind of tease him and he would feed off that and play more." By focusing on "atmosphere" with Miles, Airto expanded his abilities to provide color with percussion.

This role expansion would change Airto's musical direction and influence almost all jazz drummers and percussionists to follow. "He was playing stuff that couldn't be played by anybody else here," reported jazz keyboardist George Duke. "I'd never heard a percussionist play like that, that free, and understanding how to play the right thing at the right moment." Airto's success would begin a northerly migration: "After I played for Miles, a lot of Brazilian percussionists started coming to the States and bringing all kinds of stuff and making their own instruments."

Meanwhile, in between gigs with Davis, Airto found time for his first solo albums, *Natural Feelings* (1970) and *Seeds on the Ground* (1971). The next year, he and Flora joined bassist Stanley Clarke, saxophonist-flutist Joe Farrell, and keyboardist Chick Corea for the latter's seminal

fusion LP *Return to Forever* (the album's name would become the group's moniker). "When Chick heard the rhythms I was playing, it was a whole new thing for him. Brazilian music has a very different beat, and he really liked the way Flora was singing and phrasing. It was different from both jazz and Latin music." In the band, Airto had an uncharacteristic role, playing only drums while Flora handled the percussion. Airto and Flora also played on Return to Forever's 1973 album *Light As a Feather*, and they gave both albums a strong Brazilian edge.

Airto then left the group. "Chick wanted to go more into electronics and I didn't want to do that, to play loud," Moreira said. Instead, with producer Creed Taylor's backing, Airto formed his own band Fingers, which included David Amaro on guitar and lasted for two years. In 1975 came Airto's tour-de-force solo album *Identity*, considered one of the seventies' finest fusion recordings and which inspired musicologist John Storm Roberts to effuse in *The Latin Tinge*, "The texture of *Identity* was extraordinarily dense. Driving Afro-Brazilian percussion, berimbau musical bow, bossa nova vocals, almost purely Congo-Angola melodies, Amerindian wooden flutes, rich strings, rock drumming and guitar, shimmering free-rhythm bells and strikers, a kind of manic avant-garde scatting, were interwoven through multiple tracking in a series of compositions so rich in their references that they took on deeper meaning on every listening."

After Moreira's performances with Miles Davis, Weather Report, and Chick Corea, many bands added a percussionist, and percussive coloration became standard in jazz and fusion.

In 1979, Airto traveled down to Brazil with George Duke, Ndugu Chancler, Stanley Clarke, Raul de Souza, Roland Batista, and other fusion stars to give a concert in Rio. Recalled Duke, "It was the first time Airto had been back to Brazil in a long time. He was nervous because everybody was waiting to hear him. And he played a solo that night by himself that was the most incredible, magnificent percussion solo I've ever heard, bar none. It was an experience."

In 1972 *down beat* magazine added a percussion category to its annual awards, and Moreira took top honors that year and in many subsequent years. Over the next two decades, Airto continued to release his own solo albums, team with wife Flora for releases together, and record and tour with the Crusaders, Freddie Hubbard, Carlos Santana, Herbie Hancock, Gil Evans, Mickey Hart, and Babatunde Olatunji.

NANÁ VASCONCELOS

Along with Airto, Naná Vasconcelos has arguably been the most creative and influential percussionist of the last two decades. Naná (whom Airto calls "the best berimbau player in the world") gained international critical acclaim through his work with Egberto Gismonti, Codona, and the Pat Metheny Group.

Born in Recife in 1945, Naná was part of Quarteto Livre (with Geraldo Azevedo) in the late 1960s, then lived in Europe throughout much of the 1970s. While there he toured with saxophonist Gato Barbieri and

PERCUSSION IN BRAZIL

Some of Brazil's top drummers and percussionists include João Parahyba, a knowledgeable ethnomusicologist and in-demand player who has recorded and toured with Ivan Lins, Dori Caymmi, and Alemão; Téo Lima, who has played with Djavan, Maria Bethânia, Martinho da Vila, Yutaka, and many more; Robertinho Silva, known worldwide for his work with Milton Nascimento; Oswaldinho da Cuíca (Little Oswald of the Cuíca); Carlinhos Brown, a Bahian percussionist and noted composer; Djalma Correa; Pascoal Meirelles; Paulinho Braga; Chico Batera; Marcelo Salazar, and Repolho. There are hundreds more Brazilian rhythm masters and many of them have worked in other countries (see page 169).

Brazilian drummer/percussionist João Parahyba demonstrating his berimbau technique.

Naná Vasconcelos with berimbau slung over his left shoulder.

The back of Codona's 1979 album jacket cover. Pictured are members Colin Walcott, Don Cherry, and Naná Vasconcelos.

others and also spent a few years in Paris working with disturbed children in a psychiatric hospital, using music as a form of creative therapy. Back in Brazil, he was part of the notable Som Imaginário band, then toured and recorded with Egberto Gismonti in the late seventies. In 1979, he formed Codona with trumpeter Don Cherry and percussionist Collin Walcott. The trio released three highly regarded albums that mixed free jazz and cross-cultural improvisation.

Naná played percussion and sang with the Pat Metheny Group in the early eighties. He added a significant amount of rhythmic density and atmosphere to the albums, especially 1981's *As Falls Wichita, So Falls Wichita Falls*, on which Naná was part of a trio with guitarist Metheny and keyboardist Lyle Mays. "He was a total joy to work with," said Mays. "One of the things that I most enjoyed about playing with Naná was that he was interested in working with me as a synthesizer player to come up with combination textures that neither of us could do alone. He took things a step further, using his voice together with his instrument and with my instruments. Naná broadened our soundscape, and he added charisma, another focal point of attention on stage."

Like Airto, Naná can create a dense musical atmosphere of rustles, rattles, whispers, and rumbles, moving with an irresistible groove, or clashing in unearthly cacophony. And, as Airto noted, Naná can wield the berimbau like no other, turning it into a unique solo voice. His best works, among them the 1989 solo album *Rain Dance*, are like sound encyclopedias, beautiful expansions of rhythmic and textural possibilities.

FLORA PURIM

Airto's wife Flora Purim was arguably the most successful jazz-fusion singer of the 1970s, both artistically and commercially. Many were the jazz fans in that decade who tuned in to one of Flora's songs on the radio and were astonished and delighted by what they heard. She sang with great passion (both in Portuguese and accented English), and utilized an extended array of vocal effects: squeaks, moans, cries, electronic distortions, free-form scatting, and precipitous glissandi (slides). Her voice, alternately smooth and husky, was sensuous and rhythmic. She could serve as a lead vocalist or as another instrument interacting with the flute, guitar, or percussion. Flora was ideally suited to collaborate with the creative talents of Airto, George Duke, Chich Corea, Hermeto Pascoal, and Stanley Clarke. She seemed both a force of nature and a new type of jazz singer.

Born in 1942, Flora grew up listening to jazz, blues, samba, and classical music. She sang in various clubs in and around Rio in the sixties, during which time she met her future husband Airto, and Hermeto Pascoal (who suggested she try wordless vocal improvisation). After moving to New York in 1968, she sat in on jam sessions with the likes of Herbie Hancock and Thelonious Monk. Her first gigs involved touring Europe with Stan Getz (singing jazz-bossa) and recording and performing with Duke Pearson and Gil Evans.

Then Corea invited Flora and Airto to play on the aforementioned *Return to Forever* album, and she stayed with that band for two years, singing and writing lyrics for songs such as "Light As a Feather." Recalled

Flora Purim.

George Duke, "She was so free melodically that she sounded like a horn player. It was absolutely new music. I don't think there's anybody that sings quite like her. Free as a bird."

Calamity struck in 1971 when Flora was arrested for cocaine possession. She fought the charge but was convicted, then spent a year and a half appealing the conviction, during which time she continued her musical career and recorded her solo debut in 1973, *Butterfly Dreams*. The LP's opening notes—Airto's cuíca and Stanley Clarke's funky bass playing off each other—give the listener a hint of the hot jazz-fusion that follows. The album's personnel also included keyboardist Duke, guitarist Amaro, flutist Joe Henderson, and zither-player Ernie Hood. Collectively they mixed funk-Brazilian grooves with uninhibited free-form solos creating one of the era's most noted works. Highlights included Purim's lovely rendition of Jobim's beautiful "Dindi" and the ballad "Love Reborn," notable for its bossa-nova-flavored guitar, Flora's romantic vocals, and Henderson's languid sax.

Flora cut a live album in Montreux and then finished another studio work, *Stories to Tell*, just before starting her sentence in 1974 at the Terminal Island Prison in Long Beach, California. While there she was awarded *down beat* magazine's 1974 award for best female

Flora Purim giving a goodbye concert at the Terminal Island Prison. Also visible in the photo are Hermeto Pascoal (flute), David Amaro (guitar), and Airto (drums).

jazz vocalist—an award she would win the next two years as well.

Following her release from Terminal Island in 1975, Flora recorded *Open Your Eyes, You Can Fly* (1976), whose title song became one of her most popular standards. That LP featured Duke, Airto, bassist Alphonso Johnson, drummer Ndugu, drummer Robertinho Silva, Pascoal, and Egberto Gismonti. Since then, Flora has recorded many albums in the United States and Europe, and has been a frequent performer at events such as the Montreux Jazz Festival.

THE BRAZILIAN WAVE

On the prolonged interchange between Brazilian and American music, Sérgio Mendes commented, "It's interesting for me today to see Herbie Hancock doing things with Milton Nascimento. It's a kind of mutual curiosity between two different worlds. I still listen to Horace Silver

Milton Nascimento and Wayne Shorter.

Charlie Byrd in 1989. He was one of the first U.S. jazz artists to incorporate Brazilian melodies and rhythms in his music.

and Bud Powell. And Stevie Wonder, Henry Mancini, Burt Bacharach, Pat Metheny—who has not been influenced by Brazilian music?"

Latin American and Caribbean music in general has strongly influenced American jazz and popular music throughout the twentieth century, as was painstakingly documented by musicologist John Storm Roberts in his book *The Latin Tinge*. Jelly Roll Morton used the habanera rhythm in many songs; Cole Porter incorporated the rumba; Professor Longhair and Fats Domino both had Latin-influenced piano styles; rocker Bo Diddley's trademark beat was a pounding rumba rhythm (with Jerome Green on maracas); and the jazz musicians Dizzy Gillespie, Duke Ellington, Stan Kenton, George Shearing, and Bud Shank experimented with Latin (especially Cuban) rhythms, percussion, and song styles in the 1940s and 1950s. Machito, Gato Barbieri, Tito Puente, Willie Bobo, Cal Tjader, Mongo Santamaria, Paquito D'Rivera, Daniel Ponce, Jorge Dalto, and Eddie Palmieri were all important figures in the Latin-jazz interchange that occurred from the fifties through the eighties.

Brazilian music—its rhythms, instruments, harmonies, melodies, and textures—would have an enormous influence in the U.S. from 1962 on. Percussionists were a large part of that impact. Brazilian music helped create a new rhythmic emphasis in jazz and was an important element in the new style called "jazz fusion." Airto personified this rhythmic revolution.

BRAZILIAN PERCUSSION OUTSIDE BRAZIL

The following is a sampling of the feverish recording and touring activity of Brazilian drummers and percussionists beyond their native shores in recent decades. The Brazilian artist's name is followed by the artist(s) with whom they toured or recorded.

Milton Banana: Stan Getz.

Cyro Baptista: David Byrne, Ambitious Lovers, Herbie Mann, and Ryuichi Sakamoto.

Chico Batera: Lee Ritenour.

Paulinho Braga: Lee Ritenour.

Café: Elements.

Djalma Correa: Peter Gabriel and the Manhattan Transfer.

Mayuto Correa: Charles Lloyd, Gabor Szabo, Hugh Masakela, Freddie Hubbard, Donald Byrd, and many others.

Paulinho da Costa: Dizzy Gillespie, Milt Jackson, Ella Fitzgerald, Joe Pass, Michael Jackson, Madonna, Barbra Streisand, Lionel Richie, and many more.

Alyrio Lima Cova: Webster Lewis and Weather Report.

Reinaldo Fernandes: John Zorn, Arto Lindsay, and David Byrne.

Guilherme Franco: Gato Barbieri, Keith Jarrett, McCoy Tyner, Elvin Jones, and Paul Winter.

Téo Lima: Yutaka.

Édison Machado: Herbie Mann and Stan Getz.

Armando Marçal: The Pat Metheny Group.

Hélcio Milito: Solo album *Kilombo* released in 1987 in U.S.

Carlinho de Oliveira: Herbie Mann.

Airto Moreira: Miles Davis, Weather Report, Return to Forever, Paul Simon, George Duke, Paul Desmond, and many more.

Laudir de Oliveira: Chicago, Nina Simone, and many more.

João Palma: Sérgio Mendes.

João Parahyba: Michel LeGrand.

Roberto Pinheiro: Al Di Meola.

Carlos Pinto: Al Di Meola.

Portinho: Manfredo Fest.

Dom Um Romão: Cannonball Adderley, Paul Horn, and Weather Report.

Jorge Da Silva: John Zorn, Arto Lindsay, and David Byrne.

Naná Vasconcelos: Codona, Gato Barbieri, the Pat Metheny Group, Paul Simon, B.B. King, Talking Heads, and many others.

"In all fusion bands, the drummers slip into a jazz-Brazilian groove almost automatically," observed jazz flutist Herbie Mann. And, in the 1970s, "it became almost matter of fact for every band to have a percussionist. But all the colors were Brazilian-influenced. Before that, the Latin drummers just played congas, timbales, and bongos."

Along with bossa, samba is a favored Brazilian rhythm (often played by Americans at an accelerated tempo). Sambas have been recorded by many North Americans: Joni Mitchell ("Dreamland" in 1978), Earl Klugh and George Benson ("Brazilian Stomp" in 1988), John Patitucci ("Our Family" in 1988), David Byrne ("Office Cowboy" in 1989), among others. As George Duke said, "You can find these Brazilian rhythms everywhere, they've gone into TV and [film] scoring. And percussion has become so strong in dance music, and all that came from Latin American music in general. But all that stuff on top is Brazilian stuff that sounds like a batucada—shakers, agogôs, and those kind of rhythms. In a strange sort of way, [Brazilian music] infiltrated the modern pop world without them even knowing it. Nowadays, when you turn in a contemporary record, the first thing the A&R guy will tell you is 'Don't you think it needs more percussion?' "

"I think Brazilian music has affected jazz musicians and songwriters a lot, including how they melodically approach their music," continued George Duke. "I know that when I was in Brazil in 1970, I bought every Milton, Ivan [Lins], and Edu Lobo record I could find. I brought them back and played them for my friends. And then I sat down and tried to emulate those songs, to compose in that area, and you can hear that on some of my early records. The same way I learned to play jazz, I learned to play Brazilian music; you have to learn the fundamentals first. And I know that Cannonball Adderley was totally immersed in that music before he died. He felt the same way."

One of Duke's most Brazilian albums was *Brazilian Love Affair* (1977), which featured Milton, Airto, and Flora Purim. He, like many jazz artists, turned to Brazil for material in the 1970s and 1980s for great melodies to cover because so much of the music sounded fresh and original. Perhaps Duke and his peers were searching abroad because American composers were no longer writing music comparable in quality to the standards produced by the likes of Gershwin and Ellington in the 1930s and 1940s. "The U.S. is becoming more of a rhythm nation than a melodic nation," noted Duke, speaking of popular music. "Brazil is both."

Lyle Mays and Pat Metheny

"You have to credit Brazilian music with harmonic innovation. Their harmonies have definitely influenced me, starting with Jobim," admitted Lyle Mays. An even greater influence on the keyboardist-composer was Milton Nascimento, whom Lyle had first heard on Wayne Shorter's landmark 1975 album *Native Dancer*.

"It was a watershed record, a classic, and I think it turned a lot of jazz musicians onto Milton," said Mays. "Even to this day it stands as one of the best blends of Brazilian music and American jazz. When I first heard it, I didn't know what to think, it was so different. I thought it was like magic, and I just couldn't imagine that music. I simply had to listen again as I couldn't quite grasp it. I had never heard those kinds of tunes [that Milton composed] before." Not only were the melodies remarkable (starting with the opening track, "Ponta de Areia"), but the breathtaking dialogue between Shorter's sax and Nascimento's voice was symbolic in a way of the growing musical interchange between American and Brazilian musicians.

Mays and Pat Metheny were profoundly affected by Nascimento's two *Clube da Esquina* double albums (especially the second one), which featured other Mineiro musicians such as Lô Borges, Wagner Tiso, Tavinho Moura, and Beto Guedes in strong collaborative roles (see Chapter 5). Mays recalled listening to the *Clube* albums for the first time with Metheny: "I remember how excited we were. It was an amazing, unpredictable combination of cultural influences of the Western classical harmonic sense and the African rhythmic sense, done in a completely different way from jazz.... Listening to it gave me the same kind of excitement as when I first heard jazz. I don't think there's any parallel to those records in any music I've come across. The *Clube da Esquina* records have things in common with the Beatles and Miles Davis, a combination of hipness, accessibility, and exoticness. That was the start of me getting into unfiltered Brazilian music, searching for imports."

The Pat Metheny Group in 1989 (Lyle Mays is on far left; Brazilian percussionist Armando Marçal is standing behind him, wearing dark shirt; Pat Metheny is front center).

One of the key *Clube da Esquina* participants was guitarist Toninho Horta, who would have a strong influence on Metheny's playing and harmonic sense. Metheny in turn would later perform on Nascimento's *Encontros e Despedidas* in 1985 and on two of Toninho's albums that decade.

The Pat Metheny Group incorporated many Brazilian elements into its sound. "During the first half of the group's history, one hundred percent of the music we did had that straight-eighth rhythm, which comes from Brazilian music," noted Mays (most jazz has the characteristic "swing eighth note").

Toninho Horta and Pat Metheny.

"You can hear it in *San Lorenzo, Phase Dance,* and then it is even more evident in the album *Watercolors.* We played [our music] on electric guitar and keyboards, but under the surface the actual rhythms had a whole lot to do with Brazilian music. I don't mean that to sound like we were pioneers. It was a thing happening in jazz in general, such as with Gary Burton, which is where Pat got it from. There was some Latin influence going around too, all the way back to Dizzy Gillespie. But the Brazilian rhythms are a little more subtle and translated into a music that sounded like a hybrid. It wasn't so obvious it was Brazilian based."

While such influences were rather covert, as Lyle saw it, a more overt impact began when Brazilian musicians such as Airto and Flora began to join American bands. In 1981, Metheny and Mays began to work with Vasconcelos, who stayed with them through *Travels* (1983). As mentioned above, Naná made a profound atmospheric contribution to their sound; and, rhythmically, some of their tunes became more obviously samba-based, as in "Are You Going with Me?" and "Straight on Red."

After Vasconcelos left the band, they gained a new percussion phenomenon: Armando Marçal. "Naná and Armando can both do rhythm, but I think that Naná was more interested in sounds and textures,

Dave Grusin.

Don Grusin.

while Armando is more interested in rhythms. Armando is almost like an entire samba school," enthused Mays. "He has maybe the strongest rhythmic clock of anybody I've ever heard, just relentless, incredible. He does everything from rock tambourine parts to more traditional samba."

Don and Dave Grusin

Keyboardist-composer Don Grusin and his brother Dave Grusin have both been strongly influenced by the Brazilian sound. "It started in the 1960s when I first heard Astrud Gilberto and Stan Getz and João Gilberto," reported Don, who in the seventies and eighties would produce or arrange albums for Gilberto Gil, Simone, Rique Pantoja, and other Brazilian artists. He sees Brazilian music as having helped create the "hybrid" North American music of the 1980s. "I hear a kind of hybrid sound in my music and that of Dave, Lee Ritenour, Ronnie Foster, Harvey Mason. I hear Bill Evans changes, Oscar Peterson right-hand licks, all combined with Brazilian rhythmic content, such as the way the caxixi [shaker] works. That stuff all fits together and that's part of where we're headed. I'm hearing some of that in a lot of pop too, such as the Thompson Twins."

OTHER MUSICIANS GOING BRAZILIAN

Among the international jazz and pop artists who often collaborated with Brazilian artists in the 1970s and 1980s were: Ronnie Foster, Herbie Hancock, Harvey Mason, Ernie Watts, Ron Carter, Clare Fischer, Cannonball Adderley, Paquito D'Rivera, John Patitucci, Lalo Schifrin, and Patti Austin.

Talking Heads leader David Byrne became so enamored with Brazilian music that he released four Brazilian music compilation albums beginning in 1989, shot a documentary on candomblé (*Ilê Aiyê*), recorded two sambas on his Latin-inspired *Rei Momo* CD, and toured with Margareth Menezes.

Paul Simon released *The Rhythm of the Saints* in 1990, which mixed Brazilian, West African, and American musical elements and instruments. Among the Brazilians on it were Milton Nascimento, accordionist João Severo da Silva, the groups Olodum and Uakti, and the percussionists Naná Vasconcelos, Gordinho, Wilson das Neves, and Sidinho.

Don's 1989 solo album *Raven* featured Brazilians such as Ricardo Silveira and Djavan, and included the choro-inspired "Catwalk" and other Brazilian-flavored tunes.

Paul Winter

Paul Winter, who began his long association with Brazilian music in the bossa era, continued recording Brazilian songs and working with Brazilian musicians through the 1980s. On the *Paul Winter Consort* album (1968) he covered Jobim and Villa-Lobos; on *Common Ground* (1978) he recorded imaginative renditions of Dorival Caymmi's "Iemanjá" ("The Promise of a Fisherman") and Ivan Lins' "Velho Sermão" ("Common Ground"). That album and many others by Winter were co-produced by Oscar Castro-Neves, whose acoustic guitar work was an integral part of the Consort sound. Castro-Neves also co-wrote songs for Winter's *Earthbeat* and *Missa Gaia*. On the album *Earth: Voices of a Planet* in 1990, Winter was joined by vocalist-percussionist Gaudencio Thiago de Mello and percussionist Guillherme Franco.

Paul Winter.

KEYBOARDS

One of the most influential Brazilian musicians in North America in the 1970s was Eumir Deodato, a pianist-arranger born in Rio in 1943. Eumir scored a hit with his funky-jazzy rendition of Richard Strauss's "Also Sprach Zarathustra" in 1973 (which at the time the public was humming because of Stanley Kubrick's film *2001: A Space Odyssey*). Deodato's hip version went to number two on Billboard's pop singles chart and the album it was from, *Prelude* (1972), hit number three.

Deodato was also an accomplished arranger. As mentioned earlier, he played an important part in launching Milton Nascimento's career in Brazil by arranging Milton's songs for his debut at the International Song Festival in Rio. In the United States, Eumir helped shape the pop sound of the 1970s and 1980s through his work as a producer and/or arranger for Kool and the Gang, Earth, Wind and Fire, Roberta Flack, Bette Midler, Stanley Turrentine, Aretha Franklin, and others.

Singer-songwriter-pianist Tânia Maria was a familiar figure on international jazz radio in the 1980s, achieving great success with a spicy

Tânia Maria in a 1988 photograph.

Jazz ensemble Cama de Gato performing at Jazzmania in Rio (l. to r.): Rique Pantoja, Arthur Maia, Mauro Senise, and Pascoal Meirelles.

Eliane Elias.

Husband-and-wife team Randy Brecker and Eliane Elias as pictured on their 1986 album *Amanda*.

combination of Brazilian and Cuban rhythms, funk and rock influences, a percussive piano attack, and vigorous vocalese. Tânia started her career in France by launching several albums there in the 1970s, then moved to the U.S. and released her first album there in 1981, *Piquant*, produced by Latin-jazz legend Cal Tjader. Later came a string of hit LPs in the 1980s, notably *Come with Me* and *Love Explosion*, that established her as a compelling new voice.

Keyboardist Rique Pantoja made his mark in the late 1980s. Born in Rio in 1955, Pantoja studied at the Berklee School of Music in Boston, then relocated to Europe, where he played with a French-Brazilian jazz group called Novos Tempos (New Times). For a few years, that band toured Europe with cool-jazz trumpeter Chet Baker. Off and on, between 1984 and 1987, Chet and Rique recorded tracks for what would be the album *Rique Pantoja and Chet Baker* (Pantoja penned all the compositions). In the latter half of the eighties, Pantoja was also a member of the "Brazilian fusion" instrumental quartet Cama de Gato, and in 1986 he recorded his first solo work *Rique Pantoja*.

Pianist-composer Eliane Elias was another acclaimed young Brazilian keyboardist of the 1980s but more steeped in traditional jazz than most of her Brazilian musical peers. Based in New York City, she has had many hit jazz albums, and her impressive piano technique, harmonic inventiveness, and compositional skill have won her kudos from jazz critics.

Born in 1960 in São Paulo, Eliane was a child prodigy who at the age of twelve could play jazz standards by Bud Powell, Art Tatum, and Bill Evans. At age seventeen, she started playing behind Vinícius de Moraes and Toquinho, and stayed with their group for three years. In 1981, in Paris, she met bassist Eddie Gomez, then a member of the fusion group Steps Ahead. She subsequently moved to New York and began a year-long stint with Gomez's band. She married American trumpet-player Randy Brecker, with whom she recorded *Amanda* (named for their daughter) in 1985.

On her first solo album, *Illusions* (1987), Elias delved into bop, ballads, and choro, backed by Eddie Gomez, Al Foster, Stanley Clarke, Lenny White, and Toots Thielmans. *Cross Currents* (1988) was also heavily jazz-oriented, while *So Far, So Close* (1989) included more samba, choro, and bossa.

MORE KEYBOARDISTS

Other important Brazilian contemporary piano and synthesizer players include: Antonio Adolfo, Nelson Ayres, Cido Bianchi, João Carlos Assis Brasil, João Donato, Luis Eça, Manfredo Fest, Amílson Godoy, Amilton Godoy, César Camargo Mariano, Gilson Peranzzetta, Dom Salvador, and Wagner Tiso.

Players from a younger generation include Marcos Ariel, Luiz Avellar, Marinho Boffa, Ricardo Bomba, Lígia Campos, Nando Carneiro, Hugo Fattoruso, Ricardo Leão, Túlio Mourão, Lincoln Olivetti, Marcos Silva, and Guilherme Vergeiro.

On the accordion keys, Brazil has many hot players as well. Some of the best are Dominguinhos, Severo, Baú dos Oito Baixos, Renato Borghetti (a gaúcho who mixes music from southern Brazil with samba and forró in fiery blends), and Chiquinho do Acordeon.

Baú dos Oito Baixos and his accordion.

Renato Borghetti.

WIND INSTRUMENTS

Cláudio Roditi is a trumpeter who has been part of the United States jazz scene since the early 1970s, appearing on albums by Charlie Rouse, Slide Hampton, Herbie Mann, and Paquito D'Rivera. His solo albums *Gemini Man* and *Slow Fire* display his unique bebop-Brazilian blends. Raul de Souza is a trombonist who was a strong presence in the jazz world in the 1970s, recording with the Crusaders and Sonny Rollins, among others.

Trumpeter Márcio Montarroyos has been a valued session man, and his solo albums such as *Samba Solstice* have found an international audience. Saxophonist Leo Gandelman's Brazilian fusion albums found great commercial success in the late 1980s in Brazil, and some have been released internationally.

Also notable are harmonica-player Maurício Einhorn; saxophonist-flutists Nivaldo Ornellas, Roberto Sion, Mauro Senise, and Raul Mascarenhas; flutist Danilo Caymmi; trumpeter Guilherme Dias Gomes; and flutist-guitarist Edson Alves.

Cláudio Roditi.

GUITAR

If there is a musical instrument that most typifies Brazil, it is probably the guitar. Brazil has produced many greats on that instrument, from Laurindo Almeida and Bola Sete to Baden Powell, Luiz Bonfá, João Gilberto, Toquinho, and Oscar Castro-Neves.

Heraldo do Monte is a veteran whose playing spans several decades, but who only began his solo recording career in the 1980s. Born in Recife in 1935, Heraldo was a member of Quarteto Novo with Airto Moreira and Hermeto Pascoal. He is a master of the guitar and of many other stringed instruments as well, including the mandolin and cavaquinho. Mixing both regional styles (baião, xaxado) with choro and Tal Farlow influences, Heraldo cut the albums *Cordas Vivas* (Live Strings) and *Cordas Mágicas* (Magic Strings) in the 1980s, both of which show off his dazzling electric and acoustic guitar work.

Andre Geraissati, Ulisses Rocha, and Marco Pereira have recorded together in the acoustic guitar trio D'Alma and have also released outstanding solo efforts. Pereira's *Círculo das Cordas* (Circle of Strings) in 1988 was a

Heraldo do Monte.

remarkable meeting of classical guitar, jazz improvisation, and standards by Villa-Lobos, Egberto Gismonti, and Chick Corea.

Ricardo Silveira.

Ricardo Silveira has added his impressive jazz-fusion guitar licks to albums and shows by Milton Nascimento, Herbie Mann, Sonny Fortune, Don Grusin, and Jon Hassell, and cut instrumental solo LPs that were released internationally in the late eighties.

Some of the other talented Brazilian guitarists of recent years are Olmir "Alemão" Stocker, also an excellent composer and arranger, as shown on his 1987 album *Alemão Bem Brasileiro*; Hélio Delmiro; Toninho Horta (see Chapter 5); Dori Caymmi (see Chapter 4); Heitor T.P., who joined the Simply Red band in the late 1980s; Victor Biglione; Almir Sater; Rafael Rabello; José Neto; Fredera; Pepeu Gomes; Carlos Barbosa-Lima; Sérgio Assad; Odair Assad; Turíbio Santos; Paulinho Soledade; Natan Marques; Paulo Bellinati; and Tavinho Bonfá.

Some of Brazil's best bassists include Artur Maia (a member of Cama de Gato who made his solo debut in 1990 with *Maia*), Luis Alves, Nico Assumpção, Jorge Degas, Arismar do Espírito Santo, and Jamil Joanes.

COMBOS

The trio Azymuth was a popular international act in the 1980s that blended jazz, samba, and funk. The members of the band are José Roberto Bertrami on keyboards, Ivan Conti on drums, and Alex Malheiros on bass (all three were born in 1946). In 1979, they had their first United States release, *Light As a Feather*, and in the 1980s they recorded ten more albums in the United States. *Telecommunication* (1982) was a top-ten U.S. jazz album and "Jazz Carnival" (from *Light As a Feather*) was a gold single in England. And, separately, they each recorded notable solo albums.

Other groups from the 1980s included Nó Em Pingo D'Água (Knot in a Drop of Water), Aquarela Carioca (Carioca Watercolor), Cama de Gato (Cat's Cradle), Zil, Orquestra de Cordas Dedilhadas de Pernambuco (Plucked String Orchestra of Pernambuco), Pau Brasil (Brazilwood), Orquestra de Música Brasileira, ZonAzul (BlueZone), and Homem de Bem (Man of Good).

Uakti

Arguably the most innovative Brazilian instrumental group of the seventies and eighties was Uakti, named after a mythological figure of the Toucan tribe in the Amazon rain forest. His story was recounted in the liner notes of the band's eponymous United States debut album. Uakti's body was perforated with holes and when the wind blew through them an irresistible sound was produced that attracted all the Toucan women. Jealous, the men killed Uakti, burying his body in the ground in a place where tall palms later grew. From the wood of the palms, the Indians fashioned instruments that could produce melodious

Progressive-jazz ensemble Azymuth (l. to r.): Ivan Conti, José Roberto Bertrami, and Alex Malheiros.

and seductive tones like those once made by the wind passing through Uakti's body. It was absolutely forbidden to play these flutes outside of secret male ceremonies.

The group Uakti, which also makes its own instruments, was formed in the mid-seventies by Marco Antonio Guimarães, who had studied at the University of Bahia with composer Walter Smetak (born in 1913 in Switzerland), a sort of Swiss-Brazilian Harry Partch who created new musical systems and instruments. One of Smetak's creations was A Grande Virgem (The Big Virgin), a giant flute played by twenty-two persons.

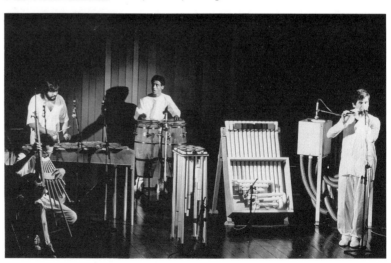

The members of Uakti in performance.

When Guimarães returned home to Belo Horizonte, Minas Gerais, he gathered together a group of like-minded, adventurous musicians, each of whom had classical training: Paulo Sérgio dos Santos, Artur Andres Ribeiro, and Décio de Souza Ramos. The foursome designed an orchestra of wholly original string, wind, and percussion instruments. Among them are the *planetário* (planetarium), a wooden box strung with latex bands, the *marimba de vidro*, a two-octave glass marimba, and the *trilobita* (trilobite), a cluster of tuned PVC tubes topped with drum skins. The sounds that come from them are as mesmerizing as what might have come from their mythological namesake. Commented the Manhattan Transfer's Tim Hauser, who worked with the quartet in 1987 on the Transfer's *Brasil* album, "The sounds are very spiritual. It makes you feel like you're in a band two thousand years ago."

Uakti also made appearances on several Milton Nascimento albums (most notably on *Anima*) and on Paul Simon's *The Rhythm of the Saints*, but it is their solo work, on 1984's *Tudo e Todas As Coisas* (All and Everything) for example, that is most remarkable. They mix together maracatu, samba, jazz, minimalism, and elements of medieval, Hindu, and Andean music; all this is then played upon their strange-looking and beautiful-sounding instruments. Uakti's songs sound like chamber music from some lost Asian civilization.

ON THE INTERNATIONAL STAGE

Uakti was part of a strong Brazilian instrumental music scene in the 1980s. Such music had received a big boost with the debut of annual international jazz festivals in São Paulo and Rio, including the Free Jazz Festival (launched in 1985). And, just as importantly, there was also a boom in the release of instrumental music by small independent labels. This was partly due to veteran keyboardist Antonio Adolfo.

In 1977, frustrated with the indifference of the major record companies, Adolfo financed and released his own LP, *Feito em Casa* (Homemade), and its success proved there was a small but eager market for instrumental recordings. Many other artists subsequently launched their own albums. And in the 1980s, the independent Brazilian record labels Som da Gente, Kuarup, Visom, Chorus, and Eldorado were launched and provided an aficionado's forum for artful instrumental blends of choro, jazz, samba, bossa, and more.

As the nineties began, considering the international music community's infatuation with Brazilian musicians, songs, and rhythms, it was indeed a question of "Who has not been influenced by Brazil?," as Sérgio Mendes put it. The links between the music of Brazil and other countries have become so numerous that in the decades to come it will probably become increasingly difficult to separate them. As Herbie Mann said, "It gets to the point where you have Djavan recording in Los Angeles, and Manhattan Transfer in Brazil, and they are all using people who have been listening to Herbie Hancock and Ivan Lins. That is, it all gets so crossed that each in turn re-influences the other."

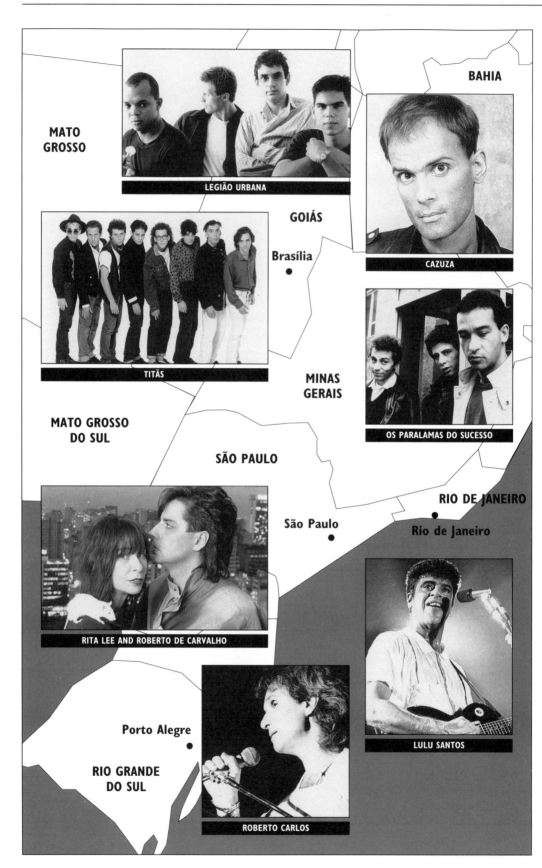

MATO GROSSO

BAHIA

LEGIÃO URBANA

GOIÁS

Brasília

CAZUZA

TITÃS

MINAS GERAIS

OS PARALAMAS DO SUCESSO

MATO GROSSO DO SUL

SÃO PAULO

RIO DE JANEIRO

São Paulo

Rio de Janeiro

RITA LEE AND ROBERTO DE CARVALHO

LULU SANTOS

Porto Alegre

RIO GRANDE DO SUL

ROBERTO CARLOS

TROPICAL ROCK

O ver the last four decades rock has undergone as complex an evolution in Brazil as it has in the United States, its country of origin. Two song lyric quotations illustrate the range, in attitude at least, of Brazilian rock and roll since the fifties. In 1958, Celly Campello recorded Fred Jorge's giddy "Banho da Lua" (Moonlight Bath): "I take moonlight showers/ And turn snow-white/ Moonlight is my friend." By the late 1980s, Cazuza and Arnaldo Brandão were snarling in "O Tempo não Pára" (Time Doesn't Stop): "Your swimming pool's packed with rats/ Your ideas do not correspond to facts/ Time doesn't stop."

Paula Toller, lead singer of Kid Abelha. The band was part of the commercial Brazilian rock boom in the mid-eighties.

In the sixties, seventies, and eighties a great deal happened in Brazilian rock. Brazilian musicians produced their own versions of bubble-gum rock, Beatles-styled pop rock, hard rock, punk rock, folk rock, and heavy metal— most of which went unnoticed by the outside world. They also fused rock with Brazilian genres and came up with new musical hybrids.

As a whole, Brazilian rock came of age in the eighties. One reason for this, perhaps, was that this new generation of *roqueiros* (rockers) had grown up listening to rock— American, English, and Brazilian—their entire lives. "It was like our generation was eating the whole rock history," commented singer Paulo Ricardo, ex-leader of RPM, the first rock act to sell more than two million units of a single album in Brazil. "We had all that information in our minds and we couldn't wait to put it all together. We felt we were equal in some sense with rock in the rest of the world."

By the 1980s Brazilian roqueiros possessed quality electric guitars and keyboards, high-tech recording equipment, and demonstrated greater professionalism in staging shows. Starting around 1982, the rockers began to benefit from increased music company support. Once they had this infrastructure, added Ricardo, "It took us just two or three years to go from Elvis to the Talking Heads."

Brazilian rock acts were recording songs of remarkable creativity and quality in the eighties. The most musically accomplished of them—the Paralamas, Lulu Santos, and Lobão—like their English and American counterparts, are highly innovative. And the top Brazilian rock wordsmiths—Cazuza, Titãs, the Engenheiros do Hawaii, and Legião Urbana—carried on the MPB tradition of great lyric writing, albeit with an angrier, more outspoken edge. This new generation would prove to be enormously successful in Brazil in the late eighties.

Milton Nascimento and members of the rock group RPM (Paulo Ricardo is on Milton's left).

Two other factors may have also contributed to producing so many great rock artists in that decade: the lifting of censorship imposed by the government and the arrival of the socio-economic crisis that slammed Brazil in the 1980s. During the military dictatorship's heaviest repression, roughly between 1968 and 1978, lyrics had to be free of political content or heavily coded, and the great MPB artists crafted elegant and metaphoric verses to voice their discontent. But in the eighties songwriters (whether in MPB or rock) were by and large free to question the government and criticize Brazil. Many rock groups used raw, direct, and openly aggressive language to express their generation's dismay with the country's horrific problems.

And those problems were very serious indeed, as Brazil plunged into the most intense economic and moral crisis of its history. Hyper-inflation struck (topping 1,700 percent in 1989), widespread corruption hit all levels of government and society, and quality of life plummeted for both the poor and the middle class. Crime skyrocketed, as did the numbers of abandoned children, homeless people, and starving poor.

Brazilians in the 1980s were cynical and bitter. People had the feeling that "they" (the government) had been making fools of everyone for quite a long time and no one had noticed. They were impatient for a return to democracy; they were sick and tired of governmental corruption and repression. This feeling was strongest among the youth, and the form of art that best reflected it, for the middle class, was rock. In their song "Estado Violência" the Titãs growled: "Violent state, hypocritical state/ The law that isn't mine, the law I didn't want/... Man in silence, man in prison/ Man in darkness, future of the nation."

Yet, diversity was also a hallmark of Brazilian rock in the 1980s. It wasn't completely angry. After all, Brazilians have a remarkable capacity to make do with new circumstances, as well as to seize the moment and leave their sorrows behind—at least for a night of partying or an afternoon of soccer. And because Brazil has absorbed so many influences— national and international—there is not one uniform Brazilian rock style.

1957-1981: FROM COPACABANA TO THE UNDERGROUND

Brazilian rock dates back to 1957, when Cauby Peixoto recorded the first domestically composed rock tune, "Rock 'n' Roll em Copacabana." After that singers like Celly Campello, Tony Campello, Demetrius, Sérgio Murilo, and Ronnie Cord recorded a string of Portuguese-language covers of American and European rock tunes. In 1965 the Jovem Guarda (Young Guard) movement arrived, led by Roberto Carlos and Erasmo Carlos. Roberto, a singer and composer, had established a rock career two years earlier with "Calhambeque" (Old Heap) and a cover of "Splish Splash." By that time, bossa nova had largely turned to social and political themes, singing about the poverty and suffering of rural and urban Brazilians. But a great portion of urban youth did not care about droughts in the Northeast or peasants without land. They worried about more simple things: cars, romance, clothes, school. Jovem Guarda's rock 'n' roll reflected these concerns.

Roberto and Erasmo

Born in 1943, Roberto Carlos had started out singing bossa nova, but then met Erasmo Carlos (real name Erasmo Esteves, born in 1941), a true Carioca rocker, and a long and fertile songwriting partnership was born. Roberto's romanticism and Erasmo's naive aggressiveness blended perfectly, shaping the format of Jovem Guarda music: upbeat, simple rock and roll. They recorded separately and together, but most of their many successes came through Roberto singing their cowritten tunes.

Cauby Peixoto in 1969. The crooner is not a *roqueiro* but has nevertheless earned a place in Brazilian rock history.

Fame resulted from the "Jovem Guarda" show on the TV Record network, a massive success that lasted from 1965 to 1968. Recorded live in São Paulo, the show was watched all over the country by means of a recent technological innovation: videotape. And on videotape the nation saw girls crying hysterically, boys dancing madly, and on stage, under Roberto and Erasmo's command, young singers like Wanderléia, Eduardo Araújo, Rosemary, Ronnie Von, and Jerry Adriani. Roberto and Erasmo scored hits with songs like "Parei na Contramão" (I Parked the Wrong Way), "É Proibido Fumar" (No Smoking), "Garota do Baile" (Dance Girl),

Roberto Carlos in the eighties.

and the most important one—Jovem Guarda's anthem—"Quero que Tudo Mais Vá Pára o Inferno" (I Want All the Rest to Go to Hell). It was a reply to the more nationalistic critics and musicians who didn't accept any pop mixture that defiled the "purity" of Brazilian music.

Erasmo Carlos, Wanderléia, and Roberto Carlos at the microphone in 1968.

Roberto Carlos in concert. He switched from rock to boleros and ballads in the seventies.

By 1969 the music business phenomenon of the Jovem Guarda TV show was over, and each artist went off on his or her own path. In the 1970s, Roberto made a transition from rocker to romantic singer and has since typically recorded boleros and ballads on his albums. He achieved artistic respectability with sentimental songs like "Detalhes" (Details), "Proposta" (Proposal), "Eu Disse Adeus" (I Said Goodbye), all written with old partner and friend Erasmo.

Roberto was the best-selling recording artist in Brazil in the seventies and eighties. In Brazil alone he sold an annual average of a million units (quadruple-platinum) with *each* new album. Roberto also achieved success in Europe and Latin America; his foreign releases often hit the top ten in many countries. His main international competition as a crooner has come from Spanish ballad-singer Júlio Iglesias, the most popular global star of his time. But in Brazil, Roberto was number one.

The Jovem Guarda movement translated and adapted rock to Brazil, to its language and culture. While its roots were in American rock, Jovem Guarda was undoubtedly Brazilian— Brazilian singers, composers, arrangers, and instrumentalists.

The Mutants and Tropicália

The next big step for Brazilian rock came with the Tropicália movement, in which anything went, artistically speaking, and which mixed rock freely with native genres. The rock side of the movement was represented by a group called Os Mutantes (The Mutants). Sérgio Dias Baptista (guitar and vocals), his brother Arnaldo Dias Baptista (bass, keyboards, and vocals) and Rita Lee (flute and vocals) formed the basic lineup of the first artistically important rock band in Brazil. On their debut album, *Os Mutantes*, they fused rock and roll with sertaneja music, baião, mambo, and irreverent, sometimes surrealistic lyrics. "A mixture of Bosch and Salvador Dali," is how Arnaldo described it.

Good humor was always part of the group's personality; their philosophy was "yes" to non-conformism, "no" to anger. This spirit was maintained in their next several albums, as evidenced by the titles: *A Divina Comédia ou Ando Meio Desligado* (The Divine Comedy or I'm Kind of Spaced-Out, 1970), *Jardim Elétrico* (Electric Garden, 1971), and *Mutantes e Seus Cometas no País dos Bauretz* (The Mutants and Their Comets in Bauretz Country, 1972).

Their song "Caminhante Noturno" (Night Walker) illustrates the band's Tropicalista tendency to create musical salads: it opens with a fanfare leading into a waltz. Then a strong bass enters, introducing a rock pulse. The melody takes surprising twists and turns, the vocals sometimes sound natural and at other times are quite artificially pitched, and the waltz rhythm comes and goes. A Mexican-flavored interlude is introduced by a Herb Alpert Tijuana Brass-like arrangement. The song keeps throwing out surprises until it ends in a burst of sonorous paraphernalia that includes a soccer-stadium crowd chant and the voice of the robot in the "Lost in Space" TV series repeating (in Portuguese): "Danger, danger, red alert . . . ."

Os Mutantes performing in 1968 (l. to r.): Sérgio Dias Baptista, Rita Lee, and Arnaldo Dias Baptista.

Rita Lee left the band in 1973 to embark on a solo career, and Arnaldo departed the next year. But Sérgio Dias, one of the best Brazilian guitarists of his time, stayed, added new players, and kept the band going. This new incarnation of Os Mutantes, with a bassist named Liminha, made two more albums, then disbanded. Liminha would go on to become one of Brazil's top rock producers and to produce foreign acts such as Sigue Sigue Sputnik in the late eighties.

Meanwhile, Dias embarked on an international career as a studio musician. He also toured and recorded with the violinist L. Shankar and was a member of the jazz-rock band Unit. In 1990, he teamed with Roxy Music veteran Phil Manzanera on *Mato Grosso*, in which the duo combined their guitar, keyboard, and production skills to create a rock-driven, new-age, Brazilian-flavored album of exotic soundscapes.

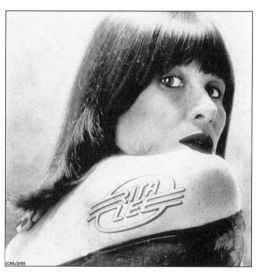

Rita Lee on her eponymous album released in 1979 by Som Livre.

Rita Lee (full name Rita Lee Jones) was born in São Paulo in 1942, the daughter of an Italian mother and a father from Alabama. In the seventies and eighties, Rita Lee was the only one of the original Mutantes to develop a commercially successful musical career. Labeled by the press as Brazilian rock's first lady, Rita continued packing her lyrics with irony and irreverence. Little by little, she moved in the direction of an upbeat, sassy, light pop-rock sound flavored with various Brazilian rhythms and touches. *Babilônia* (Babylon) in 1978

Phil Manzanera and Sérgio Dias in a photo taken in conjunction with their 1990 collaboration on *Mato Grosso*.

brought her commercial success, and her following albums went consistently gold and platinum, containing the big hits "Chega Mais" (Get Closer), "Lança Perfume" (named for a type of ether-laden perfume frequently sniffed during Carnaval), "Saúde" (Health), "Baila Comigo" (Dance with Me), and the typically playful "Mania De Você" (Mania for You), in which she sang,

> Baby, you make my mouth water
> Making up fantasies, taking your
>   clothes off
> We make love through telepathy
> On the ground, in the sea, in the
>   street, in the melody.

By that time, Rita had begun to write songs with guitarist, manager, and new husband Roberto de Carvalho. Rita and Roberto combined the sensuous and the sarcastic, and mixed catchy melodies with Brazilian rhythms, boleros, and rock beats, keeping her records at the top of the charts into the early eighties.

Europe and Japan embraced them as well. "They think we're exotic, a rock Carnaval," commented Rita. But there was often a serious undertone to their playfulness (especially in the late eighties), as shown in the 1987 tune "Brazix Muamba" ("Brazix" is a madeup word; "muamba" means contraband). In the song, they bemoan Brazil's many problems, including Angra I and II, the nuclear power plant reactors built outside of Rio:

> Long live Brazix
> Dying of pain
> AIDS for those who make love
> Angra I, Angra II, III, and afterwards
> The exterminating angel.

Rita Lee in the eighties.

Rita Lee and husband Roberto de Carvalho in 1985.

The Underground

In the 1960s, rock musicians were not considered real Brazilian musicians, and they didn't care. But then Tropicália came and absorbed the rock attitude (iconoclastic and free) and some of its musical characteristics into "authentic" Brazilian music. All of a sudden rock had lost its niche in the music scene.

At the time, rock musicians had strong musical convictions: like samba musicians, they desired to keep their musical "purity," and so they hid. Their hideout was the underground, where it was good to be anyway during the 1970s because of government repression and brutal censorship. Recording companies and radio stations didn't like to take risks with a musical genre that didn't fit the taste of the rulers.

With all doors closed, rock became music for aficionados; groups played for small audiences at small theaters. Many never secured recording contracts. Most of these groups—O Terço (led by Flávio Venturini), O Som Nosso de Cada Dia, Vímana, and A Barca do Sol for example—fell into the broad genre of "progressive rock."

In terms of public recognition, only two rock acts were really successful in the seventies. One was the short-lived (1972-1974) but very popular Secos e Molhados (Dry Ones and Wet Ones). Its androgynous lead singer Ney Matogrosso commanded attention with his high-pitched voice and provocative dancing style, and he went on to be one of MPB's most popular vocalists. Matogrosso sang lyrics and poems by the likes of Vinícius de Moraes, Manuel Bandeira, and Oswald de Andrade, surrounded by progressive rock that often used unusual fusions, such as the tune "O Vira," which mixed rockabilly with *vira*, a syncopated, high-spirited Portuguese folk style played on the accordion.

Raul Seixas (1945-89) was the most original Brazilian rocker of the seventies, and he broke many musical boundaries. He was the first, along with Alceu Valença and Gilberto Gil, to mix 1950s American-style rock and Beatles-influenced pop with northeastern styles such as baião, repente, and xote, and probably was alone in being the first to mix rock and roll with candomblé rhythms. Accordingly, his tunes often started in one rhythm and finished in another. His first hit—"Ouro de Tolo" (Fool's Gold)—was recorded in 1973 and today it would be called a rap song. On his seventeen albums (many of them big hits), he strove to provoke and challenge his audience, as in his lyrics for "Metamorfose Ambulante" (Walking Metamorphosis):

> I want to say now
> The opposite of what I said before
> I'd rather be a walking metamorphosis
> Than to have that old fixed opinion
>   about everything.

THE EIGHTIES: THE THIRD WAVE

During Brazilian rock's underground period (1972-81), its place in the hearts and minds of the youth was usurped by MPB musicians like Alceu Valença, Belchior, Fagner, Zé Ramalho,

Ney Matogrosso.

Raul Seixas in 1989.

and others who incorporated rock attitudes and instrumentation into their strongly northeastern-rooted music. Most of these artists, following the usual Brazilian musical anthropophagy, had former rock musicians in their bands.

Considering Jovem Guarda and Os Mutantes as the first generation of Brazilian rock and the underground groups the second, the 1980s saw the birth of the third wave: the strongest and most creative generation of rock musicians Brazil has yet seen. It was a generation that grew up listening not only to Anglo-American rock, but also had access to modern MPB that already had utilized rock and jazz elements.

There were also a few veterans of the seventies who found success in the next decade. Two of the most prominent were Lobão and Lulu Santos, who played together in a 1970s progressive group called Vímana, which featured Patrick Moraz (who had just left the English progressive-rock group Yes) on keyboards. After Vímana broke up, Lobão and Santos both went on to successful solo careers.

Lulu Santos

Lulu Santos developed his own style of "Brazilianized, tropicalized, Latinized rock" as he put it. Born in Rio in 1953, Santos mixes rock with boleros, bossa nova, reggae, and sambas. Whatever the genre, almost all his tunes have strong popular appeal due to his fluid melodies and high energy. Santos said that he wants his music to be "frantic, loud, electric, yet without losing its Brazilian-ity." He also is known for having one of the best live acts in Brazilian show business, due to his dynamic stage presence, his able guitarwork, and the topflight talent in his backup band Auxílio Luxuoso (Luxurious Assistance). "De Repente California" (Suddenly California), "Tesouro da Juventude" (Treasure of Youth), "De Leve" (Lightly) and "Areias Escaldantes" (Burning Sands) are some of Lulu's biggest hits.

"I'm a son of the Beatles, the Stones, a little of Roberto and Erasmo Carlos, a lot of Gil, Caetano, and Tropicália," Santos told us. "I'm a pop-rock artist who's had hits with boleros like 'Como uma Onda' (Like a Wave). I'm avant-garde in a popular, not academic, context. The more international I get, the more my Brazilian urban nature has to be clear."

Lulu Santos in concert.

Blitz

Before ex-Vímana member Lobão (a drummer-singer-guitarist) achieved solo fame, he also participated in a group created by underground-theater actor Evandro Mesquita and guitarist Ricardo Barreto. The band was named Blitz, and it enjoyed massive success and opened the market for a great number of new rock acts.

Most of Blitz's songs were dialogues woven into bouncy reggae, funk, rock, or pop ballads sung by Evandro and two female vocalists, Fernanda Abreu and Márcia Bulcão. Blitz created a theatrical and ludicrous atmosphere both on stage and in their records; their themes were quotidian situations described with heavy Caroica slang and presented in a fast, comic-book style. Blitz's first and biggest hit was the 1982 single "Você Não Soube me Amar" (You Didn't Know How to Love Me), which sold 700,000 copies. Then came "Weekend" and "Betty Frígida" (Frigid Betty). It was hard to listen to them without dancing to their catchy rhythms or at least smiling at the mocking irony of their lyrics.

Evandro Mesquita, former leader of Blitz.

The band's first album *Aventuras da Blitz* (Adventures of Blitz) went platinum, selling 300,000 units. They performed all over the country, including the most important concert hall in Rio: Canecão. Considered an MPB temple, Blitz were the first rock group to be allowed to play there. Their commercial success in 1982 opened record-company doors for other new Brazilian bands, and suddenly rock was mainstream. Soon came gold and platinum albums by Ritchie, Lulu Santos, Barão Vermelho, Marina, and Kid Abelha in 1983 and 1984. Talented new groups like the Paralamas do Successo (The Mudguards of Success) and Ultraje a Rigor (Formal Outrage) were also appearing on the scene. Rock wasn't underground any longer.

The *roquiero* Ritchie, who was born in England, has lived in Brazil since 1973.

But the best was yet to come: a ten-day music festival called "Rock in Rio" would draw 1.38 million fans in 1985. Staged by entrepreneur Roberto Medina and his advertising-promotion agency Artplan, Rock in Rio took place from January 11-20, in the Barra da Tijuca neighborhood on the outskirts of Rio. It was the biggest multi-day rock event to date (a fact that went largely unreported in the North American press that year) and featured international rock and pop acts James Taylor, Rod Stewart, Yes, Al Jarreau, George Benson, Ozzy Osbournè, Iron Maiden, the Go-Gos, Whitesnake, AC/DC, Scorpions, the B-52s, Nina Hagen, and Queen. Playing with them were Brazilian artists Erasmo Carlos, Ney Matogrosso, Ivan Lins, Gilberto Gil, Elba Ramalho, Blitz, Baby Consuelo and Pepeu Gomes, Rita Lee, Lulu Santos, Moraes Moreira, Eduardo Dusek, Kid Abelha, Alceu Valença, Barão Vermelho, and the Paralamas do Sucesso.

It was at Rock in Rio that Brazilian rock lost its inferiority complex for good. Brazilian and foreign bands playing together on the same bill made comparison possible, and some Brazilian bands gave better performances than the foreign acts. In addition, the festival popularized native rockers in their own country via network television and heavy press coverage. Recalls André Midani, managing director of WEA Brazil,

BABY CONSUELO
SEM PECADO e
SEM JUÍZO

Baby Consuelo as pictured on her 1985 CBS release whose title translates as *Without Sin and Without Judgment*.

"Rock in Rio helped break acts in a big way, and life has never been the same since for the music business. I think that this new generation of Brazilian youth needed a new language, something to identify with." WEA, along with EMI Brazil, signed many of these acts in the 1980s. The middle-class and upper-class youth of Brazil began to tune in to their own country's rock, listening more to it than the Anglo-American variety or to MPB's older stars.

Lobão

Blitz cut two more LPs following their auspicious debut album and then broke up in 1986. Band member Lobão (João Luis Woerdenbag, born in 1957) had left after the group's first record and launched solo albums that mixed hard-driving rock and bittersweet ballads. His sound was heavy, percussive, and energetic. He sang in a rough, growling voice, never forgetting he was a drummer: he rhythmically knocked out the words in bursts rather than fully enunciating them. Comments Lobão, "When I sing I think percussion. I'm a musician not a singer. My syllabic division is percussive." His guitarwork was also unique, showing influences of both Led Zeppelin's Jimmy Page and Spanish flamenco.

Lobão's image mirrors his music: intense, restless, *angry* (accordingly, his name means "Big Wolf"). Yet there is compassion there too—a great deal of it—and more than a little creativity. Lobão said, "I love rock, but my music is a big mixture." For instance, his hard rock is permeated by subtle samba-percussion influences. He plays tamborim for Mangueira, one of the most important samba schools in Rio. That's unusual because samba and rock musicians generally don't mix.

Lobão.

Lobão broke the invisible barrier separating samba and rock by recording with samba singers like Elza Soares and Ivo Meirelles. With Meirelles he cowrote the hard-driving funk-rock tune "Cuidado"

(Caution) in 1988, in which the two writers sang a duet and several Mangueira musicians added heavy samba percussion to close the tune. On the 1989 album *Sob o Sol de Parador* (Under the Parador Sun), pandeiros, repiques, congas, and afoxês were included in the percussive mix of the album, which ranged freely through hard rock, punk, rockabilly, and ballads (and included American jazz keyboardist Ronnie Foster on two cuts).

Paulinho da Viola performing with rocker Lobão.

One of Lobão's biggest hit tunes to date is the sad, melancholy "Me Chama" (Call Me), covered by various singers, including Marina and bossa-nova pope João Gilberto. Lobão has also penned songs charged with ironic, political criticism. On *Cuidado*, his fifth album, in the song "O Eleito" (The Elected), he and cowriter Bernardo Vilhena castigated the ineffectual and unpopular Brazilian president José Sarney, who fought against free elections when the populace demanded them in 1984:

> The palace is his most perfect refuge
> For his most secret desires
> There he thinks of himself as the elected
> Without any elections nearby.

Cazuza

Also from Rio, Cazuza (1958-1990) was one of the most incensed and incendiary songwriters/vocalists in Brazil. In the 1980s, his music mixed boleros and bossa with rather conventional blues and rock, but his lyrics were vivid attacks against deception and hypocrisy. In the romantic song "O Nosso Amor a Gente Inventa" (We Invent Our Love), for example, he displayed a bitter and desperate lyricism: "Your love is a lie/ That my vanity wants/ My love is a blind man's poem/ That you can't see."

In the electrifying "Brasil," Cazuza summed up the injustice of his country by singing, "They didn't invite me to this lousy party/ That the men put on to convince me/ To pay, before seeing, for this entire droga [drug or bummer]/ That was already cut before I was born. ("Cut" in this excerpt means to weaken a drug by adulteration.) "Brasil" is one of Cazuza's most corrosive songs, and its lyrics evoke the situation of most everyone in Brazil except the privileged upper class. The narrator of the song (the average Brazilian) has to stay outside the walls of the party (the good life from which he is excluded)—which he is taught to crave, to yearn for, to support, but will never have. Cazuza asks who was paid off, who put Brazil in its terrible present state: "Will it be that my fate is to watch color TV in the village of an Indian programmed only to say yes?" he wondered. With its combination of samba batucada and hard-rock guitar and drums, "Brasil," like Lobão's "Cuidado," was considered by some critics to be part of a new genre: heavy-samba.

Cazuza.

Cazuza, openly bisexual, discovered he had AIDS in 1987. Between treatments over the next two years, he continued performing in concert, even as his health deteriorated. Many undoubtedly came to his concerts out of curiosity, wanting to see him before he died, but many more came to appreciate his work and for the brutal honesty of his lyrics.

By 1989 he was too weak to stand in front of a microphone and sing. He had to accept the Sharp Award for best pop/rock album (*Ideologia*) and song ("Brasil") from a wheelchair. But he continued to create and to collaborate with other musicians, his natural irony and sarcasm becoming even more bitter and biting. That same year, Cazuza achieved the greatest commercial success of his career: his two last works, the live album *O Tempo Não Pára* and his final studio recording, the double album *Burguesia* (Bourgeoisie), both achieved critical acclaim and multi-platinum sales. He died the next year.

Os Paralamas do Sucesso

Perhaps the most musically inventive Brazilian rock group of the eighties was Os Paralamas do Sucesso (The Mudguards of Success), which managed to build solid musical bridges connecting Brazil, North America, Africa, and the Caribbean. They ventured far into the rock/pop/world-beat realm also explored by the U.K. and U.S. artists Peter Gabriel, Talking Heads, and Paul Simon.

The Paralamas' music is upbeat party music with an edge, a seamless weaving together of rock energy, reggae soul, and world-beat fusion. It is wrapped in a tight pop format, delivered with infectious energy, a driving rhythmic sense, and a pinch of irony. Their music, said leader Herbert Vianna, is "a collage that has created a style. Caribbean music, ska, reggae, samba. Lots of swing, very Latin, very Brazilian."

The Paralamas, based on a simple trio format, were formed in Rio de Janeiro in 1982. João Barone (drums) and Bi Ribeiro (bass) were Cariocas; Herbert Vianna (guitar) was from Paraíba. Early influences included the Specials, Madness, the English Beat, and the Clash. Their first two albums, *Cinema Mudo* in 1983 and *Passo do Lui* (Lui's Step) in 1984, featured Herbert's raw, bittersweet vocals riding atop fast, compelling rock and ska riffs and rhythms. The latter LP, coupled with exposure from the Rock in Rio festival, helped the Paralamas achieve commercial success. Herbert recalled, "With Rock in Rio we went to the top of the charts. We were known in Rio, but not in the rest of Brazil. We had seven hits out of ten songs [on *Passo do Lui*]."

Selvagem? (Wild?), released in 1986, was a creative leap forward for the trio, as they succeeded in infusing their rock and ska with a distinctively Brazilian accent, be it through suave arrangements or percussive touches. Veteran *roqueiro* Liminha produced and played keyboards on several songs. A notable tune was "Alagados," a Caribbean-Brazilian fusion that mixed elements of reggae, samba, and northeastern xaxado. It was a hint of things to come, both in its deft and natural mixing of genres and in Vianna's hard-hitting lyrics about the Alagados and Favela da Maré slums (in Salvador and Rio, respectively): "Alagados, Trench Town, Favela da Maré/ Hope comes neither from the sea nor from the TV antennas/ Art is to live out of faith/ One just doesn't know what to have faith in." The LP sold 700,000 units in Brazil alone and they followed it up the next year with a live album recorded at the Montreux Jazz Festival.

Their 1988 effort *Bora Bora* was even more accomplished, a bold expansion of their fusions. "We used a horn section for the first time, and with that we could make clear our intention and play the kind of music we wanted to play. It allowed us to use other rhythms, many from Brazil, such as lambada, afoxé, and coco," explained Vianna. With the added instrumentation, the Paralamas' new Caribbean-Brazilian blends grew heady indeed. "Um a Um" (One to One) was an infectious cover of a classic Jackson do Pandeiro tune (written by Edgar Ferreira), in which Vianna carried the coco rhythm in his voice while he played reggae chords on his guitar. "Sanfona" (Accordion), according to Herbert, was "a fusion of lambada with baião." Other highlights included the reggae-dub "Don't Give Me That," in which Jamaican Peter Metro added vocals, and the delirious Caribbean-Brazilian instrumental "Bundalelê," which incorporated the Haitian *compas* rhythm. *Bora Bora* was a rhythmic tour-de-force, a masterful fusion of Afro-based styles and rethinking of Brazilian folk genres. With it, the Paralamas drew added international attention; that album became their first United States release. Furthermore, Talking Heads leader David Byrne invited Vianna to join him for a samba duet on the song "Office Cowboy," from Byrne's solo album *Rei Momo*.

Paralamas do Sucesso in a 1989 photograph (l. to r.): Bi Ribeiro, João Barone, and Herbert Vianna.

ROCK FROM BRASÍLIA AND SÃO PAULO

Brasília—the capital of Brazil—is only three years younger than Brazilian rock, but it is already a metropolis. Inaugurated in 1960, Brasília was an instant capital, designed by

David Byrne and Herbert Vianna.

architect Oscar Niemeyer and built out in the middle of a high deserted plateau in Goiás state. Today, it is a cosmopolitan city of almost one million inhabitants which is culturally isolated from the rest of the country. Teenagers there, more than in other parts of the country, have tended to move towards the international youth language of the late twentieth century: rock. So in 1978, while the rest of the country was dancing to disco music, Brasília already had its punks.

Brasília

The best known punk bands in the capital were Aborto Elétrico (Electric Abortion) and Dado e o Reino Animal (Dado and the Animal Kingdom). Members from these two bands—Renato Russo (guitar and vocals), Dado Villa-Lobos (guitar), Renato Rocha (bass), and Marcelo Bonfá (drums)— formed Legião Urbana (Urban Legion). They came to Rio in 1983 and conquered the public with the poetic quality of their lyrics driven by their enraged energy, a reminder of their punk origins.

Legião Urbana.

Legião Urbana's songs had a hard strong beat, guitar chords reminiscent of U2, and vocals influenced by the Cure. In concert they wore jeans and T-shirts, and disheveled, unshaven lead-singer Renato Russo would whirl around on stage in a strange tribal dance, as if being stung by a thousand bees. Inspired by Legião Urbana's anti-fashion style and protest anthems, crowds went into frenzies.

Legião Urbana was the first cultural manifestation from Brasília to achieve significant national recognition. Singing about unemployment, the army, urban violence, and social disillusion, Legião summed up the life of Brazilian youth with honesty and passion. In "Geração Coca-Cola" (Coca-Cola Generation), Renato Russo sang, "Ever since we were kids/ We've been eating commercial and industrial trash/ Now it's our time/ We'll spit it all back on you."

By 1989 Legião Urbana had released three LPs. The second one, called simply "*Dois*" (Two), was a commercial success, selling 700,000 copies. Legião's third album was an anthology of their first ten years and one of its tracks became their biggest radio hit—the nine-minute song "Faroeste Caboclo"—an epic of a northeastern immigrant in Brasília who is oppressed by society.

São Paulo

São Paulo is the most important Brazilian city in terms of rock. It is a huge metropolis (fifteen million people in greater São Paulo as of the late 1980s) with immigrants from all over Brazil and the world: *sertanejos* from the Northeast, Italians, Lebanese, Portuguese, Japanese (the city's Liberdade neighborhood is the largest Japanese community outside of

Japan). There isn't a typical Paulistano, but if there is something typical about São Paulo it is work. Work and money. In terms of Paulistano rock, hundreds of bands struggle there for a place in the sun. And unlike the cities of Rio, Brasília, and Porto Alegre where bands generally have something in common, São Paulo has no dominant style. Punk, experimental, progressive, rockabilly, techno-pop, and even Japanese-influenced bands are found there.

In this setting of fierce competition few bands make it nationally. One that did, producing in 1986 the biggest-selling Brazilian rock album of all time, was RPM. A techno-pop band centered around vocalist-composer-bassist Paulo Ricardo and keyboardist-arranger Luiz Schiavon, RPM sold more than two million units of their album *Rádio Pirata Live* (Live Pirate Radio). They went Brazilian in 1988 on their last album, "Os Quatro Coiotes" (the Four Coyotes), which included special guests like Milton Nascimento and sambista Bezerra da Silva, and then broke up the next year. Ricardo now records solo, and Schiavon with his band Projeto S.

Titãs

Titãs is a Paulistano band that has multiple personalities. Titãs comprises eight individuals who all write songs and five of whom are lead singers. Their pluralistic music goes from *brega* romantic ballads to two-chord punk to reggae to funk to rap. Lyrics are evocative and often aggressively critical. During their dynamic shows, the members alternate being up front on the stage. The band has no leader. "We are not a band with only one aesthetical choice. We are not reggae, nor funk, nor heavy metal. We are nothing. We kind of confiscate everything in a free and sincere way," said Nando Reis (vocals and bass).

Titãs.

According to drummer Charles Gavin, "We inspire feelings that range from pure romanticism to repugnance." An example of the former is "Sonífera Ilha" (Somniferous Island), a romantic-existential lament: "I can't stay at your side anymore/ So I stick my ear to the radio/ To get in tune with you/ Alone on an island." "Bichos Escrotos" (Disgusting Pests) is one of their "repugnant" numbers, a rough-edged rock-funk tune whose lyrics suggest that only the pests will inherit the earth: "Animals, come out of the filth/ Cockroaches, let me see your paws/ Rats, get in the shoes of civilized citizens/ Fleas, come live in my wrinkles."

Titãs performing at Transamerica Studios in São Paulo.

On their third album, the acclaimed *Cabeça Dinossauro* (Dinosaur Head), the Titãs consolidated their musical and thematic language. The album dissected modern societal institutions with acidic fury. Nothing escaped Titãs' critical eyes. In "Porrada" (Punch), they attacked all those who uphold hypocritical society:

A mark of ten for the girls of the opposing team
Congratulations to the academics of the association
Salutations to those graduating in law
All due respect to the ladies
A punch in the face of those who do nothing.

In 1989, writer Willis Guerra Filho commented on the Titãs' lyrics: "The words of the songs are like a critical register of the Brazilian way of life, of our society nowadays, with its great insecurity where the people are attacked from all sides, from bandits and the police, from insects and DDT, from the state and social agencies."

Besides Gavin and Reis, the other members of the hydra-like band are Arnaldo Antunes (vocals), Toni Bellotto (guitar), Paulo Miklos (bass, vocals), Sérgio Britto (keyboards, vocals), Branco Mello (vocals), and Marcelo Fromer (guitar). The Titãs' performance in Rio's Hollywood Rock Festival in 1988 drew the attention of the international music industry, and they were invited to play in the Montreux Jazz Festival. In 1989, *Cabeça Dinossauro* was chosen as the best Brazilian album of the eighties by a poll in the Rio daily newspaper *Jornal do Brasil.*

The Engenheiros do Hawaii.

Rising young funk singer Ed Motta.

Hawaiian Engineers, Funk, and Blues

Coming from Porto Alegre—the capital of Brazil's southernmost state, Rio Grande do Sul—are the Engenheiros do Hawaii (Hawaiian Engineers). An art-school band that performed together at college parties, they're influenced by Caetano Veloso, Led Zeppelin, and Pink Floyd, creating what they call "garage MPB." Bassist and bandleader Humberto Gessinger grounds philosophical ideas in long ballads with descriptive lyrics that build to a climax of heavy and hard instrumentation (they sound something like the rock group Rush). In some cities the Engenheiros are invited to give lectures; in Fortaleza, at the end of one particular concert, the crowd started chanting "Philosophy!"

"Ouça o que Eu Digo não Ouça Ninguém" (Listen to What I Say Don't Listen to Anyone) advised, "If they tell you not to flip the table/

If they tell you attacking is the worst defense/ If they tell you to wait for dessert/ Listen to me, don't listen to anyone." In "Alívio Imediato" (Immediate Relief) they warned of contemporary dangers "The best hideout, the greatest darkness/ No longer serve as shelter, no longer give protection/ Libya bombarded, the libido and the virus/ The lips and the lipstick." A trio that also includes Carlos Maltz (drums) and Augusto Licks (guitar), the Engenheiros made their international debut in the USSR in 1989, playing in an event sponsored by the Brazilian embassy there.

Funk music is also very popular in Brazil, and in some places in the country it is not unusual to find clubs that have samba meetings on Saturdays and funk on Sundays. The pioneer in Brazilian funk and soul music is vocalist Tim Maia (born in Rio in 1942), who masters the mixture of American black music with Brazilian musical spices. A hit-maker either with romantic ballads or heavy funk, Tim Maia is the godfather of a whole generation of soul-influenced musicians that includes his cousin Ed Motta, Sandra de Sá, Cláudio Zoli, Luni, Skowa e Mafia, and Hanói Hanói.

Though the instruments and musical elements used by roqueiros in Brazil are similar to those utilized by other rock musicians all over the world, the country's bands sing in Portuguese and add uniquely Brazilian ingredients to the internationally known rock format. The native element may be a different kind of percussion, an attitude in the lyrics, a blend of Brazilian rhythms, or an original way of placing words in the melody. Rock-based acts like the Paralamas do Sucesso, Lulu Santos, Lobão, and Titãs have achieved the artistic level of the best rock bands in the world and have already embarked on international careers. Over thirty years old now, Brazilian rock seems here to stay.

MORE ROCK AND BLUES

The wide spectrum of Brazilian pop also includes blues artists Celso Blues Boy, André Christovam, and Blues Etilicos. Other artists and groups that deserve mention are Robertinho de Recife, a master of frevo, rock and other styles on guitar; Fausto Fawcett, the bard of Copacabana low-life; Eduardo Dusek, a theatrical, satirical crooner who fuses rock, MPB and tacky love songs; Barão Vermelho (Red Baron), a successful R&B group with whom Cazuza played before going solo; and Marina, a talented interpreter with a sensual, husky voice.

Vinícius Cantuária, Ritchie, Leo Jaime, Capital Inicial (Initial Capital), Ultraje a Rigor, Ira! (Anger!), Os Mulheres Negras (The Male Negresses), Kid Abelha (Kid Bee), and Heróis da Resistência (Heroes of the Resistance) are other notable rock/ blues artists.

Marina in concert.

THE NINETIES AND BEYOND

In the late 1980s, the Brazilian pop charts were dominated largely by Brazilian rock, *brega* romantic ballads, and international artists. Many Brazilian musicians and critics worried that their country's popular music was declining, overwhelmed once again by the "Americanization" of alienated Brazilian youth whose musical tastes were being manipulated through the adroit marketing of Anglo-American pop by the multinational music companies. But despite the omnipresence of songs by Madonna, Phil Collins, and Michael Jackson at discos and parties attended by middle-class teenagers, Brazilian music had lost none of its creative energy. It was just moving in new directions, not all of them yet reflected in major record sales.

Of course, samba was always a strong musical presence, fortified somewhat by the big commercial boost the genre received in the 1980s from "pagode," born in Ramos. Regional music, especially forró and *música sertaneja*, was doing as well as ever. The new Brazilian-Caribbean hybrid of *lambada*, which spread from the North to the rest of Brazil, had become yet another ingredient in the "caldron into which enters everything spicy," as critic Zuza Homem de Mello described music in Bahia. There, musicians were working with a multiplicity of hot new musical recipes, *samba-reggae* being one of the more notable examples (few critics have complained about the "Jamaicanization" of Brazilian music however).

Instrumental music also gained momentum heading into the nineties, as Brazilian artists artfully combined choro, jazz, samba, and other genres, discovering a large international market for their work. MPB artists continued to stay busy touring the world. And rock, so often derided by nationalists as more "cultural imperialism," was being mixed with various Brazilian styles by domestic rock groups and used as a base for a new generation of brilliant, thoroughly Brazilian lyricists.

As it moves into the 1990s, Brazilian music is still as playful, open, cannibalistic, vibrant, lyrical, imaginative, and self-renewing as ever.

GLOSSARY

aboio: wordless song used by cowboys of the northeastern sertão to call cattle.

acalanto: lullaby (from Portugal).

afoxé: song form/rhythm derived from candomblé ritual music; also bloco afro that plays afoxé during Carnaval (mainly in Salvador).

afoxê: a gourd with beads strung on cords or wire around it; sometimes called cabaça.

afro-samba: samba mixed with additional Afro-Brazilian elements (such as afoxé).

agogô: double cowbell (each bell is a different size) struck by wooden stick.

apito: any whistle; whistle used by the bateria's director in an escola de samba.

atabaque: generic name for conical single-headed drums played with the hands, similar to Cuban conga drum.

auto: dramatic form that includes dances, songs, and allegorical characters, often processional. Autos are performed during December and January, and came to Brazil from Portugal, where they date back to medieval times. Jesuits introduced religious-themed autos to Brazilians as a method of instruction and conversion, but over the years autos incorporated local themes and musical elements. Examples of autos include reisado, chegança, and bumba-meu-boi.

Bahia: state in northeastern Brazil; common nickname for Salvador, the capital of Bahia state.

baiano: (masculine noun or adjective) someone or something from Bahia state (feminine: baiana); archaic Afro-Brazilian circle dance.

baião: binary northeastern song style (popularized by Luiz Gonzaga) featuring syncopated melody, instrumental refrains in short arpeggios, and often, raised fourths and flattened sevenths.

baixo: bass.

banda: group of people who celebrate Carnaval together, generally with marcha music, attempting to bring atmosphere of club festivities out onto the street; any musical group.

bandolim: mandolin.

baqueta: drumstick.

bateria: drums; drum-and-percussion section of an escola de samba.

batucada: drumming session or percussion-playing involving different instruments.

batuque: archaic Afro-Brazilian music/dance observed as early as eighteenth century; generic name for Afro-Brazilian dances in general; type of Afro-Brazilian religion in northern Brazil; type of drum used in jongo.

berimbau: wooden bow with metal string and gourd resonator, common in Bahia and used especially to accompany capoeira.

bloco: group of people who parade during Carnaval.

bloco afro: Afro-Brazilian Carnaval group, primarily in Salvador; plural: blocos afro.

bloco de empolgação: (or bloco) Carnaval group whose members wear the same costume and parade to samba music.

bloco de enredo: Carnaval group structured as a small escola de samba.

bombo: (or bumbo) the largest Brazilian bass drum.

bossa nova: genre of music developed in Rio de Janeiro in late 1950s that included rhythmic elements of samba, a highly syncopated style of guitar playing developed by João Gilberto, a generally subdued vocal style (when sung), and harmonic influences from both cool jazz and classical music.

brega: pejorative word for tacky romantic songs.

bumba-meu-boi: processional dance (an auto) of Portuguese origin with added Brazilian

elements. It celebrates the death and resurrection of a bull and involves elaborate costumes and choreography. Also known as boi-bumbá (in the Amazonian region), boi-de-mamão (in Paraná), and boi-surubi (in Ceará).

caboclinho: northeastern Carnaval group that parades dressed as Amerindians and plays flutes and pífanos.

cachaça: Brazilian sugar-cane liquor.

caixa: snare drum.

caixeta: wood block with deep indentation or hollow, struck with drumstick.

calango: popular dance in Minas Gerais and Rio de Janeiro states, performed by couples with simple steps and 2/4 meter.

calunga: fetishistic doll carried by the dama de passo in a maracatu procession.

cambará: fusion of cumbia, mambo, carimbó, and lambada invented by Paraense guitarist Vieira in late 1980s.

cana-verde: dance from southern and central Brazil performed by couples; the men and women sing to each other, change places, and form pairs; probably of Portuguese origin.

canção praieira: fisherman's song.

candomblé: Afro-Brazilian religion of Gegê-Nagô and Bantu derivation, practiced to greatest extent in Bahia. It is the closest to the old West African practices of all the Afro-Brazilian religions. Its ritual music utilizes three different atabaques (the rum, rumpi, and lê) and pentatonic and hexatonic scales.

cantador: troubadour from northeastern and central Brazil who sings improvised or memorized songs.

cantiga: generic term for ballad or popular song.

cantoria: singing; act of performing a desafio.

capoeira: Afro-Brazilian dance/martial-arts form brought to Brazil by Bantu slaves from Angola.

carimbó: Afro-Brazilian song/dance from Pará that dates back at least to nineteenth century. It features a 2/4 meter, a fast tempo, and heavy percussion dominated by the carimbó drum (a hollow tree-trunk section covered with deer skin). The dance is a circle dance, with couples taking turns soloing in center of circle.

carioca: someone or something from city of Rio de Janeiro.

Carnaval: (Carnival in English) four days of celebration before Ash Wednesday, observed primarily in Roman Catholic countries. Mardi Gras is the American version.

cateretê: rural dance of probable Amerindian origin, performed by couples who are accompanied by a singer and two violas.

catira: common alternate name for cateretê.

cavaquinho: four-stringed, ukulele-like instrument with 17 frets, usually tuned D-G-B-D.

caxambu: Afro-Brazilian song/dance accompanied by drums and handclapping; type of drum used in it.

caxixi: small, closed wicker basket filled with seeds, used as a shaker in capoeira.

cearense: someone or something from Ceará state.

chegança: (chegança-de-mouros; cristãos-e-mouros) popular pageant (an auto) about the Christians fighting the Moors; lascivious and sensual dance from eighteenth century.

chocalho: (xocalho) wooden or metal shaker in the shape of two cones united at the base.

choro: (or chorinho) binary instrumental genre of music that features rapid modulations, melodic leaps, and improvisation by lead instrument, developed in late nineteenth century in Rio.

cinema novo: Brazilian film movement in 1950s and 1960s that sought to create an authentically Brazilian cinema.

ciranda: children's circle dance of Portuguese origin; rural samba in Rio de Janeiro state; folkloric song/dance from Pernambuco.

coco: Afro-Brazilian song/dance in 2/4 time from northeastern littoral.

congada: (or congo) processional dance that incorporates both African traditions and Iberian elements, and that often includes characters who represent African royalty; congada is found in southern and central Brazil, while congo is generally found in northern and northeastern Brazil.

cordão: originally an all-male group that danced and celebrated Carnaval to accompaniment of batucada, and that first appeared in late nineteenth century.

cozinha: an ensemble of bass, drums, and assorted percussion; rhythmic mix.

cuíca: small friction drum with thin stick inside attached to drumskin. A moistened cloth is used to rub the stick and one hand applies pressure to the drumskin, producing grunting, groaning, and squeaking noises.

deboche: synonym for fricote; playing with a musical form.

desafio: poetic improvisational contests between two vocalists, usually unaccompanied while sung but with short instrumental passage in between question and answer.

embolada: poetic-musical form from northeastern littoral with stanza-and-refrain structure, 2/4 meter, fast tempo, declamatory melody, short note values, small musical intervals, and stanzas that are often improvised.

entrudo: rude, chaotic style of celebrating Carnaval that originated in Portugal and was popular in Brazil until the mid-nineteenth century.

escola de samba: organization that plans and puts on samba parades during Carnaval. It typically has many other social functions and may serve as the community center in its neighborhood (usually a poorer area of the city).

fado: melancholy, guitar-accompanied Portuguese ballad that derived from lundu. Some scholars believe it actually originated in Brazil, but was fully developed in Portugal.

favela: slum.

fluminense: someone or something from Rio de Janeiro state.

fofa: voluptuous Portuguese dance of eighteenth century.

forró: generic name for dance-oriented northeastern musical styles; dance at which they are played; also used by some to signify a certain variation of the baião.

frevo: fast, syncopated marcha that originated in Recife.

fricote: song form that mixes ijexá and reggae, invented by Luiz Caldas.

frigideira: percussion instrument shaped like a frying pan and played with a stick.

galope: folk song/dance style; six-verse martelo (same as agalopado or martelo-agalopado).

ganzá: single, double, or triple tubular metal shaker; wooden or metal square with cymbals.

gaúcho: (masculine noun or adjective) someone or something from Rio Grande do Sul state. Feminine: gaúcha.

Gegê: (Jeje) Brazilian word for the Africans who came from Dahomey (Benin), such as the Ewe people.

guitarra: electric guitar.

habanera: slow Cuban song/dance in duple time.

ijexá: rhythm of afoxé song form; also a sub-group of the Yoruba people.

jongo: type of rural samba from southeastern Brazil.

Ketu: sub-group of the Yoruba people.

lambada: a fusion of merengue and carimbó with other Caribbean accents, featuring a rhythm in 2/4 time, syncopation, and a fast tempo; also a close, sexy dance for two partners that evolved at the same time and that incorporates dance elements of merengue, samba, maxixe, and forró.

lundu: (lundum) song/dance of Angolan origin, brought to Brazil by Bantu slaves; ancestor of many urban Brazilian song forms.

maculelê: Afro-Brazilian stick-fighting war dance.

macumba: generic name for various Afro-Brazilian religions (candomblé, umbanda, xangô, pajelança, catimbó, batuque, caboclo); name of specific Afro-Brazilian religion practiced in Rio de Janeiro.

malandro: man who makes his living by exploiting women, gambling or playing small confidence tricks; scoundrel, vagabond, loafer.

maraca: hollow gourd with dried seeds or pebbles inside, commonly used by Brazilian Indians.

maracatu: slow, heavy Afro-Brazilian processional music and accompanying dance from northeastern Brazil, featuring many characters including a king, queen, and dama de passo; groups that perform maracatu during Carnaval.

marcha: (marchinha) binary Afro-Brazilian form with strong accent on downbeat and fast tempo, first made famous by Chiquinha Gonzaga. In the 1920s the marcha was influenced by one-step and ragtime.

marcha-rancho: slower and more melodically developed variation of the marcha.

martelo: northeastern poetic form with ten syllables per line, and six to ten lines per stanza.

maxixe: song/dance that was a fusion of lundu with tango, polka, and habanera. It was created in late nineteenth century and was first original Brazilian urban dance.

merengue: Caribbean song/dance in 2/4 time that originated in the Dominican Republic in early nineteenth century.

mestre-sala: master of ceremonies who symbolically protects porta-bandeira in escola de samba parade.

mineiro: (masculine noun or adjective) someone or something from Minas Gerais state. Feminine: mineira.

moda: sentimental song from Portugal.

moda de viola: rural folk song with simple melody, often performed by two guitarist-vocalists singing in thirds, found in central and southeastern Brazil.

modinha: sentimental Brazilian song style derived from moda and lundu.

morro: in Rio used to mean one of the hills around the city upon which are located poor neighborhoods (the favelas); any hill.

MPB: (música popular brasileira) general term for post-bossa Brazilian urban popular music that combined many different musical elements and whose artists did not fall into individual categories such as samba, forró, jazz, or rock.

mulato: (masculine noun) mulatto. Feminine: mulata.

música sertaneja: pop music versions of Brazilian rural idioms such as toada, moda da viola, cana-verde, and catira, with influences from Bolivian and Paraguayan music and, in the late twentieth century, from American country music.

Nagô: name by which Yoruba descendents in Brazil refer to themselves.

nordestino: (masculine noun or adjective) someone or something from northeastern Brazil. Feminine: nordestina.

one-step: American dance in simple duple time.

orixá: deity in Afro-Brazilian religions.

pandeiro: similar to tambourine, but with jingles inverted.

pagode: party or gathering where samba is played; type of samba popularized in 1980s by composers who gathered in Ramos, a neighborhood in Rio's Zona Norte.

paraense: someone or something from Pará state.

partido alto: type of samba with short, light refrains that the singers must follow with improvised verses.

passista: person who masters samba steps.

paulista: someone or something from São Paulo state.

paulistano: (masculine noun or adjective) someone or something from city of São Paulo. Feminine: paulistana.

pífano: (pífaro) primitive flute; fife.

polka: a round dance and musical form in uptempo 2/4 time that originated in Bohemia around 1830.

pontos de candomblé: invocation songs for deities in candomblé religion.

pontos de umbanda: invocation songs for deities in umbanda religion.

porta-bandeira: standard-bearer (a woman) in escola de samba parade.

pratos: cymbals.

quadrilha: quadrille, a square dance popular in France in early nineteenth century.

quilombo: settlements founded by runaway slaves in colonial Brazil.

rancho: Carnaval group that parades to marcha-ranchos. Highly influential on early escolas de samba.

reco-reco: a notched instrument (often made of bamboo or metal) that is scraped with a stick and produces a crisp sound.

repente: improvised stanza sung by a repentista.

repentista: a troubadour, generally from northeastern Brazil, who sings improvised stanzas as he tells stories or performs in a desafio.

repique: (repinique) two-headed tenor drum in samba.

rock tupiniquim: nickname, often pejorative, for Brazilian rock.

rojão: baião; faster-tempo baião.

roqueiro: rocker.

samba: the most famous Brazilian song/dance, musically characterized by 2/4 meter and interlocking, syncopated lines in melody and accompaniment.

samba-canção: slower, softer type of samba in which melody and lyrics are emphasized more than the rhythm.

samba de breque: type of samba with a "break" in which singer dramatizes a situation or improvises dialogues.

samba de gafieira: a dance-hall style of samba, generally instrumental and with horn arrangements influenced by American big-band jazz.

samba de morro: name used by Brazilian media in 1940s and 1950s to characterize samba that kept essential characteristics of the style developed by Estácio composers such as Ismael Silva and Bide, and to differentiate this style from others such as samba-canção and sambolero.

samba de roda: circle-dance samba, accompanied by hand-clapping and batucada.

samba-enredo: samba based on pre-selected theme, played by escola de samba and written for Carnaval.

samba-reggae: mixture of samba and reggae developed in Salvador in 1980s.

sambista: someone who sings, writes, plays, or dances samba almost exclusively.

sambolero: mixture of samba with bolero.

sanfona: accordion; button-accordion.

saudade: longing or yearning for someone or something.

schottische: ballroom dance similar to polka introduced to England in mid-nineteenth century, also called "German polka."

sertão: general term for remote interior regions of Brazil; also specific name for the arid backlands of northeastern Brazil.

sertanejo: (masculine noun or adjective) somone or something from sertão. Feminine: sertaneja.

sétima nordestina: the northeastern flattened seventh note.

siriá: folkloric music from Cametá region of Pará played in marujada and boi-bumbá dramatic dances; a couples dance with elements of maxixe and forró.

surdo: drum played in samba with wooden stick topped by velvet-covered wooden head. Surdos come in three sizes and function as the bass in the samba bateria.

tambor: any drum.

tamborim: small tambourine without jingles played with single or double stick.

tango: Argentinian song/dance that derived its rhythm from the Cuban habanera and Argentinian milonga.

tan-tan: deep drum similar to an atabaque. It substitutes for the surdo in pagode samba.

tarol: shallow two-headed drum with strings across skin and played with two wooden sticks.

teclados: keyboards.

toada: generic term for a stanza-and-refrain song with a simple, often melancholy melody and short lyrics of a romantic or comical nature.

trio elétrico: musicians playing electrified instruments; the decorated truck atop which they play during Carnaval in Salvador.

triângulo: triangle.

Tropicália: (Tropicalismo) arts movement in the late 1960s, led in musical area by Gilberto Gil, Caetano Veloso, and others.

umbanda: Afro-Brazilian religion developed in twentieth century which has considerable influence from Spiritist beliefs.

umbigada: movement in lundu, samba, and other Afro-Brazilian dances in which one dancer touches navels with another as an invitation to dance.

viola: guitar-like instrument whose number of strings (five, seven, eight, ten, twelve, or fourteen) varies according to the region.

violão: guitar.

violeiro: guitarist; especially, troubadors of rural Brazil who play guitar or viola and perform improvised or memorized songs.

violino: violin.

virada: change in percussion pattern.

xaxado: northeastern song/dance reportedly popularized by the famed bandit Lampião.

xerém: song/dance from northeastern Brazil, similar to polka and xote, generally accompanied by accordion.

xique-xique: a type of cactus; a type of chocalho.

Yoruba: an African people from Nigeria; also their language.

xote: a northeastern dance in 2/4 time derived from the schottische.

zabumba: type of bass drum, popular in northeastern music.

Zona Sul: Southern zone of Rio. It is the area in Rio that is closer to the beaches and includes neighborhoods such as Flamengo, Botafogo, Copacabana, Ipanema, Leblon, Jardim Botânico, and Gávea.

Zona Norte: Northern zone of Rio that includes neighborhoods such as Estácio, Tijuca, Vila Isabel, and Ramos.

SELECT BIBLIOGRAPHY

Almeida, Laurindo. *Latin Percussion Instruments and Rhythms*. Sherman Oaks, Calif.: Gwyn Publishing Company, 1972.

Alvarenga, Oneyda. *Música Popular Brasileira*. Rio de Janeiro: Editora Globo, 1950.

Andrade, Mario de. *Danças Dramáticas do Brasil*. São Paulo: Livraria Martins Editora, 1959.

———. *Dicionário Musical Brasileiro*. 2nd ed. São Paulo: Editora da Universidade de São Paulo, 1989.

Appleby, David P. *The Music of Brazil*. Austin: University of Texas Press, 1983.

Assumpção, José Teixeira de. *Curso de Folclore Musical Brasileiro*. Rio de Janeiro: Livraria Freitas Bastos, 1967.

Bahiana, Ana Maria. *Nada Será Como Antes*. Rio de Janeiro: Editora Civilização Brasileira, 1980.

Barsante, Cássio Emmanuel. *Carmen Miranda*. Rio de Janeiro: Editora Europa, 1985.

Behague, Gerard. *Music in Latin America: An Introduction*. Englewood Cliffs, N.J.: Prentice-Hall, 1979.

Bello, José Maria. *A History of Modern Brazil: 1889-1964*. Stanford: Stanford University Press, 1968.

Bramly, Serge. *Macumba*. New York: St. Martin's Press, 1977.

Burns, E. Bradford. *A History of Brazil*. 2nd ed. New York: Columbia University Press, 1980.

Cabral, Sérgio. *As Escolas de Samba: O Que, Quem, Como, Quando e Por Que*. Rio de Janeiro: Fontana, 1974.

Calado, Carlos. "Lambada Vai Dividir Com 'Negões' a Folia Baiana." *Folha de São Paulo* (February 11, 1990): E-4.

Campos, Augusto de. *Balanço da Bossa e Outras Bossas*. São Paulo: Editora Perspectiva, 1978.

Castro, Ruy. "Bossa fora da Cápsula." *Veja* (May 30, 1990): 48-54.

Cascudo, Luis da Câmara. *Dicionário do Folclore Brasileiro*. 5th ed. Belo Horizonte: Editora Itatiaia Limitada, 1984.

Caúrio, Rita, ed. *Brasil Musical*. Rio de Janeiro: Art Bureau, 1988.

Caymmi, Dorival. *Cancioneiro da Bahia*. 5th ed. Rio de Janeiro: Editora Record, 1978.

Civita, Victor, ed. *Nosso Século*. Abril Cultural, 1980.

Damante, Hélio. *Folclore Brasileiro: São Paulo*. Rio de Janeiro: FUNARTE, 1980.

Feather, Leonard. *The Encyclopedia of Jazz in the Sixties*. New York: Horizon, 1966.

Feather, Leonard, and Gitler, Ira. *The Encyclopedia of Jazz in the Seventies*. New York: Bonanza, 1976.

Frade, Cascia. *Folclore Brasileiro: Rio de Janeiro*. Rio de Janeiro: FUNARTE, 1979.

Freyre, Gilberto. *The Mansions and the Shanties*. 2nd ed. Westport, Conn.: Greenwood Press, 1980.

Giron, Luis Antonio. "Carnaval de 90 Promete 'Lambadear'." *Folha de São Paulo* (February 11, 1990): E-1.

———."Obra de Câmara Cascudo Omitiu Ritmos do Pará." *Folha de São Paulo* (February 11, 1990): E-3.

Goes, Fred de. *O País do Carnaval Elétrico*. Salvador: Editora Corrupio, 1982.

Gontijo, Ricardo. "Oi…Milton." *Canja* (October 1, 1980).

Graham, Ronnie. *The Da Capo Guide to Contemporary African Music*. New York: Da Capo Press, 1988.

Gridley, Mark C. *Jazz Styles*. Englewood Cliffs, N.J.: Prentice-Hall, 1978.

Kernfield, Barry, ed. *The New Grove Dictionary of Jazz*. New York: MacMillan Press Ltd., 1988.

Lacerda, Regina. *Folclore Brasileiro: Goiás*. Rio de Janeiro: FUNARTE, 1977.

Lockhart, James, and Schwartz, Stuart B. *Early Latin America: a History of Colonial Spanish America and Brazil*. Cambridge: Cambridge University Press, 1984.

Lody, Raul Giovanni da Motta. *Cadernos de Folclore: Afoxé*. Rio de Janeiro: FUNARTE, 1976.

McGowan, Chris. "Brazilian Instrumental Music." In "Viva Brazil" special supplement to *Billboard* (November 7, 1987): B6.

———. "Brazilian Music Industry: Challenging the Cross-Currents of a Volatile World Market." In "Viva Brazil" supplement to *Billboard* (Nov. 7, 1987): B-4.

———. "Brazilian Talent: A Deep Reserve of Musical Greatness to Come." In "Viva Brazil" supplement to *Billboard*. (Nov. 7, 1987): B-3.

———. "The Brazilian Wave Comes Ashore." In "Viva Brazil" supplement to *Billboard* (Nov. 7, 1987): B-1.

———. "Gilberto Gil: Cultivator of the Spirit." *The Beat* (Vol. 10, No. 2, 1991).

———. "Industry Struggles Uphill Against Four-Year Recession, Aided by Strong Musical Heritage." In "Viva Latino" supplement to *Billboard* (January 26, 1985): VL-22.

———. "In Quotes: Perspectives on Brazilian Music." In "Viva Brazil" supplement to *Billboard* (Nov. 7, 1987): B-4.

Marcondes, Marco Antonio, ed. *Enciclopédia da Música Brasileira: Erudita, Folclórica e Popular*. São Paulo: Art Editora, 1977.

Mariz, Vasco. *A Canção Brasileira*. 5th ed. Rio de Janeiro: Editora Nova Fronteira, 1985.

Mello, José Eduardo Homem de. *Música Popular Brasileira*. São Paulo: Editora da Universidade de São Paulo, 1976.

Motta, Nelson. *Música, Humana Música*. Rio de Janeiro: Salamandra, 1980.

Moura, Roberto M. *Carnaval: Da Redentora a Praça do Apocalipse*. Rio de Janeiro: Jorge Zahar, 1986.

Navarro, Jesse, Jr., ed. *Nova História da Música Popular Brasileira*. 2nd ed. São Paulo: Abril Cultural, 1977.

Nettl, Bruno. *Folk and Traditional Music of the Western Continents.* Englewood Cliffs, N.J.: Prentice-Hall, 1973.

Neves, Guilherme Santos. *Folclore Brasileiro: Espírito Santo.* Rio de Janeiro: FUNARTE, 1978.

Nketia, J.H. Kwabena. *The Music of Africa.* New York: W.W. Norton & Company, 1974.

Omari, Mikelle Smith. *The Art and Ritual of Bahian Candomblé.* Los Angeles: UCLA Museum of Cultural History, Monograph Series No. 24, 1984.

Palmer, Robert. "Eastern Brazil Exports Influential Pop to the World." *New York Times* (May 4, 1986).

Perrone, Charles A. *Masters of Contemporary Brazilian Song: MPB 1965-1985.* Austin: University of Texas Press, 1989.

Pessanha, Ricardo. "Margareth Menezes: She's Not the Girl from Ipanema." *The Beat* (Vol. 10, No. 2, 1991).

Poppino, Rollie E. *Brazil—the Land and People.* 2nd ed. New York: Oxford University Press, 1973.

Rawley, James. *The Transatlantic Slave Trade.* New York: W.W. Norton & Co., 1981.

Ribeiro, Maria de Lourdes Borges. *Cadernos de Folclore: O Jongo.* Rio de Janeiro: FUNARTE, 1984.

Risério, Antonio. *Carnaval Ijexá: Notas sobre a Re-africanização do Carnaval Baiano.* Salvador: Editora Corrupio, 1982.

Roberts, John Storm. *Black Music of Two Worlds.* New York: William Morrow and Company, 1974.

———. *The Latin Tinge.* Oxford: Oxford University Press, 1979.

Rocca, Edgard. *Ritmos Brasileiros e Seus Instrumentos de Percussão.* Rio de Janeiro: Europa Editora, 1986.

Rock, a Música do Século XX. Edited by Pedro Paulo Popovic Consultores Editoriais Ltda. Rio de Janeiro: Rio Gráfica, 1983.

Sabanovich, Daniel. *Brazilian Percussion Manual.* Van Nuys, Calif.: Alfred Publishing Company, 1988.

Seraine, Florival. *Folclore Brasileiro: Ceará.* Rio de Janeiro: FUNARTE, 1978.

Sousa, José Geraldo de, Padre. *Cadernos de Folclore: Características da Música Folclórica Brasileira.* Rio de Janeiro: FUNARTE, 1969.

Sousa, Tárik de. *O Som Nosso de Cada Dia.* Porto Alegre: L&PM, 1983.

———, and Andreato, Elifas. *Rostos e Gostos da Música Popular Brasileira.* Porto Alegre: L&PM, 1979.

Tinhorão, José Ramos. *Pequena História da Música Popular—Da Modinha ao Tropicalismo.* 5th ed. São Paulo: Art Editora, 1986.

Ventura, Zuenir. *1968, O Ano que não Terminou.* Rio de Janeiro: Nova Fronteira, 1988.

SELECT DISCOGRAPHY

Brazilian Artists

The following recordings comprise a representative list of contemporary popular Brazilian music, focusing primarily on the 1980s, with some titles from other decades also included. It is a *starting* point for listeners interested in exploring Brazilian sounds. The discography is arranged alphabetically by artist's last name. If more than one recording for an artist is included, the subsequent recordings are listed chronologically (except for the heading "Various Artists"; these compilations are listed alphabetically by album title). If titles were released in both Brazil and the United States, the latter release is listed; the date of a U.S. release is often one or more years after the original Brazilian release. Abbreviations: (rpt.) indicates reprint; (n.d.) indicates we could not confirm date of release; BR = Brazilian release. No country noted = U.S. release.

Adolfo, Antonio. *Jinga.* Happy Hour 5011, 1990
Alcione. *A Cor do Brasil.* BR/RCA 103.0627, 1984
———. *Fruto e Raiz.* BR/RCA 103.0673, 1986
———. *Nosso Nome: Resistência.* BR/RCA 130.0015, 1987
Alf, Johnny. *Diagonal.* RCA BBL 1271, 1964
Almeida, Laurindo, & Carlos Barbosa-Lima, Charlie Byrd. *Music of the Brazilian Masters.* Concord Picante CCD-4389, 1989
Almeida, Laurindo, & Charlie Byrd. *Brazilian Soul.* Concord CJP-150, 1981
Almeida, Laurindo, & Bud Shank. *Brazilliance, Vol. 1,.* World Pacific 1412, 1961
———. *Artistry in Rhythm.* Concord CJ-238, 1984
Alves, Ataulfo. *Ataulfo Alves: 80 Anos.* BR/EMI 062 792602, 1989
Andrade, Leny. *Luz Neon.* BR/Eldorado 130.88.0536, 1988
Ariel, Marcos. *Terra de Índio.* Tropical Storm/WEA WH 55942, 1989
Assad, Sérgio and Odair. *Alma Brasileira.* Elektra/Nonesuch 79179, 1988
Ayres, Nelson. *Mantiqueira.* BR/Som da Gente SDG 009, 1981
Azevedo, Geraldo. *A Luz do Solo: Geraldo Azevedo.* BR/Barclay 827 904, 1985
Azevedo, Geraldo, & Naná Vasconcelos. *De Outra Maneira.* BR/Echo/RCA 109.0157, 1986
Azymuth. *Telecommunication.* Milestone M-9101, 1982
———. *Rapid Transit.* Milestone M-9118, 1983
Banda Mel. *Banda Mel do Brasil.* BR/Continental 1.01.404.376, 1989
Barão Vermelho. *Maior Abandonado.* BR/CBS 412.082, 1984
Barbosa, Beto. *Beto Barbosa.* BR/Continental 1.73.405.016, 1988
Barbosa-Lima, Carlos, & S. Isbin. *Brazil, with Love.* Concord CCD-4320, 1987

Baú dos 8 Baixos. *Bucho com Bucho.* BR/Som da Gente SDG 011, 1982
Belchior. *Alucinação.* BR/Philips 634 9160, 1976
Ben, Jorge. *Grandes Successos de Jorge Ben.* BR/Som Livre 402.0012, 1988
———. *Benjor.* Tropical Storm/WEA WH56619, 1989
Bethânia, Maria. *Alibi.* BR/Philips 836 001, 1988 (rpt.)
———. *Maria.* RCA 8585, 1988
———. *Memória Da Pele.* BR/Philips 838 928, 1989
Biglione, Victor. *Baleia Azul.* Tropical Storm/WEA WH 55999, 1989
Blitz. *As Aventuras da Blitz.* BR/EMI 064 422 919, 1982
Bomba, Ricardo. *Ultralight.* BR/Tropical Jazz/BMG 131 0007, 1988
Bonfá, Luiz. *Recado Novo de Luiz Bonfá.* Odeon MOFB 3310, 1965
———. *Non-Stop to Brazil.* Chesky JD29, 1989
Borges, Lô. *Lô Borges.* BR/EMI SC 10112, 1977 (rpt.)
Borghetti, Renato. *Renato Borghetti.* BR/RCA 103.0705, 1987
Bosco, João. *Caça a Raposa.* BR/RCA 103 0112, 1975
———. *Gagabirô.* BR/Barclay 823 694, 1984
———. *Ai Ai Ai de Mim.* BR/CBS 138292, 1986
———. *Bosco.* BR/CBS 231 218, 1989
Brasil, João Carlos Assis. *Jazz Brasil.* BR/Kuarup KLP-022, 1986
Buarque, Chico. *Meus Caros Amigos.* BR/Philips 6349 189, 1976
———. *Vida.* BR/Philips 6349 435, 1980
———. *Francisco.* RCA 9628, 1987
———. *Construção.* BR/Philips 836 013, 1989 (rpt.)
Caldas, Luiz. *Magia.* BR/PolyGram 826 583, 1985
———. *Flor Cigana.* BR/Polydor 831 268, 1986
Cama de Gato. *Guerra Fria.* BR/Som da Gente SDG 036, 1988
Carlos, Erasmo. *Mulher.* BR/Polydor 2451-176, 1981
Carlos, Roberto. *Roberto Carlos.* BR/CBS 230 105, 1986
Cartola. *70 Anos.* BR/RCA 103 0278, 1978
Carvalho, Beth. *Beth Carvalho Ao Vivo.* BR/RCA 713 0018, 1987
———. *Alma do Brasil.* BR/Philips 836 695, 1988
———. *Saudades de Guanabara.* BR/Philips 842 084, 1989
Castro-Neves, Oscar. *Oscar!* Living Music LM 0010, 1987
Caymmi, Dori. *Dori Caymmi.* Elektra Musician 60790, 1988
Caymmi, Dorival. *Saudades da Bahia.* BR/EMI 036 422.593, 1985
Caymmi, Nana. *Atrás da Porta.* BR/CID 8014, 1977
Caymmi, Nana, & Dori, Danilo and Dorival Caymmi. *Caymmi's Grandes Amigos.* BR/EMI 064 422.963, 1986
———. *Família Caymmi.* BR/EMI 064 748 788, 1987
Cazes, Henrique, et al. *Orquestra Brasília: Pixinguinha.* Kuarup 035, 1989

Cazuza. *Burguesia.* BR/Philips 838 447, 1989

Chiclete Com Banana. *Tambores Urbanos.* BR/Continental 1.01.404.360, 1988

Chiquinho do Acordeon. *Chiquinho do Acordeon.* BR/Visom 026, 1989

Consuelo, Baby. *Sem Pecado e Sem Juízo.* BR/CBS 138272, 1985

Costa, Gal. *Gal Canta Caymmi.* BR/Philips 836 014, 1988 (rpt.)

————. *Fantasia.* BR/Philips 836 015, 1988 (rpt.)

————. *Tropical.* BR/Philips 836 016, 1988 (rpt.)

————. *Aquarela do Brasil.* BR/Philips 836 017, 1988 (rpt.)

D'Alma. *D'Alma.* BR/Som da Gente SDG 019, 1983

Delmiro, Hélio. *Chama.* BR/Som da Gente SDG 020, 1984

Deodato, Eumir. *Prelude.* CTI 6021, 1972

Deodato, Eumir, & Airto Moreira. *Deodato/Airto In Concert.* CTI 6041, 1974

Djavan. *Luz.* BR/CBS 138.251, 1982

————. *Meu Lado.* Japan/Epic-Sony 32 8P-144, 1986

————. *Bird of Paradise.* Columbia CK 44276, 1988

————. *Seduzir.* World Pacific 48206, 1990 (rpt.)

Dodô & Osmar. *O Melhor do Trio Elétrico.* BR/Continental 1.04.405.266, 1979

Donato, João. *Muito à Vontade.* Polydor 4085, 1963

Donato, João, & Eumir Deodato. *João Donato.* Muse MR 5017, 1973

Dougllas, Betto. *O Rei da Lambada.* BR/Continental 1.73.405.017, 1988

Elias, Eliane. *Illusions.* Blue Note BLJ 46994, 1987

————. *So Far So Close.* Blue Note 91141, 1989

————. *Eliane Elias Plays Jobim.* Blue Note 93089, 1990

Elomar, & A.M. Lima, P. Moura, H. do Monte. *ConSertão.* BR/Kuarup KLP 008/9, 1981

Elomar, & G. Azevedo, V. Farias, Xangai. *Cantoria.* BR/Kuarup KLP-018, 1984

————. *Cantoria 2.* BR/Kuarup KLP-032, 1987

Engenheiros do Hawaii. *Alívio Imediato.* BR/RCA 150.0004, 1989

Fafá de Belém. *Tamba-Tajá.* BR/Polydor 2451 073, 1976

————. *Atrevida.* BR/Som Livre 530 032, 1986

Fagner. *Raimundo Fagner.* BR/CBS 137.964, 1976

Falcão, Fernando. *Memória das Águas.* BR/Poitou 001, 1981

Farney, Dick. *30 Sucessos.* BR/EMI 162 421194/5, 1978

————. *Feliz de Amor.* BR/Som da Gente SDG 017, 1983

Fest, Manfredo. *Jungle Cat.* DMP CD-470, 1989

Fredera. *Aurora Vermelha.* BR/Som da Gente SDG 006, 1981

Geraissati, André. *Dadgad.* Tropical Storm/WEA WH 55998, 1989

Gil, Gilberto. *Louvação.* BR/Philips R 765 005L, 1967

————. *Refazenda.* BR/Philips 6349 152, 1975

————. *Refavela.* BR/Philips 6349 329, 1977

————. *Raça Humana.* Tropical Storm/WEA WH52122, 1984

————. *Em Concerto.* BR/WEA 670.9001, 1987

Gilberto, Astrud. *The Astrud Gilberto Album.* Verve 68608, 1965

Gilberto, João. *Chega de Saudade.* BR/EMI MOFB 3073, 1959

————. *Brasil.* WEA BSK 3613, 1981

————. *Interpreta Tom Jobim.* BR/EMI 052 422005, 1985

————. *João Gilberto: Live in Montreux.* Elektra Musician 9 60760, 1987

————. *João Gilberto.* Verve 837 589, 1988 (rpt.)

————. *The Legendary João Gilberto.* World Pacific 93891, 1990 (rpt.)

Gismonti, Egberto. *Sol do Meio Dia.* ECM 1116, 1978

————. *Solo.* ECM 1136, 1979

————. *Sanfona.* ECM 1203, 1981

————. *Dança dos Escravos.* ECM 1387, 1989

Gismonti, Egberto, & N. Vasconcelos. *Dança das Cabeças.* ECM 1089, 1977

————. *Duas Vozes.* ECM 1279, 1984

Godoy, Amílson. *Amílson Godoy.* BR/Som da Gente SDG 040, 1989

Gomes, Manoel, & et al. *Brasil, Flauta, Cavaquinho e Viola.* Marcus Pereira 9301, 1968

Gomes, Pepeu. *Energia Positiva.* BR/CBS 138 284, 1985

Gonzaga, Luiz. *De Fia Pavi.* BR/RCA 109 0159, 1987

————. *O Melhor de Luiz Gonzaga.* BR/RCA 10032, 1989

Gonzaga, Luiz, & Fagner. *Gonzagão & Fagner.* BR/RCA 130 0050, 1988

Gonzaguinha. *É.* World Pacific 91688, 1990 (rpt.)

Grupo Fundo de Quintal. *Samba É No Fundo de Quintal.* BR/RGE 308.6133, 1987

Guedes, Beto. *Página do Relâmpago Elétrico.* BR/EMI EMCB 7021, 1977

Guineto, Almir. *Almir Guineto.* BR/RGE 308.6118, 1986

Horta, Toninho. *Diamond Land.* Verve Forecast 835 183, 1988

————. *Moonstone.* Verve Forecast 839 734, 1989

————. *Toninho Horta.* World Pacific 93865, 1990 (rpt.)

Jobim, Antonio Carlos. *Wave.* A&M SP-9-3002, 1967

————. *Tide.* A&M SP-9-3031, 1970

————. *Stone Flower.* CTI 6002, 1971

————. *Terra Brasilis.* WB 3409, 1980

————. *Tom Jobim e Convidados.* BR/Philips 826 665, 1985

————. *Urubu.* BR/WEA 610 7044, 1985 (rpt.)

Jobim, Antonio Carlos, & Gal Costa. *Rio Revisited.* Verve 841 286, 1989

Joyce, & G. Peranzetta. *Jobim.* BR/CBS 106002, 1987

Kenia. *Initial Thrill.* MCA ZBC 5967, 1987

Leão, Nara. *Girl from Ipanema.* Philips 826 348, 1985

————. *Meus Sonhos Dourados.* BR/Philips 832 639, 1988

Lee, Rita. *Tratos à Bola.* BR/Philips 830 374, 1986

————. *Rita Lee.* BR/Som Livre 530 035, 1986 (rpt.)

Lee, Rita, & R. de Carvalho. *Flerte Fatal.* BR/EMI 064 422971, 1987

Legião Urbana. *Dois.* BR/EMI 064 422961, 1986

————. *Que País É Este?* BR/EMI 068 748 8201, 1987

Lima, Arthur Moreira, & A. Ferreira. *Chorando Baixinho.* BR/Kuarup KLP 005, 1979

Lins, Ivan. *Juntos*. BR/Philips 822 672, 1984
————. *Mãos*. BR/Philips 832 262, 1988
————. *Amar Assim*. BR/Philips 836 613, 1988
————. *Awa Yiô*. Reprise 9 26499, 1991
Lobão. *Cuidado*. RCA 9633, 1988
————. *Sob o Sol de Parador*. BR/RCA 150.0001, 1989
Lobo, Edu. *Camaleão*. BR/Philips 6349 350, 1978
Lobo, Edu, & A.C. Jobim. *Edu e Tom*. BR/Philips 6328 378, 1981
Lyra, Carlos. *O Sambalanço de Carlos Lyra*. Philips 630492L, 1962
————. *Pobre Menina Rica*. CBS 37360, 1964
————. *Carlos Lyra, 25 Anos de Bossa Nova*. 3M 900006, 1987
Malheiros, Alex. *Atlantic Forest*. Milestone M-9131, 1984
Marçal, Nilton Delfino. *A Incrível Bateria do Mestre Marçal*. BR/Polydor 835 123, 1987
Maria, Tânia. *Come with Me*. Concord CCD-200, 1983
————. *Love Explosion*. Concord CJP-230, 1984
Marina. *Fullgas*. BR/Philips 818 380, 1984
————. *Próxima Parada*. BR/Philips 838 298, 1989
Martins, Alípio. *Eu Chego Lá*. BR/Continental 2.73.405.157, 1989
Mascarenhas, Raul. *Raul Mascarenhas*. Tropical Storm/WEA WH 56214, 1989
Matogrosso, Ney. *Ney Matogrosso Ao Vivo*. BR/CBS 231.222, 1989
Melodia, Luiz. *Pérola Negra*. BR/Fontana 6488 151, 1982 (rpt.)
————. *Claro*. BR/Continental 1.35.404.032, 1987
Mendes, Sérgio. *Sérgio Mendes & Brasil '66*. A&M 4116, 1966
————. *Arara*. A&M SP 5250, 1989
Menezes, Margareth. *Elegibô*. Mango 539 855, 1990
Milito, Hélcio. *Kilombo*. Antilles 90629, 1987
Miranda, Carmen. *Carmen Miranda*. BR/RCA 103 0651, 1989
Miúcha. *Miúcha*. BR/Continental 1.35.404.035, 1988
Miúcha, & A.C. Jobim. *Miúcha & Tom*. BR/RCA 130 0060 (rpt.)
Montarroyos, Márcio. *Terra Mater*. Black Sun 15004, 1989
Monte, Heraldo do. *Cordas Vivas*. BR/Som da Gente 015, 1983
————. *Cordas Mágicas*. BR/Som da Gente SDG 030, 1986
Monte, Marisa. *Marisa Monte*. BR/EMI 791 761, 1988
Moraes, Vinícius de, & Toquinho. *Vinícius and Toquinho*. BR/Philips 6349 090, 1985
Moreira, Airto. *Identity*. Arista 4068, 1975
————. *Free*. CTI 8000, 1979 (rpt.)
Moreira, Airto, & Flora Purim. *The Colours of Life*. W. Germany/In + Out 001, 1988
Moreira, Moraes. *Mancha de Dendê Não Sai*. BR/CBS 138264, 1984
————. *Mestiço É Isso*. BR/CBS 138294, 1986
Moreira, Wilson. *Peso Na Balança*. BR/Kuarup KLP-026, 1986
Moura, Paulo. *Gafieira, Etc. & Tal*. BR/Kuarup 992 320, 1986

————. *Mistura e Manda*. Braziloid BR 4012, 1988
————. *Confusão Urbana, Suburbana e Rural*. Braziloid BR 4013, 1988
Moura, Tavinho. *Tavinho Moura*. BR/RCA 103.0334, 1989
Nascimento, Milton. *Clube da Esquina*. BR/EMI MOAB 6005-6, 1972
————. *Minas*. BR/EMI 064 82325, 1975
————. *Gerais*. BR/EMI 064 422806D, 1976
————. *Clube da Esquina 2*. BR/EMI 164 422831-32, 1978
————. *Travessia*. BR/Sigla 403 6152, 1978 (rpt.)
————. *Sentinela*. BR/Ariola 201 610, 1980
————. *Missa dos Quilombos*. BR/Ariola 201 649, 1982
————. *Anima*. Verve 813 296, 1982 (rpt.)
————. *Milagre dos Peixes*. Intuition/Capitol C1-90790, 1988 (rpt.)
————. *Miltons*. Columbia FC 45239, 1989
Nunes, Clara. *O Canto da Guerreira*. BR/EMI 066 792177, 1989
Obina Shok. *Obina Shok*. BR/RCA 103 0691, 1986
Olodum. *From the Northeast of Sahara to the Northeast of Brazil*. Soundwave/WEA 89004, 1991
Quarteto Negro. *Quarteto Negro*. BR/Kuarup KLP 031, 1987
Quinteto Armorial. *Do Romance ao Galope Nordestino*. BR/Marcus Pereira MPL 9306, 1975
Quinteto Violado. . . . *Até a Amazônia?* BR/Philips 6349 362, 1978
Orquestra da Cordas Dedilhadas de Pernambuco. *Orchestra da Cordas Dedilhadas de Pernambuco*. BR/Som da Gente SDG 031, 1987
Oswaldinho. *Céu e Chão*. BR/Som da Gente SDG 016, 1983
Pagodinho, Zeca. *Zeca Pagodinho*. BR/RGE 308.6104, 1986
Pandeiro, Jackson do. *Isso É Que É Forró!* BR/PolyGram 2494 622, 1981
Pantoja, Rique. *Rique Pantoja*. Sound Wave/WEA WH 56325, 1989
Pantoja, Rique, & Chet Baker. *Rique Pantoja & Chet Baker*. Tropical Storm/WEA WH 55155, 1989
Parahyba, João. *The New Lambadas*. Happy Hour 5010, 1990
Paralamas do Sucesso. *Selvagem?* BR/EMI 062 421 273, 1986
————. *Bora Bora*. Intuition/Capitol CDP 7 90554, 1989
Pascoal, Hermeto. *Slaves Mass*. WEA BS 2980, 1977
————. *Só Não Toca Quem Não Quer*. Intuition/Capitol C4-90559, 1988
————. *Por Diferentes Caminhos*. BR/Som da Gente SDG 039, 1988
————. *Lagoa da Canoa*. Happy Hour 5005, 1988
————. *Brasil, Universo*. Happy Hour 5007, 1989
————. *Hermeto Pascoal & Grupo*. Happy Hour 5009, 1989
Pau Brasil. *Cenas Brasileiras*. BR/Continental 1.01.404.316, 1987
Pena Branca, & Xavantinho. *Canto Violeiro*. BR/Continental 1-71-405-657, 1988

Pereira, Marco. *Círculo das Cordas*. BR/Som da Gente SDG 038, 1988

Pérola Negra, Jovelina. *Pérola Negra*. BR/RGE 738.6107, 1986

Pinheiro, Leila. *Benção Bossa Nova*. BR/Philips 842 036, 1989

Powell, Baden. *Afro Sambas*. BR/Philips FE 1016, 1966

———. *A Arte de Baden Powell*. BR/Fontana 6470 533, 1975

———. *Estudos*. W. Germany/MPS 821 855, 1979

———. *Felicidade*. France/Adda 581011, 1987 (rpt.)

Purim, Flora. *Butterfly Dreams*. Fantasy OJC-315 (rpt.)

———. *Open Your Eyes, You Can Fly*. Milestone 9065, 1976

———. *500 Miles High*. Milestone 9070, 1976

Quarteto Negro. *Quarteto Negro*. BR/Kuarup KLP-031, 1987

14 Bis. *Sete*. BR/EMI 064 422972, 1987

RPM. *Rádio Pirata Ao Vivo*. BR/CBS 144.500, 1986

Rabello, Rafael. *Rafael Rabello Interpreta Radamés Gnattali*. BR/Visom VO 006, 1987

Ramalho, Elba. *Do Jeito Que a Gente Gosta*. BR/Barclay 823 030, 1984

———. *Elba ao Vivo*. BR/Philips 842 336, 1989

Ramalho, Zé. *Zé Ramalho*. BR/Epic 44231, 1978

Banda Reflexu's. *Reflexu's da Mãe África*. Mango 162-539 901, 1987

Regina, Elis. *Elis*. BR/Philips 836 009, 1988 (rpt.)

———. *Falso Brilhante*. BR/Philips 836 010, 1988 (rpt.)

———. *Essa Mulher*. WEA WH 55900, 1988 (rpt.)

Regina, Elis, & A.C. Jobim. *Elis & Tom*. Verve 824 418, 1974

Robertinho de Recife. *Satisfação*. BR/Philips 6328 342, 1981

Rocha, Ulisses. *Alguma Coisa a Ver Com o Silêncio*. BR/Visom VO 002, 1986

Roditi, Cláudio. *Slow Fire*. Milestone M-9175, 1989

Romão, Dom Um. *Dom Um Romão*. Muse MR 5013, 1974

———. *Spirit of the Times*. Muse MR 5049, 1975

Rosa, Noel. *Noel por Noel*. BR/Imperial 30.205, 1971

Santos, Lulu. *Tudo Azul*. BR/WEA BR 26126, 1984

———. *Amor à Arte*. BR/RCA 140.0009, 1988

Santos, Moacir. *Maestro*. Blue Note LA007-F, 1972

Santos, Turíbio. *Valsas e Choros*. BR/Kuarup KLP 001, 1980

Sargento, Nelson. *Encanto da Paisagem*. BR/Kuarup KLP-025, 1986

Sater, Almir. *Instrumental*. BR/Som da Gente SDG 025, 1985

Seixas, Raul. *Raul Rock*. BR/Fontana 826 189, 1985

Sete, Bola. *Autêntico!* Fantasy OJC 290, 1987 (rpt.)

———. *Bossa Nova*. Fantasy OJC 286, 1987 (rpt.)

Severo. *Machucando Gostosinho*. BR/EMI 036 422 636, 1987

Silva, Bezerra da. *Justiça Social*. BR/RCA 103 0701, 1987

Silveira, Ricardo. *Sky Light*. Verve Forecast 837 696, 1989

Simone. *Amar*. BR/CBS 138.247, 1981

———. *Corpo e Alma*. BR/CBS 138.267, 1982

———. *Delírios e Delícias*. BR/CBS 138.277, 1983

Sivuca. *Cabelo de Milho*. BR/Copacabana 12528, 1980

———. *Forró e Frevo*. BR/Copacabana 12859, 1984

———. *Som Brasil*. Norway/Sonet SNTF-942, 1985

Souza, Raul de. *Colors*. Milestone 9061, 1974

Stocker, Olmir (Alemão). *Alemão Bem Brasileiro*. Happy Hour 5008, 1988

———. *Longe dos Olhos*. Happy Hour 5006, 1989

Tamba Trio. *Tamba Trio*. Philips 632129, 1962

———. *20 Anos de Sucessos*. BR/RCA 103 0548, 1984

Tapajós, Sebastião. *Painel*. BR/Visom VO 0001, 1986

Tiso, Wagner. *Os Pássaros*. BR/EMI 064 422948, 1985

———. *Giselle*. Verve 831 819, 1987

———. *Manú Çaruê, Uma Aventura Holística*. BR/Philips 834 632, 1988

Titãs. *Cabeça Dinossauro*. BR/WEA 6106014, 1986

———. *O Blesq Blom*. BR/WEA 229257032, 1989

Toquinho. *A Luz do Solo*. BR/Barclay 827 823, 1985

———. (w. Sadao Watanabe). *Made in Coração*. BR/RCA 140 0007, 1988

———. *À Sombra de um Jatobá*. BR/RCA 150 0002, 1989

Toquinho & Vinícius. *Dez Anos de...* BR/Philips 634 940, 1979

Uakti. *Uakti*. Verve 831-705, 1987

Ultraje a Rigor. *Nós Vamos Invadir Sua Praia*. BR/WEA 28128, 1985

Vale, João do. *João do Vale*. BR/CBS 138237, 1981

Valença, Alceu. *Espelho Cristalino*. BR/Som Livre 403 6140, 1977

———. *Cavalo de Pau*. BR/Ariola 201 647, 1982

———. *Mágico*. BR/Barclay 823 693, 1984

———. *Ao Vivo*. BR/Barclay 825 738, 1986 (rpt.)

Various Artists. *Afros e Afoxés da Bahia*. Mango 539 893, 1990

———. *Asa Branca: Accordion Forró from Brazil*. Rykodisc 20154, 1990

———. *Ataulfo Alves: Leva Meu Samba...* BR/Som Livre 407 0006, 1989

———. *Black Orpheus* [soundtrack]. Verve 830 783, 1990 (rpt.)

———. *Bossa Nova*. BR/CBS 231 083, 1988

———. *Bossa Nova*. BR/Fontana 826 666, 1985

———. *Bossa Nova Story*. France/Carrere CA 96-405, 1986

———. *Bossa Nova: Trinta Anos Depois*. BR/Philips 826 870, 1987

———. *Brazil Classics 1: Beleza Tropical*. Fly/Sire 9 25805, 1989

———. *Brazil Classics 2: O Samba*. Luaka Bop/Sire 9 26019, 1989

———. *Brazil Classics 3: Forró Etc*. Luaka Bop/Sire 9 26323, 1991

———. *Brazil Classics 4: The Best of Tom Zé*. Luaka Bop/Sire 9 26396, 1990

———. *Brazil: Forró*. Rounder 5044, 1989

———. *Brazilliance! The Music of Rhythm*. Rykodisc 20153, 1990

———. *Brazil-Roots-Samba*. Rounder 5045, 1989

———. *Cartola: Bate Outra Vez*. BR/Som Livre 406 0034, 1988

——. *Grandes Autores: Ary Barroso*. BR/Philips 838 337, 1989

——. *Grandes Autores: Dorival Caymmi*. BR/Philips 838 336, 1989

——. *Grandes Autores: Noel Rosa*. BR/Philips 838 335, 1989

——. *Lambada*. Epic 46052, 1990

——. *Personalidade: the Best of Brazil*. BR/Philips, multiple-title series, 1987-88

——. *Raça Brasileira*. BR/RGE 308.6087, 1987

——. *Sambas de Enredo: Carnaval '86*. RCA 5637, 1985

——. *Som Especial—Clube da Esquina*. BR/EMI 052 422 158, 1985

Vasconcelos, Naná. *Saudades*. ECM 1147, 1980

——. *Rain Dance*. Island 91070, 1989

Velha Guarda da Portela. *Velha Guarda da Portela*. BR/Kuarup KLP-027, 1986

Veloso, Caetano. *Caetano Veloso*. BR/Philips R765 026L, 1968

——. *Cinema Transcendental*. BR/Philips 6349 436, 1979

——. *Totalmente Demais*. Verve 833 237, 1987

——. *Estrangeiro*. Elektra Musician 60898, 1989

Veloso, Caetano, & et al. *Tropicália ou Panis et Circensis*. BR/Philips R765 040L, 1968

Veloso, Caetano, & Gal Costa. *Domingo*. BR/Philips R765 007P, 1967

Vieira. *Lambada*. U.K./Stern's 2001, 1988

Vila, Martinho da. *Canta Canta, Minha Gente*. BR/RCA 110.0002, 1974

——. *Batuqueiro*. BR/RCA 103.0678, 1986

——. *Coração Malandro*. BR/RCA 130.0011, 1987

——. *Festa da Raça*. BR/CBS 138.310, 1988

Viola, Paulinho da. *20 Anos de Samba*. BR/EMI 052 792040, 1989

——. *Eu Canto Samba*. BR/RCA 104 0010, 1989

Xangai (**Eugenio Avelino**). *Mutirão da Vida*. BR/Kuarup KLP-019, 1984

Xangai, & Elomar. *Xangai Canta Elomar*. BR/Kuarup KLP-023, 1986

Zil. *Zil*. Verve 841 929, 1990

International Artists:
Releases With Brazilian Influence

The recordings listed below are a sampling of the many international albums that feature performances by Brazilian musicians, or have a pronounced Brazilian influence on two or more songs. Those artists in parentheses after the main artist were important contributors to the recording listed.

Adderley, Cannonball (w. S. Mendes). *Cannonball's Bossa Nova*. Landmark 1302, 1985 (rpt.)

Ambitious Lovers. *Greed*. Virgin 90903, 1989

Barbieri, Gato. *The Third World Revisited*. RCA 6995, 1988 (rpt.)

Basia. *Time and Tide*. Epic EK 40767, 1987

Benson, George. *Give Me the Night*. WB HS 3453, 1980

Brecker, Randy, & Eliane Elias. *Amanda*. Passport 88013, 1986

Byrd, Charlie. *Sugar Loaf Suite*. Concord CJP-114, 1980

——. *Brazilville*. Concord CJP-173, 1982

Corea, Chick. *Return to Forever*. ECM 811 978, 1972

Corea, Chick, & Return to Forever. *Light As a Feather*. Polydor 827 148, 1973

Codona. *Codona*. ECM 1132, 1978

——. *Codona II*. ECM 1177, 1980

——. *Codona III*. ECM 1243, 1982

The Crusaders (w. I. Lins). *Life in the Modern World*. MCA 42168, 1988

Davis, Miles (w. A. Moreira). *Live-Evil*. Columbia G 30954, 1970

Desmond, Paul (w. E. Lobo). *From the Hot Afternoon*. A&M 0824, 1969

DiMeola, Al. *Tirami Su*. Manhattan MLT-46995, 1987

D'Rivera, Paquito. *Tico! Tico!* Chesky JD34, 1989

Elements (w. Café, A. Moreira). *Spirit River*. Novus 3089, 1990

Fitzgerald, Ella. *Ella Abraça Jobim*. Pablo 2630-201, n.d.

Franks, Michael. *Sleeping Gypsy*. Warner BS 3004, 1977

Gable, Bill. *There Were Signs*. Private Music 2031, 1989

Getz, Stan. *Big Band Bossa Nova*. Verve 68494, 1962

——. (w. L. Bonfá). *Jazz Samba Encore*. Verve 68523, 1963

——. (w. A. Gilberto). *Getz Au Go Go*. Verve 68600, 1964

——. (w. C. Corea, S. Clarke, A. Moreira). *Captain Marvel*. Columbia KC 32706, 1972

——. *The Girl From Ipanema: The Bossa Nova Years*. Verve 823 611, 1989 (rpts.) [Four-CD/five-LP set]

Getz, Stan, & Laurindo Almeida. *Stan Getz/Laurindo Almeida*. Verve 68665, 1966

Getz, Stan, & Charlie Byrd. *Jazz Samba*. Verve 68432, 1962

Getz, Stan, & João Gilberto. *Getz/Gilberto*. Verve 68545, 1964

——. (w. Miúcha). *The Best of Two Worlds*. CBS PC 33703, 1976

Grusin, Dave, & Lee Ritenour (w. I. Lins). *Harlequin*. GRP 9522, 1986

Grusin, Don. *Raven*. GRP 9602, 1990

Guaraldi, Vince. *Cast Your Fate to the Wind*. Fantasy 607 8089, 1965

Guaraldi, Vince, & Bola Sete. *Vince Guaraldi, Bola Sete and Friends*. Fantasy 8356, 1963

Guedes, Carlos, & Desvio. *Churun Meru*. Oxymoron 3006, 1990

Haden, Charlie & Jan Garbarek, Egberto Gismonti. *Mágico*. ECM 1151, 1980

——. *Folk Songs*. ECM 1170, 1981

Hart, Mickey, & Airto Moreira, Flora Purim. *Dafos*. Rykodisc RCD 10108, 1989

Hawkins, Coleman. *Desafinado*. Impulse LP AS-28, 1962

Horn, Paul, & Egberto Gismonti. *The Altitude of the Sun*. Black Sun 15002, 1989 (rpt.)

Kaoma. *World Beat*. Epic EK 40610, 1989

L.A. Four. *The L.A. Four Scores!* Concord CJ-8, 1975

The Manhattan Transfer (w. Uakti, Djavan, M. Nascimento). *Brasil*. Atlantic 81803, 1987

Mann, Herbie (w. S. Mendes, A.C. Jobim). *Do the Bossa Nova with Herbie Mann*. Atlantic 1397, 1962
———. (w. C. Roditi). *Jasil Brazz*. RBI 1401, 1987
———. (w. R. Silveira). *Opalescence*. Mocca/Gaia 13-9020, 1989
Manzanera, Phil, & Sérgio Dias. *Mato Grosso*. Black Sun 15010, 1990
Mays, Lyle (w. N. Vasconcelos). *Lyle Mays*. Geffen 24097, 1986
Pat Metheny. *Pat Metheny Group*. ECM 1114, 1978
———. (w. N. Vasconcelos). *As Falls Wichita, So Falls Wichita Falls*. ECM 1190, 1981
———. (w. N. Vasconcelos). *Offramp*. ECM 1216, 1982
———. (w. N. Vasconcelos). *Travels*. ECM 1252, 1983
———. (w. A. Marçal). *Still Life (Talking)*. Geffen GHS 24145, 1987
———. (w. A. Marçal). *Letter From Home*. Geffen GHS 24245, 1989
Modern Jazz Quartet (w. L. Almeida). *Collaboration*. Atlantic 1429, 1964
Montoliu, Tetê. *Temas Brasileños*. Ensayo 3951, n.d.
Murphy, Mark. *Brazil Song (Canções do Brasil)*. Muse MR 5297, 1984
———. (w. Azymuth). *Night Mood*. Milestone M-9145, 1987
Pass, Joe (w. P. da Costa). *Tudo Bem*. Pablo 2310-824, 1977
Pearson, Duke (w. F. Purim). *It Could Only Happen to You*. Blue Note LA317, 1970
Ritenour, Lee. *Rio*. GRP 1017, 1979
———. *Portrait*. GRP GRD-9553, 1987
———. (w. J. Bosco). *Festival*. GRP GR-9570, 1988
Sade. *Diamond Life*. CBS FR 39581, 1985
Shank, Bud (w. M. Silva). *Tomorrow's Rainbow*. Contemporary C-14048, 1989
Shank, Bud, & Laurindo Almeida. *Brazilliance, Vol. 2*. World Pacific 1419, 1962
———. *Brazilliance, Vol. 3*. World Pacific 1425, 1963
Shearing, George. *Bossa Nova*. Capitol 1873, n.d.
Shorter, Wayne, & Milton Nascimento (w. H. Hancock). *Native Dancer*. Columbia PC 33418, 1975
Simon, Paul. *The Rhythm of the Saints*. WB26098, 1990
Sinatra, Frank, & Antonio Carlos Jobim. *Francis Albert Sinatra & Antonio Carlos Jobim*. Reprise FS-1021, 1967
Slagle, Steve (w. R. Silveira). *Rio Highlife*. Atlantic 81657, 1986
Steps Ahead (w. E. Elias). *Steps Ahead*. Elektra 9 60168, 1983
Thielemans, Toots, & Elis Regina. *Aquarela do Brasil*. Philips 830 931, 1969
Thielemans, Toots & Sivuca. *Chiko's Bar*. Norway/Sonet SNTF-944, 1985
Various Artists. *Wild Orchid* [soundtrack]. Sire 9 26127, 1990

Vaughan, Sarah. *I Love Brazil!* Pablo 2312-101, 1979
———. (w. Dori Caymmi). *Brazilian Romance*. CBS FM 42519, 1987
Vaughan, Sarah & Hélio Delmiro. *Copacabana*. Fantasy 2312 137, 1987 (rpt.)
Watanabe, Sadao. *Birds of Passage*. Elektra 9 60748, 1987
———. (w. Toquinho). *Elis*. Elektra 9 60816, 1988
Weather Report (w. A. Moreira). *Weather Report*. Columbia 30661, 1971
———. (w. D.U. Romão). *Mysterious Traveller*. Columbia 32494, 1974
Winter, Paul. *Jazz Meets the Bossa Nova*. Columbia CS 8725, 1962
———. *The Winter Consort*. A&M SP-4170, 1968
———. (w. L. Bonfá, R. Menescal, L. Eça). *Rio*. Columbia JCS 9115, 1973 (rpt.)
———. (w. O. Castro-Neves). *Common Ground*. A&M SP-4698, 1978
———. (w. O. Castro-Neves). *Missa Gaia: Earth Mass*. Living Music LMR-2, 1982
———. (w. O. Castro-Neves). *Earthbeat*. Living Music 0015, 1987
———. (w. G. Thiago de Mello). *Earth: Voices of a Planet*. Living Music 0019, 1990
Winter, Paul & Carlos Lyra. *The Sound of Ipanema*. Columbia CL 2272, 1964
Yutaka (w. O.Castro-Neves). *Brazasia*. GRP GRD 9616, 1990

SELECT VIDEOGRAPHY (U.S.)

[LD = laserdisc]
Airto & Flora Purim: the Latin Jazz All-Stars. VIEW 1311. (LD: Image ID7736VW)
Antonio Carlos Jobim, Gal Costa: Rio Revisited. Verve 081 331-3 (LD: Verve 081 331-1)
Black Orpheus. Connoisseur CVC 1001 (LD: Criterion 2002L)
Djavan, Ivan Lins: Brazilian Knights and a Lady. Verve 081 343-3 (LD: Verve 081 343-1)
Carnaval 89. Globo GVE 8900
Carnaval 90. Globo GVE 8904
Egberto Gismonti Live. Proscenium 10006
Ópera do Malandro. Virgin 70074 (LD: Image ID6157VV)
The Three Caballeros. Walt Disney 91 (LD: WD 091 AS)

SOURCES

Billboard Buyer's Guide/international guide to music and video companies (Billboard Directories, P.O. Box 2016, Lakewood NJ 08701; (800) 223-7524).
Globo Video/distributes Globo Video titles from Brazil (10-30 44 Drive, Long Island City NY 11101; (718) 784-5544).
Musicrama/recorded-music importer (164 Driggs Ave., Brooklyn NY 11222; (718) 389-7818).
PolyGram Imports/imports PolyGram Brazil titles (825 Eighth Ave., New York NY 10019; (212) 333-8000).

PHOTO CREDITS

Agência Jornol de Brasil (AJB), 29, 38, 134b, 185a
Conceição Almeida/RCA (BMG), 98, *135, 136
Atlantic Records, 111
Mabel Arthou/AJB, 157b

André Barcinski/AJB, 187b
Luis Bettencourt/AJB, 100b
courtesy **Black Sun Records**, 185b
courtesy **BMG**, 48b, *61, 94, 134a, *144b, 175b, 190b
Marcos Bonisson/Polygram, *192
Phil Bray/Fantasy Records, 163b
Buckmaster/Polygram, *117b

Livio Campos/BMG, *145b, 146a, 146b; **/Braziloid**, 88; **/Polygram**, *82, 87, 91, 189a, 189b, 197
courtesy **Casa Editrice Libraria, Ulrico Hoepli, S.p.A.**, 25
courtesy **CBS Records**, *49b, 77, *101b, 102
courtesy **Cebitur**, 120b, *126a, 126b, 141
courtesy **Concord Jazz Records**, *155, *163a, 168b
Ivan Cordeiro, *142

Ines Daflon, 128b
Mircea Dordea/CBS, *183b, 184b, 187a

courtesy **ECM**, *157a
courtesy **Embratur**, 12, 15, 28, 39, 42a, *42b, 54, 70
courtesy **EMI**, 129b, 193b
courtesy **Epic Records**, 131

Márcio Ferreira, 14, 107, 171b; **/Quilombo**, 112a, 168a
Walter Firmo/BMG, 47

Paulo Rubens Fonseca, 76 (Ben photo)
Carol Friedman/Blue Note, 174c

David Gahr/Milestone, 176a
Galeao/AJB, 183a
Karl Garabedian, 63
Isabel Garcia/EMI, *194
Ari Gomes/AJB, 78
Cristina Granato/BMG, 45, 191
courtesy **GRP Records**, 172a, 172b

Antonio Guerreiro/Polygram, 93

Hamilton/AJB, 85
Hans Harzheim/MPS Records, *65
Hugo/AJB, *138a

Jacob/AJB, 31
Ana Lontra Jobim, 59
courtesy **JVC**, 75

Chris Kehoe/Geffen, 171a
courtesy **Kuarup Records**, 143a, 177a

courtesy **Herbie Mann**, *58a, 58b
Jim Marshall/Fantasy Records, 167b
Chris McGowan, 17, 23, 105, *109, 133, 154b, 174a
Frederico Mendes/CBS, 100a, 140, 182
courtesy **Milestone**, 178a
Wilton Montenegro, 86a, 86b, 86c, *121

Campanella Neto/AJB, *34b

Lidio Parente/CBS, *106; **/WEA**, 196b
José Pederneiras/CBS, 124
Luis Pederneiras/EMI, *112b
Ricardo Pessanha, 13a, 18, 36, 71, 73, 84, *99, *128a, 165
courtesy **Polygram**, 92, *97, 129a, *130a

Andrew Putler/Retna, 164
Cristiano Quintino/Verve, *178b

Márcia Ramalho/EMI, 96
courtesy **RCA (BMG)**, *188
Márcio Rodrigues/Som Livre, 149a
Mick Rock/Capitol, 173b
Joseph A. Rosen/Retna, 116a, 151

Alex Salim/WEA, 181
Wilson Santos/AJB, 184a
Fernando Seixas/RCA (BMG), 143b
courtesy **Som da Gente**, *159, 175a, 176b
courtesy **Som Livre**, 33,

Felipe Taborda/Som Livre, *186b
Antonio Teixeira/AJB, *32, *46
Ronaldo Theobald/AJB, 144a
courtesy **Tropical Storm**, 85b

Maurício Valladarez/Intuition, *193a
Paulo Vasconcellos/Som da Gente, 160
courtesy **Verve Records**, 13b, 114, 116b
Cláudio Vianna, 120a
Delfim Vieira/AJB, 158
courtesy **Virgin Records**, 167a
courtesy **The Voyager Company**, 64

courtesy **WEA**, 90a, 95, *195a, 195b
Nick White/Island Records, *166a
Timothy White/Verve, 177b
courtesy **Paul Winter**, 68, 173a
Bob Wolfenson/EMI, 186a

Chico Ybarra/Braziloid, *154a

Dario Zalis/BMG, 196a

INDEX